T0121916

MARGOT MORRELL

Reagan's Journey

Lessons from a Remarkable Career

THRESHOLD EDITIONS

New York London Toronto Sydney

Threshold Editions
A Division of Simon & Schuster, Inc.
1230 Avenue of the Americas
New York, NY 10020

First Threshold Editions hardcover edition May 2011

Designed by Ruth Lee-Mui

Manufactured in the United States of America

10 9 8 7 6 5 4 3 2 1

Library of Congress Cataloging-in-Publication Data

Morrell, Margot.
Reagan's journey: lessons from a remarkable career / Margot Morrell.
p. cm.
Includes bibliographical references and index.
1. Reagan, Ronald. 2. Presidents—United States—Biography. 3. Governors—California—Biography. 4. Motion picture actors and actresses—United States—Biography. I. Title.
E877.M65 2011
973.927092—dc22
[B] 2010045808

ISBN 978-1-4516-2399-4
ISBN 978-1-4516-2086-3 (ebook)

For

JUDITH R. HABERKORN

Wonderful Mentor, Dear Friend

They used to say about him that he could charm anybody, but for people who really hated him it took ten minutes.

—Caspar Weinberger,
Secretary of Defense,
Reagan Administration

Contents

INTRODUCTION

RONALD REAGAN decided he was going to college.

He got a summer position as a lifeguard, worked odd jobs throughout the year, and started saving. His father had explained to him and his older brother Neil that he couldn't help them finance their education. At the time college was for the fortunate few; only 7 percent of Americans continued their education past high school. Neil, convinced college was out of the question, finished high school and went to work as a laborer in a local cement factory. Ronald Reagan, armed with determination and persistence, pursued a different path.

Fresh-faced and eager, he graduated from college in 1932 and ran head-on into the worst economic downturn in the nation's history. Unemployment hit an all-time high of 24 percent that summer, but rather than look for whatever job—if any—might be available, he drilled down on a life-defining question: "*What do you want to do?*" The answer focused him on a career path that would eventually lead to extraordinary success.

Though he would one day be hailed as the Great Communicator,

Reagan was fired from his first job as a radio announcer for being "plain awful" at reading a script. Downcast and discouraged, he confided his troubles to a colleague who counseled him to find another line of work, "I can tell in five minutes whether a fellow should be in show business or not." Then he sadly shook his head.

At that first career setback at radio station WOC in Davenport, Iowa, fate stepped in to give Reagan a reprieve when a conversation with a friend snapped him out of his "mental block." Four years later, he moved on to an acting career in Hollywood. There the stardom he sought remained forever, tantalizingly, beyond his grasp. In the next phase of his career, after eight successful years as corporate ambassador he was unceremoniously dumped by General Electric, with scarcely a moment's notice. When success finally found him, he rejected it out of hand. He had no interest in politics. As he put it in his 1965 autobiography, "That hat didn't fit."

In the course of his sixty-year career, Reagan faced challenges and hardships. Four times his life slammed into a brick wall. He was heartbroken by his divorce from first wife, Jane Wyman, the collapse of his long-standing relationship with Warner Bros., the termination of his eight-year association with General Electric, and a hard-fought loss to President Gerald Ford in the 1976 primary campaign. Yet after every disaster, he picked himself up and kept moving forward.

How did he do that? How, during his wilderness years—when his movie career was on life support—did he manage to stay in the public eye and keep going? How did he handle the hurdles involved in transitioning from actor and union leader into political star? What can we learn from the way he muscled through adversity, maintained his focus, and achieved his goals? What traits did he possess that helped a young kid from America's heartland become one of history's most influential leaders?

Reagan's Journey had its origins in my experience working in Presidential Personnel on the 1980–81 Reagan Transition Team—on loan from an executive search firm. For six intense weeks I worked with people who had been Reagan's closest associates for years. They thought the world of him and invariably referred to him as "Governor" right up to Inauguration Day. Far from being a disengaged figurehead, the Reagan insiders knew he was driven, ambitious, hardworking, and no-nonsense but, at the same time, thoughtful and kind to his staff. I left with a very different impression of Reagan than was commonly offered in the press.

I hadn't always been a Reagan fan. A small incident triggered a change in my thinking. One April day in 1980, as Reagan and George Bush were still battling through the primary campaigns, I was lying on a chaise longue by a pool in Monte Carlo reading when a dignified matron, with a blue-blazer-clad son in tow, drifted into my field of vision. Huge REAGAN buttons sprouted from their lapels. I rolled my eyes—what on earth were they thinking!—and went back to my book.

Try as I might, though, to refocus on the page in front of me, my brain was buzzing. What was it about that man—a washed-up actor, for crying out loud!—that inspired such passion in his supporters? What could they possibly see in him?

That was typical eastern thinking from the land of "Me Too" Republicans such as Governor Nelson Rockefeller and

Senators Jacob Javits and Edward Brooke. Reagan had come to conservatism from a different path—the rugged individualism of the West. Considered a moderate in California, he was hysterically characterized in the East as a right-wing extremist. He often joked that as he crossed the Mississippi, he grew horns.

He had started out in his political thinking as a hard-core Democrat—as he phrased it, "a hemophiliac liberal who bled for causes." Experiences with federal bureaucrats, communists, and exorbitant tax rates forced him to reconsider his views. Over the course of about fifteen years, from the late 1940s to the early 1960s, he moved slowly across the political spectrum from staunch Democrat to committed Republican. He often joked about the Democratic Party that "I didn't leave the party, the party left me." In his soul he always remained a classic liberal who held tight to a handful of cherished principles—individual rights and limited federal government—in the mold of the Founding Fathers.

Back home, I picked up a copy of *Time* with Reagan's photo on the cover. That year, George Bush's election strategy was to avoid taking stands on issues—a source of frustration to his supporters. As I read through Reagan's well-thought-out, long-held, principled positions, the scales fell from my eyes. The article[1] quoted him as saying, "Government causes inflation, and Government can make it go away." The solution, he believed, was to cut income taxes. He believed in ending controls on agriculture and energy and said, "If we turn both of them loose in the marketplace, they will produce the food and fuel we need." He said Washington had weakened our national defenses through a "foreign policy bordering on appeasement." On one point after another, I found myself thinking, Hmmm . . . I agree with that. Suddenly I was yearning for one of those huge Reagan buttons. That fall, I worked on the Reagan campaign.

I arrived in D.C. on December 8, 1980, and started at the Transition office the next day. Assigned to a desk outside the office of long-term Reagan aide and eventual White House Director for Personnel Helene von Damm, I had a front-row seat as luminaries of the new administration passed through: Ed Meese, Drew Lewis, Bill Casey, and Don Regan were a few I recognized.

Presidential Personnel was tasked with filling the "plum jobs"—the top thirteen hundred roles in the administration. I was charged with processing résumés forwarded by top Republicans—former president Ford, vice president–elect George H. W. Bush, Elizabeth Dole, and on and on. The supply of résumés was endless, the piles around my desk seemingly bottomless.

Maximizing the advantages offered by my temporary perch, I raced across the street to the Mayflower Hotel to watch press conferences, attended inaugural festivities and, by chance, arrived on Capitol Hill on Inauguration Day just in time to see President and Mrs. Reagan leaving the Capitol on their way to the White House. People often describe Reagan as "larger than life." That's because he was.

Waving from the open-top car, he exuded joy and confidence. A few weeks later he told a long-term associate, "I'm having a ball." That's exactly how he looked. In his graceful way, he had been working toward the presidency with single-minded determination for years. Grounded by firmly held views and lifelong values, he focused on reviving the economy, spreading freedom and democracy around the world, and containing the mushrooming growth of the federal government.

At the time, there was great press interest in the efforts of the Transition Team, and particularly in the mysterious workings of Presidential Personnel. Major media outlets wrote articles, filmed news stories, and produced a one-hour TV special. Though well-intentioned, they failed to capture anything that remotely resembled my firsthand experience working there. *Reagan's Journey* seeks to capture the man Reagan insiders knew, the man I caught a glimpse of during those days on the Transition Team.

In 1983, I met Reagan advance man Rick Ahearn, who talked about life on the 1980 campaign trail. During the early primaries, the Reagan campaign was so short of funds that the advance team was reduced to eating "moldy sandwiches." They collected leftover box lunches—"a roast beef sandwich, a peanut butter cookie, and an apple"—from a campaign event, stored them in the trunks of their cars, and ate them for the next several days. I was left wondering, What would someone have to be like, what would you have to see in him, that you'd be willing to work for moldy sandwiches?

There things stood for twenty years, until 2003, when I met Reagan's 1980 debate advisor, Myles Martel. Myles shared memories of spending days in a Virginia stable that had been converted into a television studio in preparation for the debates with Congressman John Anderson and President Jimmy Carter. A few years later, at a New Year's Eve party, I was introduced to 1940s-era MCA agent Richard Steenberg, who worked with Reagan when he was still making movies. Chatting about that bygone era, Richard painted a vivid picture of Hollywood in its glory days. Then, at a business conference in Washington, D.C., in May 2007, I met White House photographer Bill Fitzpatrick. Over lunch, we talked about his career. Bill's admiration for his long-ago boss was contagious. I was finally catapulted into action and began working on *Reagan's Journey* in earnest.

Today the name Ronald Reagan is synonymous with great leadership. He led by example—at a time when few thought it possible, and against the advice of experts, he went to the Berlin Wall and demanded it be torn down. He worked at keeping up the morale of his fellow citizens in honoring the sacrifices at Pointe du Hoc in Normandy, relighting the Statue of Liberty, and giving a magnificent speech for the children of the country on the occasion of the *Challenger* disaster. In the face of a tremendous personal crisis, he maintained a positive attitude. The world watched in wonder and amazement as he joked his way through the assassination attempt that very nearly killed him. And above all else, in his signature style—friendly, avuncular, easygoing—from the Oval Office, in auditoriums large and small, and on his Saturday radio programs, he communicated with us.

Please join me in exploring Reagan's Journey.

Chapter I

Discovering Talents, Developing Strengths

Early Years in Tampico, Dixon, and Eureka, Illinois, 1911–32

What does the YMCA mean to Dixon? . . . [I]t is the place where future Americans receive training, morally, mentally, physically. The future of the country rests with the boys of today. They will be the men of tomorrow.

—*Dixon Evening Telegraph,* November 10, 1922

He was a gifted athlete with a powerful build and a straight-A student, when he put his mind to it. He had a streak of independence his mother termed "brassiness"[1] and an offbeat sense of humor. Widely considered a natural leader and talented actor, friends and neighbors predicted he was headed for a promising career on the stage. His name was Neil Reagan and he had a shy, scrawny, insecure, little brother named Ronald.

Neil was nicknamed "Moon" by schoolmates. He reminded them of "Moon Mullins"—a tough-talking but good-natured cartoon character who parted his hair in the center. Moon, like his father, was a strong extrovert. He loved pool halls and hanging out with his gang.

At Ronald's birth, his father declared him "a little bit of a fat

Dutchman!" The name stuck. As a child, Dutch Reagan spent hours staring at birds' eggs and butterflies—he was mesmerized by the mysteries of nature—and made regular trips to the library. But while still in their teens, the Reagan boys, in effect, swapped birth-order positions when Dutch, the thoughtful, "doggedly determined,"[2] initiator, set his sights on going to college and dragged Moon along in his wake.

In a rare introspective mood in his seventies, Moon reminisced about his college days, "It's a funny thing, and I guess I've really never gotten over it completely. I automatically became the younger brother."[3] The diffident but persistent younger child had overtaken his more gifted sibling—in a biblical twist of fate, Jacob was again chosen over Esau.

The boys were children of America's heartland, born and raised—but for one brief urban interlude—in towns that rise like beacons amid the seemingly endless cornfields and farms of northwestern Illinois. The Reagan brothers grew up in a world of unlocked doors; a world of we and us, not they and them. Ronald Reagan long remembered those towns as places where "almost everybody knew one another, and because they knew one another, they tended to care about each other."[4]

Early on, Dutch absorbed values that stayed with him for a lifetime. As a little boy with no living grandparents, he was "adopted" by kind neighbors. Local druggist "Uncle Jim" Greenman and his wife, "Aunt Emma," gave Dutch daily doses of chocolate and cookies, a generous weekly allowance of ten cents, and a plump rocking chair for after-school reading as his parents clerked in a store nearby. With the skewed perspective of childhood, Reagan, in his 1965 autobiography, described the Greenmans as "elderly." They were in their midfifties when he lived next door to them—his age at the time he was just starting to think about running for public office.

In the close-knit communities of his youth, the future governor and president witnessed "how the love and common sense of purpose that unites families is one of the most powerful glues on earth and that it can help them overcome the greatest of adversities. I learned that hard work is an essential part of life—that by and large, you don't get something for nothing—and that America was a place that offered unlimited opportunity to those who did work hard."[5] Early in life, Dutch Reagan came to appreciate there are universal values. He believed everyone wanted "freedom and liberty, peace, love and security, a good home, and a chance to worship God in our own way; we all want the chance to work at a job of our own choosing and to be fairly rewarded for it and the opportunity to control our own destiny."[6]

Today the one-block commercial district of Tampico, Illinois, is lined with boarded-up businesses and shuttered storefronts. But once upon a time a wave of prosperity flooded the tiny town and drew a young couple named Reagan there in search of a brighter future.

The town's burst of affluence was an unlikely outgrowth of the 1825 opening of New York's wildly successful Erie Canal. Overnight the canal transformed New York into an economic powerhouse by connecting the vast natural resources of the Midwest with the insatiable markets of the East Coast. Illinois businessmen and farmers were soon conjuring up ways to get their goods to market faster, cheaper, and more profitably.

In 1832, a proposal was put forth to connect Chicago directly to the nation's premier port, New Orleans, via a superhighway of rivers. Budget concerns, competing interests, and war delayed the start of construction until canals were obsolete. The Hennepin Canal was doomed before the first shovel of dirt was finally dug in 1892. By then, railroads had superseded canals. Still the project pressed forward with construction of two canals that linked three rivers—the Illinois, the Mississippi, and the Rock. Tampico, ideally situated halfway along the shorter canal, seemed poised for an all-but-inevitable explosion of growth.

As digging started, Tampico's soon-to-be-tycoons were gleeful. They dreamed of rising profits and real estate values and planned extravagant building campaigns. Up went a "costly and imposing" church, a string of new houses, and the grandest home for miles around. Overeager investors built a railroad but failed to secure the necessary rights of way. Their stunted fourteen-mile effort only succeeded in connecting Tampico—peak population fourteen hundred—to two even smaller towns.

For a while the future looked bright. Tampico's energetic entrepreneur Henry C. Pitney combined and enlarged two existing stores. In 1906, at the peak of the bubble, he hired twenty-three-year old John (Jack) Reagan, who arrived from nearby Fulton with eight years of retail experience and a wife, Nelle Wilson Reagan.[7] Shortly after the couple settled in, the town's population started a slow decline as construction teams moved on and the canal failed to lure business from the railroads that rushed past on tracks laid a few miles to the north of the tiny enclave. Dreams of glory withered and died and Tampico shrank back to a small-market town serving the needs of farms that circled the once, ever so briefly, prosperous community.

Ronald Reagan's ancestors arrived in northwestern Illinois when it was still the edge of America's frontier. Like many immigrants, they were drawn to the arable land the federal government was giving away for free to settlers willing to farm it. The Wilsons made their way to Whiteside County from Scotland through Canada in the early years of the nineteenth century when the area's economy consisted of subsistence farming, with little cash changing hands. The Reagans arrived from Ireland via England in the 1850s just as the intricate iron web spun by the railways changed the rural landscape forever. Emerging technologies were sweeping away the old world order and sparking developments in farming and commerce. In Whiteside County, a young blacksmith, John Deere, worked late nights to develop a plow that cut through the area's "sticky" soil. Across the river in Iowa, an enterprising immigrant named Friedrich Weyerhaeuser started a lumber business.

Though very different in personality, Nelle Wilson and Jack Reagan had a strong common bond: early loss. Jack's parents died in their thirties of tuberculosis, leaving behind four young children to be raised by their grandmother Catherine Reagan and aunts Margaret (Maggie) and Mary. Fortunately, the Reagan women had a flair for business. They established a millinery business in Fulton in the 1880s. When Maggie married, she moved away and expanded the business to other locations. In Fulton, their shop did well enough to hire a clerk. While working in the Reagans' shop in Fulton, Nelle Wilson met Jack Reagan.

Nelle's father, Thomas Wilson, walked away from his farm and deserted his wife and children in 1889 when Nelle was six. Her mother packed up her family and moved to Fulton where Nelle, the youngest, grew up with the support of her siblings. Nelle's mother, Mary Anne Wilson, died when Nelle was seventeen. Her father lived until December 1909, but it was her brother Alexander who gave her away when she married John Edward Reagan on November 8, 1904, at Fulton's Immaculate Conception Catholic Church. They were both twenty-one.

Ronald Reagan remembered his father as "burning with ambition to succeed."[8] Jack was handsome, dapper, expansive, flamboyant, and charming. Dutch admired his flair for telling jokes and stories and considered him "the best raconteur I ever heard." It was a talent Dutch worked hard to emulate and used to great effect in his own career. But Jack was also a "cynic who expected the worst in people." A "one match a day man," he smoked three packs of cigarettes daily, lighting one from the end of another.

Jack's outward bravado concealed an inner weakness: he was a binge drinker who disappeared for days at a time. Nelle drilled into her boys that their father's problem was a sickness that he couldn't help and that they shouldn't hold it against him. But Jack's drinking was a source of embarrassment and concern to his family. One evening Jack staggered home drunk, his car nowhere in sight. Dutch backtracked his father's path and found the car in the middle of a street with the motor still running. Moon said Jack was "his own worst enemy. He talked or worked himself out of nearly every job he had. . . . He spent it as fast as he made it. He was quite a gambler and he liked the bottle."[9] Jack Reagan burned through a string of jobs. His earnings peaked at fifty-five dollars a week as a shoe salesman. Nelle helped out by taking in sewing and working as a salesclerk.

Despite Jack's failings, as a small businessman with an entrepreneurial spirit, he managed to teach his sons the value of hard work, initiative, and enterprise. From Jack, the boys picked up a love of sports. An ardent Democrat, he was passionate about the rights of the working man and loathed bigotry in any form, having borne the brunt of much of it as an Irish Catholic. To his older son, he passed along his convivial nature and drinking problem. He had the opposite effect on his younger son. Jack's example of squandering opportunities instilled in Dutch a steely determination and self-discipline that led to extraordinary success.

Ronald Reagan attributed his success to his wiry, auburn-haired mother, who had "a sense of optimism that ran as deep as the cosmos."[10] From Nelle, Reagan learned "the value of prayer" and "how to have dreams and believe that I could make them come true." In the 1960s, Reagan summed up Nelle's outlook on life in a note sent to Nancy Reagan: "God has a plan and it isn't for us to understand, only to know that He has His reasons and because He is all merciful and all loving we can depend on it that there is a purpose in whatever He does and it is for our own good. What you must understand without any question or doubt is that I believe this and trust Him and you must, too."[11]

For Nelle, faith wasn't something to talk about or do on

a Sunday morning; it was a way of life. She was lively and spunky, with a can-do attitude, and no one ever described her as "preachy." She was too much fun for that. "She simply served God by serving people."[12] Raised in an era when people's only source of entertainment was one another, she made weekly visits to hospitals to read to patients and play her banjo. With funds provided by her sons, she brought patients "food, candy, pens, and pencils." More important, she brought hope and encouragement. Nelle took hot meals to prisoners and gave them practical help. The Reagans took in newly released convicts, giving them a place to stay and help finding jobs. Nelle firmly believed that "no matter what a person had done, he should be given the chance to pick himself up again."[13]

When Moon's Bel Air home burned to the ground in a 1961 wildfire, with scarcely a moment's notice, the only belongings his wife thought to save were a box of silverware and Nelle's well-thumbed, held-together-by-tape Bible. When Ronald Reagan took the oath of office as president of the United States on January 20, 1981, his hand was on Nelle's Bible, opened to II Chronicles 7:14: "If my people, which are called by my name, shall humble themselves, and pray, and seek my face, and turn from their wicked ways; then will I hear from heaven, and will forgive their sin, and will heal their land." In the margin, Nelle had jotted, "A most wonderful verse for the healing of nations."[14] On his desk in the Oval Office, Ronald Reagan kept a small maroon leather plaque with his mother's mantra embossed in gold, "It CAN be done." Nelle's granddaughter Maureen Reagan recalled, "She had the gift of making you believe that you could change the world."[15]

At the time of her marriage, though, Nelle was an indifferent Protestant. By heritage, the Wilsons were Scots Presbyterian. While living on the farm, they attended a local Methodist Episcopal church. When Nelle married Jack in the Catholic Church, she was required to promise to raise their children as Roman Catholics. When her first son, John Neil Reagan, was born on September 16, 1908, she dutifully took him to be baptized. But by the time Ronald was born on February 6, 1911, something had changed. St. Mary's pastor, Father Du Four, came to see her about having Ronald baptized. She had no memory of any discussion, much less a promise, to raise the children as Roman Catholics. Jack backed her up.

Between the births of her boys, Nelle had developed a stronger sense of faith. In February 1910, four years after moving to Tampico, she joined the Disciples of Christ. The Disciples[16] believe Christians should be united as one big family. Founded as "a faith which is socially relevant and intellectually sound," the Disciples pride themselves on being open-minded, independent thinkers who believe in community and providing practical care to the needy. Where Jack Reagan failed, the Disciples stepped in and provided Dutch with a nurturing support system of role models, friends, and mentors.

In late 1913, as business in Tampico slowed and receipts ebbed, H. C. Pitney, Jack Reagan's employer, decided to sell his store and thereby triggered the wild roller-coaster ride through towns, jobs, and homes that defined Ronald Reagan's childhood. Over the next five years, the Reagans lived in five communities and the boys attended five separate schools.

Their first stop was Chicago, where Jack worked for The Fair Store, a twelve-story, discount department store—a forerunner of Kresge and Kmart—at the corner of State and Adams streets in the Loop. The family, used to the space and grass of rural life, moved to an apartment on the city's South Side. The experiment in urban living didn't last long. For the first time, but not the last, Jack was fired for drinking.

By May 1915, the family was on a train heading to Galesburg, Illinois. Thanks to family connections, Jack got a job as a shoe salesman at O. T. Johnson's Big Store, the "biggest, best and busiest store" in town. Galesburg, population twenty-four thousand, offered the Reagans a life right out of a Norman Rockwell painting. The Big Store sponsored employee picnics and costume parties. The town had a minor league baseball team, opera house, YMCA, and a good-size library. Everything was in walking distance: school for the boys, work for Jack, and church for Nelle.

With his mother's encouragement, Dutch learned to read before starting school—"One evening all the funny black marks on paper clicked into place."[17] His proud parents dragged neighbors over to witness their five-year old's first public performance. In Galesburg, Dutch completed first grade with a 95 percent overall average and 97 percent in reading.

Life in Galesburg sparked Dutch's "great naturalist" phase. Nearby there was an open field to explore. Tucked away in the wonderful, dusty attic there was a fascinating collection of birds' eggs and butterflies that inspired Dutch to set about gathering his own collection. The idyll in Galesburg lasted for less than four years. In 1918, Jack was again fired for drinking.

Their next stop was twenty miles to the southwest, Monmouth, Illinois, a pocket edition of Galesburg. There, Dutch skipped a grade in school and caught a glimpse of college life. Monmouth College was down the street. In Monmouth, Jack developed a taste for dealing with luxury goods while working at high-end department store E. B. Colwell. And Nelle almost died.

They'd arrived in Monmouth as the second wave of the 1918 flu epidemic erupted in Boston and raced across the country. In October alone, 195,000 Americans died of the virus. Young women of childbearing age were particularly hard hit; one was Nelle Reagan. Dutch's abiding memory of their stay in Monmouth was the QUARANTINE signs hanging from doorways. For days Nelle hovered close to death. Then, unexpectedly, she survived. She was certain she had been saved to spread the gospel—love God and love one another.

That spring, Jack's former employer H. C. Pitney bought back his old business in Tampico and contacted Jack with the offer of a raise and an expanded role as buyer and manager of the shoe department. The Reagans had made a complete circle. They were back to where Jack and Nelle had started out, in an apartment on Main Street in Tampico. The *Tornado* heralded their return: "Mr. Reagan and family formerly resided in Tampico and have many friends who will welcome them back."

Jack's career seemed poised for growth. He was traveling on business, attending conventions, and building a network of industry contacts. He now billed himself as a graduate of Dr. Scholl's school of "Practipedics." He was earning a dollar a day at Pitney's. The Reagans' apartment cost ten dollars a month and they had close to one hundred dollars in savings in the bank. Nelle clerked at Pitney's, taught Sunday school, and helped the needy. In May 1920, Dutch made his stage debut at a church event reciting a poem, "About Mother." In June, he was back with another poem, "The Sad Dollar and the Glad Dollar."

During the summer of 1920, nine-year-old Dutch learned to swim and a new industry—radio—was emerging. Both had far-reaching consequences for Ronald Reagan. That summer, Tampico businessmen taught Dutch how to swim in the recently completed Hennepin Canal. The canal's shallow waters had proven unexpectedly treacherous, especially for young children. When a distant, unseen lock was opened up to let a barge through, the normally placid water suddenly switched to raging. After a couple of small children drowned, local fathers banded together to teach youngsters how to protect themselves against the turbulence.

Swimming gave Dutch his first taste of athletic success. He hadn't realized yet that he had terrible eyesight. Team sports were difficult for him, because he couldn't see the ball coming toward him. He was always the last picked for any team. Swimming, though, took advantage of his innate persistence. He worked at it and got better, stronger, and fitter. As a teenager he set a record in a timed race across Dixon's Rock River that stood for years.

Meanwhile, six hundred miles away, a new industry was flickering into existence in a shack on the roof of an industrial building in East Pittsburgh. A 1912 barroom bet on the accuracy of his watch prompted self-taught inventor and Westinghouse engineer Frank Conrad to build a radio capable of receiving time signals from the Naval Observatory in Washington, D.C. Conrad won the bet, kept tinkering and, in the summer of 1916, started playing records on Saturday nights from his garage. His "regularly scheduled" broadcasts were picked up by fellow experimenters twirling their dials along the spectrum of radio waves. Conrad's broadcasts sparked a demand for radio receivers in the Pittsburgh area.

Ironically, at the time, Westinghouse researchers were wrestling with how to keep "radio phone calls" private. Glancing at a newspaper one day, Conrad's boss, H. P. Davis, noticed an ad for ten-dollar "receiving sets." In a flash of inspiration, he saw that the opportunity lay in the opposite direction from the company's research efforts. Future profits would come from making access to radio broadcasts widely available, not in trying to contain them. Westinghouse was soon in the business of manufacturing radios.

The next challenge was to create a demand—a market—for their invention. They hit on the strategy of making a splashy debut on election night 1920, broadcasting the voting results of the contest between Republicans Warren G. Harding and Calvin Coolidge and Democrats James M. Cox and Franklin D. Roosevelt. Throughout the summer and early fall, Davis and his team worked feverishly to get licensed and up and running. With less than a week to go, they made it. Using a system designed for ships and maritime shore stations, America's first radio station got its call letters, KDKA. On election night, November 2, 1920, radio moved "out of the back pages into the front headlines."[18] KDKA Pittsburgh made its inaugural broadcast and entered history as the "first regularly scheduled, nonexperimental outlet." Dutch was enthralled by the new technology. He long remembered the excitement of huddling in a room with a dozen others, listening to the station's primitive broadcast attempts with "breathless attention."

Discovering Talents—Dixon, Illinois

A sale at Pitney's in early 1920 was a warning sign that all was not well with the business. By September, after a little more than a year back in business, Pitney announced he was closing up in Tampico and moving to Dixon, thirty miles northeast, population eight thousand. In short order he leased space in Dixon and named Mr. J. E. Reagan manager of a new store selling "high grade foot wear." It was the fifth shoe store in town. There seems to have been an unwritten agreement that eventually Jack Reagan would become a partial owner of Pitney's business with future profits that sadly never materialized. The community's booming wartime economy had stalled and farm bankruptcies were skyrocketing. Their timing could hardly have been worse.

For Dutch, the move meant yet another new school. In his autobiography, he wrote that the many moves left "a mark," and by the time they settled into a house on South Hennepin Avenue he "was a little introverted and probably a little slow in making really close friends."[19] In Dixon, though, he finally found some stability. "All of us have to have a place we go back to; Dixon is that place for me."[20] Over the next sixteen years, the Reagans moved four times within Dixon: to a busier street; to a smaller house; to a second-floor apartment where Jack and Nelle, at one point, squeezed themselves into one room and took in a boarder; and finally to a small apartment above a shoe store.

But in December 1920, they were back to living on a wide street shaded by tall trees with broad lawns for pick-up football games. The house, close to the top of a hill, was a few blocks from the grammar school where Dutch attended fifth and sixth grades and Dixon's Public Library, where Nelle took her boys to register for library cards a few weeks after moving in. Jack had an easy commute to the Fashion Boot Shop, and Nelle threw herself into church activities. Ronald Reagan recalled, "It was a good life. I never have asked for anything more, then or now." When his parents announced in early 1923 they were moving to Dixon's more fashionable North Side, Moon dug in his heels and refused to change schools.

The cloud hanging over the family was Jack's drinking. A year after moving to Dixon, Dutch was forced to deal directly with his father's alcoholism for the first time. Trudging home through the snow from the Dixon Y in the dusk, he nearly tripped over his father passed out on the front porch of their home "drunk, dead to the world. I stood over him for a minute or two. I wanted to let myself in the house and go to bed and pretend he wasn't there." Up to then, Nelle or Moon had dealt with Jack's drinking problem, but on that cold, wintry evening, it was up to a fifth-grader. Reagan later wrote: "Someplace along the line to each of us, I suppose, must come that first moment of accepting responsibility. If we don't accept it (and some don't), then we must just grow older without quite growing up."[21] It was a life-defining moment for Dutch, who proceeded to set himself consciously on a path to success.

He was becoming increasingly aware of the loud arguments between his parents, his father's bewildering disappearances, and his mother's abrupt decisions to take her sons to visit relatives. Once his eyes were opened to his father's problem, Dutch turned to books for help in figuring out who he wanted to be. He found his first role model in Gilbert Patten's wildly successful Frank Merriwell series.

Published as "dime novels," the Merriwell books flew off the shelves, selling at the rate of 135,000 copies a week. The hero's name, according to Patten, hints at his sterling qualities—frank, merry, and abounding with good health. Dutch gobbled up the stories about the Yale undergrad who attends classes, solves mysteries, and rights wrongs while racking up triumphs in football, baseball, basketball, track, and crew. Patten once joked that Merriwell "had little in common with his creator or his readers." In the case of Dutch Reagan, it wasn't for lack of trying. Handicapped by his poor eyesight (his vision was 20/200) and short of height and heft at five feet three inches and 108 pounds, Dutch was an unlikely candidate for athletic prowess. Yet, he persisted. In his 1990 autobiography, *An American Life,* he wrote: "I began to dream of myself on a college campus, wearing a college jersey, even as a star on the football team. My childhood dream was to become like those guys in the books."[22]

A few months after finding his father passed out on the porch, Dutch picked up a book his mother was reading, *That Printer of Udell's,* by a one-time Disciples of Christ minister, Harold Bell Wright.[23] The 1902 book was an enormous best seller. Wright was more than the first author to sell more than a million copies of a book and earn more than a million dollars from writing. *That Printer of Udell's* left Dutch with "an abiding belief in the triumph of good over evil."

The story was a largely autobiographical. When Wright was eleven, his mother died, leaving her three sons, the youngest of whom was two, at the mercy of their alcoholic father, who scattered his sons among reluctant caretakers and took off, seemingly without a care. Harold, the middle child, was put to work for a farmer "like an unwanted puppy." As a teenager, Wright lived with strangers, in saloons, in a brothel (with his father), plowed fields, tended sheep, slept in haystacks, and one night, in a pounding gale, under a hedge. In the fictionalized, streamlined version of his story, near starvation, scorned as a bum, he fell into the hands of a good-hearted printer who gave him a job and a life. Wright changed one letter to come up with his fictional occupation: in real life, as a youth, he'd worked on a construction crew as a painter.

In a key scene, the once dirty tramp who had "gone from door to door seeking a chance to earn a crust of bread" is now an admired citizen, a "tall, well-built figure, neatly clothed in a business suit of brown." As he walks onstage to speak in favor of establishing a young people's aid society, the audience bursts "into involuntary applause" at the sight of him. In the book's final scene, the printer, recently elected to Congress, is about to set off for Washington with his beautiful wife.

In *That Printer of Udell's,* Wright railed against organized religion and churchgoers for "pretending to be what they are not." He wrote that the church "was not touching the great problems of life; and that, while men were dying for want of spiritual bread, she was offering them only the stones of ecclesiastical pride and denominational egotism."

A few days after finishing the book, Dutch asked to be baptized. In June 1922, he and Neil, with twenty-three others, were baptized by Disciples minister Reverend David Franklin Seyster, filling in on short notice between the sudden death of Reverend Harvey Garland Waggoner and the appointment of Reverend Benjamin Cleaver. Waggoner and Cleaver were important influences on Dutch and he long remembered Seyster's words at his baptism, paraphrasing Romans 6:4: "Arise, and walk in the newness of faith."

For Dutch, navigating a lonely path through life, Dixon's faith-based organizations provided tremendous support. His church, the YMCA, a youth group called Christian Endeavor, and summer Chautauquas opened up opportunities for him to grow physically, spiritually, intellectually, and socially. After-school activities gave him a way to make friends, meet real-life role models, and start developing his strengths and testing his talents. He started to evolve into the person that he wanted to be. As he put it, "It was in Dixon that I really found myself."[24]

At the Y, Dutch joined the band, improved his swimming, got certified as a lifeguard, and participated in the Boys Hi-Y, whose motto was "Clean Speech, Clean Sports, Clean Living, and Clean Scholarship." Christian Endeavor's motto was "love and service." The organization was created to provide a network of mutual support for teenagers. Alcoholics Anonymous was modeled on CE. AA founder Bill Wilson's parents were early members. In 1928, CE provided seventeen-year-old Ronald

Reagan with a pivotal moment in his career when he was chosen to act as master of ceremonies at a CE conference in Moline, Illinois. The experience reinforced his sense that he had a flair for public speaking.

At church, Dutch met his closest friend and first love, Margaret (Mugs) Cleaver, his pastor's youngest daughter. Though they attended different high schools—the Cleavers lived on Dixon's South Side and the Reagans on the North—Dutch and Mugs got to know each other as costars in plays sponsored by the church and in the schools' joint drama club. In their senior year, they worked on the combined yearbook and served in leadership positions—Dutch as student body president, Mugs as president of her class and member of the student council.

In Reverend Waggoner's son, Garland, Dutch found a living blueprint—a real-life Frank Merriwell. Garland was active at the Y and at his father's church, where he taught Sunday school and occasionally preached a sermon. More important, in Dutch's eyes, Garland was a star football player at Dixon High and later in college at Eureka. Dutch's admiration was boundless; he once commented, "I'm a sucker for hero worship."[25] He followed in Garland's footsteps, teaching Bible lessons to younger children and leading church services. When Garland went off to Eureka College in the fall of 1922, Dutch's path was laid out for him. The only question was how to finance it.

Life for a kid in 1920s, Dixon was a predictable circuit of home, school, and after-school activities, but every summer, a festival blew into town and provided a glimpse into a bigger and broader world. Known as Chautauquas, the programs brought rural communities world-class speakers such as Mark Twain,

Will Rogers, Admiral Richard Byrd speaking on his "Antarctic Adventures," and the pre-eminent Chautauqua speaker, William Jennings Bryan. Nelle, egged on by Reverend Cleaver, was at the center of planning and organizing the programs. Set on the edge of the river to catch the flowing breezes, the Rock River Assembly theater-in-the-round, built especially for the Chautauquas, held five thousand and had room for six hundred on stage.

Jack and Nelle had their differences, but in one area they were in complete agreement: They loved performing. They had wonderful voices: Jack's singing voice was even better than Nelle's "melodic" speaking voice. Dramatics was Nelle's "first love."[26] Dutch described her as "the dean of dramatic recitals for the countryside."[27] In Tampico, Jack and Nelle starred in plays and founded a drama club. At a World War I fund-raiser in Galesburg, Jack astonished his boys by appearing onstage as a snake charmer in a wig and hula skirt.

Moon appeared to be the Reagan headed for the stage. Year after year, he starred in the Knights of Columbus's three-night fund-raiser. Always outspoken and brimming with confidence, in his seventies, he couldn't help laughing as he bragged, "I was always one of the leads. I was a song and dance man."[28]

Awed by Moon's talent, Dutch hesitated about appearing on stage. Buoyed by encouragement from Nelle, he made his Dixon debut. He couldn't recall what he had said, but he long remembered the audience's reaction, "People laughed and applauded. That was a new experience for me and I liked it. I liked that approval. For a kid suffering childhood pangs of insecurity, the applause was music. I didn't know it then, but, in a way, when I walked off the stage that night, my life had changed."[29] His aunt was so impressed that she commented to Nelle, "If he was mine, I'd take him to Hollywood if I had to walk all the way."[30]

Teaching Bible classes to young children gave Dutch a low-risk way of getting experience in front of an audience. He brought Bible verses to life by transforming the ancient parables to 1920s Dixon. He got so good at it that he was asked to lead the classes for adults when Reverend Cleaver was traveling. He got more experience and developed confidence by helping his mother entertain hospital patients. Their program was such a success that it was added to the hospital's monthly schedule.[31]

The year Dutch was a sophomore at North Dixon High School, Bernard J. Fraser joined the faculty as an English teacher and drama coach. He set about teaching his students "method" acting, "forcing them to actually 'become' the character."[32] Fraser built a theater program around Dutch's talent. Fraser encouraged his star to dig in and explore what his character was feeling and why he felt that way. In those days, Fraser remembered, Dutch was "forever asking questions." He was already self-confident and in command onstage. Dutch's dedication made an impression on his mentor and the two became lifelong friends.

Dixon had transformed Dutch from a timid little kid into a self-possessed young man. Prodded by his searching for a more promising father figure than Jack, Dutch developed a knack for attracting mentors and surrounding himself with people who encouraged and helped him be his best. It was one of his first talents to emerge and blossom. At church, at school, and in after-school activities, he nurtured his ability to be at ease in front of audiences. Sometimes consciously and sometimes just by doing what came naturally, he worked at honing his gift.

Developing Strengths—Eureka College, Eureka, Illinois

In the fall of 1928, Mugs Cleaver, following in her father and sisters' footsteps, headed off to Eureka College. Dutch went along for the ride. For him, Eureka had taken on a golden glow ever since his hero Garland Waggoner had achieved gridiron greatness there. In a tranquil, timeless town, one hundred miles south of Dixon, the school's redbrick buildings sit on a knoll flanked by trees. For Dutch, it was love at first sight. No longer shy or insecure, he jumped at the chance to live his dream of emulating Frank Merriwell and Garland Waggoner.

Exploring the campus, Dutch saw a college education could provide an escape from the dull rut that otherwise lay ahead. With some savings in the bank and a big dose of the charm and persuasiveness he'd inherited from Jack, he seized the opportunity to introduce himself to Eureka's president, Bert Wilson, and the school's football coach, Ralph McKinzie. He made the case that he'd be a great asset to the school as a football player and swimmer. His power of persuasion must have been impressive. He greatly overestimated his football ability, and the school didn't even have a swimming team—but, in short order, Wilson and McKinzie arranged a scholarship to cover half his expenses and got him a job waiting tables and washing dishes in the girls' dorm. Reagan later joked it was the best job he ever had.

Looking back, Reagan said, "One of the first things I found out about my particular college was that because of its size, we assumed a lot of assignments. Most of the time, we took a whole host of leadership roles simply because there was no one else to do it. It was my first taste of stepping forward and assuming responsibility for more than my own life, and I never forgot it. Sometimes, when I think of how little I knew about life, contrasted with how much responsibility I took on at Eureka, it makes me smile. But the college never let me do less than my best."[33] Twenty-five years after graduating, he gave the commencement address and exhorted students to "savor these moments. Keep the memories close to your heart." At Eureka he found a supportive environment that encouraged him to develop his strengths.

Years later, after visiting many top universities, Reagan wrote, "If I had to do it over again, I'd go back to Eureka or another small college like it in a second."[34] He credited Eureka with teaching him how to get things done—a lesson that stayed with him. At a small school everyone has to chip in, "There's a job for everyone, and everybody gets a chance to shine at something and build their sense of self-confidence."[35] He started and coached a swim team, won varsity letters in football, swimming, and track, won a drama contest, and, three months into his first semester, made a name for himself by leading a strike against Eureka's administration.

Founded by the Disciples of Christ in 1855, Eureka from its beginnings recruited minority students, championed social justice, and was at the forefront of campaigning for women's rights. Dutch, intending to major in economics, rapidly bonded with the college's only, and recently appointed, economics professor, A. C. Gray. Nicknamed "Daddy" Gray, he was an ordained minister and "pretty far to the left."[36] In keeping with the Disciples' philosophy of being open-minded, Gray invited one-time minister and future Socialist Party presidential candidate Norman Thomas to speak on campus. Eight hundred people showed up for the lecture. But in the classroom, Gray taught from the textbook of influential conservative Lewis Haney, who taught economics at New York University and wrote a syndicated column. "Daddy" Gray was the force behind Dutch's rise to stardom.

Perpetually underfunded, like many church schools, Eureka teetered on the edge of financial disaster. Just before Thanksgiving, the already unpopular school president, after meeting with the trustees, announced impending program cuts without consulting the faculty or explaining the situation to the students. Wilson's failure to reach out and gain the agreement of the larger community was a leadership and communication lesson that Dutch never forgot. The uproar was immediate.

Dutch, "encouraged and coached by 'Daddy' Gray whose job was at risk,"[37] was at the center of the furor. The entire student body rallied in the auditorium. As a freshman with, the thinking went, less to lose than juniors and seniors, Dutch was pushed forward as the students' spokesman. He took the stage, laid out the issues, called for a strike, and in an unforgettable moment, learned what it was like to be one with an audience. The room rocked. That night in the small world of Eureka

Ronald Reagan became a star. The peaceful but determined strike made newspaper headlines around the country. On November 29, 1928, the *New York Times* reported "Students Strike At Eureka College." The freshman waiter and dishwasher on scholarship was transformed into a Big Man on Campus.

That success, however, didn't transfer to the football field, where he spent his freshman season with his seat glued to the bench. The coach assessed him as too small, almost blind without his glasses, and with an unduly high opinion of his football talents. Dutch was so disappointed he almost didn't return. He got to play his second year, but by then Moon had followed him to Eureka and trumped him on the football field. Moon, star of an undefeated high school team, made a flashy winning play in a key game, just the sort of play Dutch daydreamed about in his fantasies of Frank Merriwell and Notre Dame star George Gipp. Moon, on the other hand, had had enough of football. He never bothered to go out for the sport again.

In academic circles there is a saying about students' career paths after graduation: "A's teach and B's work for C's."[38] At Eureka, Dutch applied himself to extracurricular activities—student government, newspaper, swimming, basketball, football, debating, dramatics, and president of the Boosters Club. He graduated with a C average. His efforts were focused on outside interests, and in those he excelled. In his senior year, he was elected president of the Student Senate, but his biggest achievement came in his junior year, when he won an "Oscar" in an acting contest sponsored by Northwestern University's Drama Department.

Under the guidance of a gifted coach, Miss Ellen Marie Johnson, for the first time Eureka's drama society entered the competition against seasoned teams such as Princeton's Triangle Club and the Yale Playhouse. In homemade costumes run up by coeds, Eureka scored an unlikely triumph, coming in second. In shock from the victory, Dutch was even more surprised to hear his own name called. For his role as a Greek shepherd boy who was strangled to death, he won the equivalent of a Best Actor award. He quipped, "Dying is the way to live in the theater."[39] Before Dutch headed back to Eureka, the head of Northwestern's Drama Department called him aside to ask if he'd given any thought to a stage career. Up to that moment he hadn't. The brief but gratifying conversation lingered in his mind and, in time, served as a spark.

The most valuable lesson he took away from his years at college was clarity about who he wanted to be. As he saw it, college was an investment that paid dividends for a lifetime. At Eureka he learned, matured, and developed the core strengths that he used for the next seventy years: a passion for fitness and sports, a deep and abiding faith, a fascination with economics, an interest in connecting with people as an entertainer, and an unshakeable conviction in the goodness of his fellow citizens. Before embarking on the unnerving project of finding a job, he spent one last summer as a lifeguard at Dixon's Lowell Park.

Lowell Park, on the bank of the Rock River, was an idyllic spot for a young man to spend summers. Bluebells and ferns frame the entrance; wildflowers grow under the shade of oaks and hemlocks. Trails for horseback riding, bicycling, and hiking weave through the park's 205 acres.

The job took advantage of his strong sense of responsibility and his ability to focus. Lowell Park gave him a way to meet successful executives and provided him with the achievement he was most proud of for the rest of his life: seventy-seven lives saved over the course of his seven years at the park, many recorded on the front page of the *Dixon Telegraph*. His father suggested he keep track of his saves by carving a notch in a log each time he rescued someone.

Watching people all day long, he became a student of human nature. An early sign of his aptitude for communicating was an article, "Meditations of a Lifeguard," that he wrote for his high school yearbook. "The lifeguard strolls by, turns and strolls by again. . . . He assumes a manly worried expression, designed to touch the heart of any blonde, brunette, or unclassified female. He has done all that is necessary. She speaks and the sound of her voice is like balm to a wounded soul." He approached his job with more wisdom than might be expected in a teenager. Employer Ruth Graybill said, "He always knew his duties and he did them well."[40]

During those summers from 1926 to 1932, Dutch added to his income by renting out a canoe and teaching young children to swim. Through the little swimmers, he got to know their grateful parents, a number of whom suggested he come see them about jobs when he finished college. But by the time he graduated from Eureka those job offers had dried up and the once-helpful executives had vanished—except for one, Sid Altschuler, an astute businessman from Kansas City, Missouri, who in that gloomy summer of 1932 offered Ronald Reagan the best advice he ever got.

REAGAN ON REAGAN

Some people called me the best football player on the worst team Dixon ever had.

—Speaking to Dixon high school students,
Dixon Telegraph, June 6, 1947

Our family didn't exactly come from the wrong side of the tracks, but we were certainly always within sound of the train whistles.

—*Where's the Rest of Me?*

I like to pay attention to one thing at a time.

—*Where's the Rest of Me?*

DISCOVERING YOUR TALENTS, DEVELOPING YOUR STRENGTHS

A man's life is what his thoughts make of it.

—Marcus Aurelius

- Make an investment in yourself by taking time to identify your core values and inner strengths. Consider what is most important to you.
- Seek out role models for yourself in literature, history, and life. Identify the attributes that you admire.
- Look for opportunities to try out your interests and strengths in nonthreatening, low-risk situations. Be prepared to practice, rehearse, fail, and try again. Sometimes you learn the most from failure.
- Rise to challenges. Take advantage of opportunities to take on new responsibilities and move out of your comfort zone.
- Develop a can-do attitude and believe in your dreams. Test your ability to achieve a goal by starting with a small project with a short time frame. Take baby steps.

Working It In

Define you. Describe yourself briefly.

____

____

____

____

____

Reflecting on your successes and accomplishments to date, what have you most enjoyed?

List your five greatest strengths and interests.

List the five personal skills you most enjoy using.

How can you put these interests and talents to use in building a career?

Chapter **2**

Finding Mentors, Setting Goals

Radio Career—Davenport and Des Moines, Iowa, 1933–37

> Those were wonderful days. I was one of a profession just becoming popular and common—the visualizer for the armchair quarterback.
>
> —Ronald Reagan, *Where's the Rest of Me?*

Choosing a Career Path

Friendly and outgoing, Reagan's mentor Sid Altschuler enjoyed horseback riding and polo. His wife was from Dixon, so every summer the Altschulers returned to be near her family. Helen and the children stayed at Lowell Park's lodge, Sid commuted back and forth for long weekends and came out for one extended stay. Dutch got to know the family while teaching the Altschuler daughters to swim. In the summer of 1932, the nation's unemployment rate stood at 24 percent, the Dow Jones Industrial Average bottomed out at 41.22, but the cheerful, business-minded Altschuler assured Dutch the economic downturn wouldn't last forever.

In a series of conversations that summer Altschuler laid out a road map for how Dutch should approach getting started on a career. Dutch followed his mentor's advice to the letter and Sid's suggestions proved farsighted and practical. The starting point was a difficult question. Altschuler urged the young man to look beyond the pressing concern of finding a job and to focus on a more important consideration: *"What do you think you'd like to do?"*

That was the problem; Dutch didn't know what he wanted to do.

Unlocking a Dream, Setting a Goal

The answer required a great deal of thought and soul-searching. It was tempting to take the easy way out and ask what's available, who's hiring, where do you have contacts? But Reagan had too much respect for Altschuler for that. Instead he spent "several days and sleepless nights" grappling with how he wanted to spend his working life. That August, as the leaves began to turn and cooler breezes blew in from the north, Dutch knew Altschuler would soon be heading back to Kansas City. Dutch wanted Sid's reaction, thoughts, and opinions before he disappeared, so he was forced to hunker down, think through his options, and make up his mind. Recognizing he was making choices that would affect the bulk of his waking hours, he didn't take the matter lightly, but within a matter of days, he came to a decision.

He pondered his experiences and successes. He knew what he enjoyed most: football and being in front of an audience—whether it was teaching Bible classes, entertaining patients, or appearing onstage. Those were the interests that came naturally to him. The things he liked to do whether he got paid or not. The challenge was how to combine those interests and leverage them into a career. His mind roamed over how thrilled he had been to win the "Oscar" at Northwestern. He thought about his flair for "patter" as he scooped ice-cream cones at Lowell Park and entertained frat brothers at Eureka. Any time he could scrounge up an audience, he'd use a broomstick as a microphone and broadcast "an imaginary football game between two imaginary teams."[1] His favorite was a Northwestern–Notre Dame game. For Dutch, nothing was more fun than launching into a "rapid-fire routine of 'Here they come out of the huddle up to the line of scrimmage . . . the ball is snapped!' "[2] Using words and imagination, he brought the games to life. His audience took sides, rooting and cheering for the teams. As Dutch considered Altschuler's question about what he would like to do and what he was good at, his goal came into focus: He zeroed in on entertainment and sports.

His dilemma was how to merge the two interests. What form would that take? Hollywood and Broadway appeared to be "as inaccessible as outer space."[3] There was a possibility, though, closer to home, a first step on the path to his long-term goal of becoming a Hollywood movie star. He decided his first job would serve as a means to an end. Chicago was a center of the radio industry and home to a number of trailblazers in sportscasting—Hal Totten, Pat Flanagan, and Quin Ryan, who loomed in Reagan's mind as legends "as famous as the great teams and athletes they described."

Mentors, Heroes, and Role Models

In May 1923—the year Dutch was eleven—a trained concert singer named Graham McNamee had jury duty in lower Manhattan. Wandering around the neighborhood at lunchtime, he noticed AT&T's new headquarters at 195 Broadway. He later said it was a whim that prompted him to go in, walk through the imposing lobby, and take the elevator to the fourth-floor office of the company's radio station WEAF.[4] He inquired about a position and took a voice test. By the time he headed back to the courthouse, he had a new job. He'd just been hired as America's first sportscaster.

Over the next year McNamee racked up a string of firsts for the fledgling industry. He broadcast a championship fight, the World Series, college football games, and President Coolidge's message to Congress. As a pioneer, he made plenty of mistakes. He readily admitted he wasn't an expert on sports and sometimes fell short on fine points and details. Despite the occasional gaffe—such as announcing the wrong winner of a regatta—he proved wildly popular.

Rival stations rapidly added sportscasters to their rosters. Scrambling to build their own audiences, McNamee's competitors set him up for embarrassment whenever they could. To their dismay, instead of cringing, he laughed. America loved him. Listeners warmed to his direct, honest style and hearty laugh. Sports-loving boys around the country were entranced by his pulse-pounding descriptions of games and events. In Dixon, Illinois, a young sports fan named Dutch Reagan was listening closely and learning.

During his years playing football in Dixon, Reagan was asked once to help broadcast a game.[5] He liked it. In seeking to combine his passion for sports with an inherent flair for expressing himself, he hit on a career he had a talent for and thoroughly enjoyed. Fresh out of college, he didn't have much experience as a broadcaster, but what he did have turned out to be enough, first to have another conversation with Altschuler about his future, then to set off in search of a job as a sportscaster.

Altschuler heard out Dutch's idea of pursuing a career in radio. He didn't have any contacts to introduce him to; what he did have to offer was advice. He approved of the choice of a "sound industry" with lots of potential and opportunities. In a few short years, listening to radio had become a habit across America. Two years after KDKA started broadcasting, a *Chicago Tribune* study found there were already one hundred thousand "radio receiving sets in Chicago." That year $350 million was spent on radios, tubes, and related hardware—a figure that doubled over the next five years. In 1926, car manufacturers started adding radios as standard equipment in automobiles, further expanding the industry. The radio business was booming. Altschuler told Dutch to start "knocking on doors, tell anyone who'll listen that you believe you have a future in the business" and take any job—"sweeping floors"—just to get a foot in the door.

Even with Altschuler's encouragement and advice, going after a job in radio seemed like a pipe dream. Nelle and Jack were supportive, but Mugs, for one, was a naysayer. Seeking a job in radio, in her opinion, with his limited experience, was an impossible quest. So when Jack arrived home for supper one night with the news of an opening for a manager in the sports department at the local Montgomery Ward, Dutch was off in a flash to apply for the job. He lined up with dozens of other applicants. The choice quickly narrowed to him and one other job seeker. The other guy got the job.

Frustrated at the near miss but filled with renewed determination, he decided—the next day—to accompany Moon, who was starting his senior year, back to Eureka. From there he would hitchhike to Chicago in search of a job, a career, and a life. The stop in Eureka would give him a chance to spend time with Mugs and the Cleavers and visit college friends and mentors. This trip turned out to be the first in a lifelong pattern. At the beginning of any major initiative or whenever he felt the need to recharge his career, he energized himself by going back to the places that meant the most to him as a youth—Dixon and Eureka. The communities provided him with a bottomless well of support.

Leaving Eureka, he headed out to the highway, got lucky, and caught a ride that took him all the way to Chicago, 150 miles away. For a week, he looked for a job during the day, slept on a frat brother's sofa at night, and set his sights high. Taking a leaf from Graham McNamee's book and following Altschuler's advice to the letter, he started knocking on doors. Monday morning he headed straight to the NBC affiliate WMAQ where Judith Waller, a bigwig in the world of Chicago radio, was the station's program manager and boss. In 1925, the enterprising Waller sold Philip Wrigley on the idea of broadcasting the Cubs' home games. Then she coaxed sportswriter Hal Totten from the *Chicago Daily News* into joining WMAQ as a sports announcer. That fall, the station chalked up an industry first with regularly scheduled broadcasts of college football games. Working at WMAQ was Dutch's dream job.

Presenting himself to the receptionist at WMAQ's new office in the Merchandise Mart, Reagan was told the program manager only met with job applicants on Thursday. Dutch left knowing more than when he'd walked in: At future stops, he would ask to see the program manager. With the optimism and naïveté of youth, he interpreted the receptionist's comment to mean he now had an official job interview scheduled for Thursday.

The Chicago transit system was a mystery to him, and being long on energy and short on funds, he walked everywhere. He tramped over to the Wrigley Building to try his luck at the CBS affiliate, WBBM. Mere mortals sat in stadiums and called games, but WBBM's Pat Flanagan, with a beguiling brogue, re-created baseball games based solely on the sketchy information passed to him by a telegraph operator. The studio engineer kept recordings of ballpark music and crowd noise on hand and used props to replicate the crack of a bat and thud of a baseball slamming into a mitt. Flanagan translated a ticker-tape report of a "home run" into "It's going. It's goinnnnng! It's GONE!" At WBBM, Dutch met with a disheartening lack of interest.

His next stop was WGN, home to another childhood hero. One-time sports announcer Quin Ryan now reigned as station manager at the *Chicago Tribune*'s radio station. WGN stood for "World's Greatest Newspaper." Ryan's "Gee Whiz" style was a hit with adults and children. Brushed off at WGN, Reagan got out the phone book to look for smaller stations, farther afield.

He was tired and discouraged, but the thought of his "interview" at WMAQ cheered him up. When he showed up at the station's office Thursday morning, a young woman, in his words, "an angel," took mercy on him. She patiently listened to his tale of winning the Northwestern drama contest and even asked a few questions. At a time when he desperately needed it, she offered him encouragement. She told him he had "every right to try for a place in radio" and, in a brief but life-changing conversation, she laid out the hard facts and set him on a path to achieving success. He was going about it all wrong, she explained. "No one in the city wants to take a chance on inexperience." She told him he'd stand a better chance of finding a job at a smaller station in "the sticks."

Hitchhiking back to Dixon in the rain, he had plenty of time to think between short rides and long waits huddled on the side of the highway. Dutch probably thought he hadn't achieved much in Chicago, but the distinguishing quality that led to his success was that he listened carefully to advice and then put it into action. Arriving home in time for supper, he told his parents about the conversation with the woman at WMAQ and her suggestions. Jack heard him out and asked if there were any radio stations within a one-day drive of Dixon. Though the Reagans listened to the Chicago stations, Dutch knew there were a handful of stations scattered around Davenport, Iowa. Jack suggested he take the family's third-hand Oldsmobile in a last-ditch effort to see if he could find a job at one of those stations.

Monday morning, Dutch got up early and drove the seventy-five miles west to Davenport. He headed to WOC, a subsidiary of the first radio station licensed west of the Mississippi and NBC's first affiliate. In the early days when it was one of just a handful of stations in the country and radio frequencies were still largely uncluttered, the station had been heard as far away as Sweden, Samoa, and Chile. Dutch walked in, asked to see the program director, and had the good luck to be introduced to Peter MacArthur, a veteran of vaudeville and early radio. MacArthur had blue eyes that twinkled, a trace of his Scottish homeland in his rolling *rrrrr*'s, and a crippling case of rheumatoid arthritis. The two hit it off immediately.

As it happened, the station had been looking to add an announcer to the staff and, after auditioning ninety-four applicants in the past month, it had just hired someone the week before. "Where the hell have ye been?" Pete bellowed. Dutch thanked Pete for his time and headed for the door. Seething with frustration as he waited for the elevator, Reagan burst out, "How in hell does a guy ever get to be a sports announcer if he can't get inside a station?" Against all odds, MacArthur heard him, hobbled down the hallway, and caught him just as the elevator door opened.

Rapping Dutch on the shin with his cane, MacArthur demanded, "What was it you said about sports?" In short order, Dutch found himself sitting in a small room draped with heavy blue velvet curtains for soundproofing and given instructions to "tell me about a game and make me see it." Hours spent practicing with ice-cream cones and broomsticks were about to pay off. Rather than invent a game, Dutch used Eureka's fourth-quarter triumph over rival Western Illinois State University the year before as inspiration. The names and details were engraved in his mind. For twenty minutes, he talked into the microphone. He brought the game to life in vivid detail—the teams battled back and forth across the playing field in "the long blue shadows." He wrapped up his performance with the flourish of a much-experienced pro, "We return you now to our main studio." He was hired for "five dollars and bus fare" to broadcast four home football games for the University of Iowa. It was a start.

The following Saturday, Dutch was waiting at the bus stop in Dixon before the sun came up. Arriving in Davenport, he met up with Pete MacArthur, who had brought along two engineers and, as a warranty against disaster, an experienced announcer. In the intervening week MacArthur had had second thoughts about entrusting his business to a twenty-one-year-old amateur. The group piled into a car for the sixty-mile drive to Iowa City.

It would have been easy, almost irresistible, for Dutch to sulk and be irritated about the seasoned announcer's horning in on his big break—for a week he'd been telling everyone in Dixon to tune in to hear him—but he had too much emotional intelligence for that. He was worried his moment in the spotlight was going to be upstaged, but he managed to put a good face on it. The sights and sounds of a Big Ten football stadium were new to him and might have been overwhelming. He was a small-town boy who had graduated from college in a class of about forty. Eureka had a simple playing field with a few benches along the sidelines. At Iowa, he rose to the occasion and found the atmosphere of the fifty-thousand-seat stadium daunting but invigorating.

Soon he heard himself being introduced for the "play-by-play." With unexpected exhilaration, he was off and running. At the end of the first quarter, he turned the microphone back over to the staff announcer, as agreed to beforehand, to call the second quarter. As Dutch listened he felt his confidence surge. He could tell his partner had only a superficial understanding of Big Ten football. The microphone was handed back to Dutch for the third quarter, and there it stayed as Pete scrawled a big note saying, "Let the kid finish the game." The kid was "overjoyed." When the day ended, he was rewarded with a 100 percent raise to ten dollars for each of Iowa's three remaining home games plus the agreed-upon bus fare. His broadcasting career was off to a good start. Iowa won that day, their only win of the season.

Dutch had an inherent talent for painting a picture of the scene in front of him for the armchair quarterback listening attentively to his radio at home. He told listeners there was "a chill wind blowing through the end of the stadium" and routinely used his signature line, "the long blue shadows." At that first game in Iowa City, he started out by telling his audience he was "high atop Memorial Stadium, looking down from the west on the south forty-yard line." He called it his "teller who" technique. He described exactly where he was sitting in the stadium so listeners could picture the game through his eyes.

His colorful phrasing came straight out of the playbook of the "dean of American sportswriters," Grantland Rice. A syndicated columnist with the *New York Herald Tribune*, Rice had immortalized a 1924 Notre Dame–Army game played at New York's Polo Grounds with the oft-quoted words: "Outlined against a blue-gray October sky the Four Horsemen rode again.

In dramatic lore they are known as famine, pestilence, destruction, and death. These are only aliases. Their real names are: Stuhldreher, Miller, Crowley, and Layden."

Rice's prose was crafted to be inspiring and heroic. This was the Golden Age of Radio and the Golden Age of Sports. It was an era when 25 million Americans—close to 25 percent of the population—tuned in to hear Graham McNamee broadcast the 1927 heavyweight championship rematch between Gene Tunney and Jack Dempsey. The fevered excitement over the impending bout had even landed McNamee on the cover of *Time* magazine. When McNamee broadcast the 1925 World Series, he had been deluged with fifty thousand letters. Between Iowa home games, Reagan spent hours at the library reading up on the Hawkeyes and their Big Ten competitors—learning names, statistics, stories. His expertise was all, as he put it, "shamelessly stolen from sports columns in the Chicago papers."[6]

But there was no job offer at the end of the season. Dutch was back to living with his parents in a cramped second-floor apartment in Dixon and waiting for the phone to ring. It wasn't an easy time, but nearby there were outlets for his energy: the YMCA, library, and church were all within a few blocks. He regularly spent time with his mentor and surrogate father, Bernard Fraser, for advice and encouragement. Fraser counseled him to pursue his talent for communication.

Staying Focused on a Goal

Shortly before Christmas 1932, as Dutch's dream of a radio career started to fade, Pete MacArthur from WOC called to say hang in there. It was the reassurance Dutch needed to hold on for two more nail-biting months. Then in early February, Pete called with the news that one of the station's announcers was leaving. He offered Dutch the job at one hundred dollars a month. Reagan's response was, "I'll be there tomorrow." He packed his one suitcase and set off for Davenport.

A big dollop of eagerness and innate talent disguised the fact that he still had a lot to learn. His first month on the job was almost disastrous. Within a few weeks of starting, he was fired. He was called in and told he was going to lose his on-air job, but not until he trained his replacement. For Dutch, it was a stomach-wrenching blow. He tried to handle it gracefully but in reality it was "the end of the world."[7] The problem was that he didn't understand how to bring a commercial to life. Station advertisers were irate about his wooden performance and way-too-casual attitude toward the products he was supposed to be hawking. The phone lines at WOC lit up with calls for management about the lousy job he was doing.

Fortunately for Reagan, the person hired to replace him was under the impression that Dutch had been working there on a temporary basis. When the new guy casually inquired how long Dutch had been in the job, he was horrified to learn he had been hired and fired in a matter of weeks. The new hire demanded a contract, which the company had no intention of giving him. He rapidly headed back to his steady job and reliable paycheck as a teacher. While WOC's interview process ramped up again, Dutch got his job back. This time it stuck.

Supportive conversations with friends and some blistering coaching sessions with Pete helped Dutch improve his on-air delivery. Dutch knew he needed help and demanded it. It didn't take much and it didn't take long. By happy coincidence, sportscasting legend Pat Flanagan's brother worked for WOC's parent station in Des Moines. With baseball season fast approaching, Pete provided Dutch with an introduction to Pat. Dutch made a trip to WBBM in Chicago where the gracious Flanagan gave the rookie a crash course on how to bring a baseball game to life for listeners with only a handful of words to work with. Flanagan took the stripling sportscaster to Wrigley Field to see the press box. Dutch soaked in the sights and embedded the memory of the ballpark and its environs in his mind for future use in "teller-who" moments.

Bringing the words of a script to life on the radio, on a movie set, or in front of an audience requires effort, training, and experience. The trick for a radio announcer, actor, or public speaker is to speak scripted words as if they've just popped into mind and to group words to make the meaning clear to listeners. Dutch needed to add emphasis to his words. With coaching he learned the effect is achieved by prolonging vowels, adding force and inflection to words, and by pausing.

Pete taught Dutch how to mark up scripts to tell him where to breathe, which words to group, and which words to emphasize in a sentence so that read-from-the-page words took on the life of just-thought-of-this-moment words. Fifty years later, Reagan was using the same techniques, and still marking up his texts to bring life to his words for live audiences, on television, and on radio.

Under Pete's coaching, he was evolving into a professional performer. He didn't know it at the time, but he was developing the skills that would make him a highly desirable asset in the yet-to-be-born television industry. As a radio announcer he acted as master of ceremonies, introducing programs, reading commercials and brief news snippets, and interviewing celebrities who were passing through town. From there it was easy to step into the role of emcee at banquets and sporting events. His liberal arts education at Eureka came in handy as he bobbed and weaved through the never-ending flow of information on the radio. Announcers have to be quick on their feet. They are called on, with no notice, to ad-lib on a wide range of topics. In years to come, his fellow actors on Hollywood sets marveled at how Reagan could reel off baseball and football statistics and expound on growing seasons and the impact of the year's climate on crops. It was all in a day's work for a radio announcer from the Midwest.

As a sportscaster, Reagan had to learn the right level of excitement to convey to his audience. The idea was not to shout or holler but to come across as enthusiastic and energized. His life was an endless round of sports. In the off-seasons, there were banquets to attend. He kept up with Mugs Cleaver via letters but they rarely saw each other. Weekends and evenings were packed with athletic events, pregame and postgame interviews, and press conferences. Spare time was spent tracking the progress and standing of athletes and teams and reading the *Sporting News, Sports Illustrated,* and the *Daily Racing Form* and keeping up with local and national newspapers.

Grace Blazer, seasoned program manager at WTKK in Boston, describes radio as "very one on one" and a "medium of intimacy." While speaking to a wide variety of people, a broadcaster has to keep in mind he's been invited into someone's home or to be a companion in a car. The trick is to talk to, rather than at, the audience and make it sound conversational. Blazer says, "Sometimes you come in a little harder and sometimes a little softer." According to media expert Roger Ailes, a speaker has five seconds to catch the listener's attention. Talk show host Michael Graham says that laying out an argument is a skill in radio: The speaker starts with a proposition, shares the evidence, and draws a conclusion. Graham notes that Reagan would artfully lead his listeners to conclusions by saying, "Let me explain . . ."

By April 1933, thanks to Pete's mentoring and encouragement, the hired-fired-rehired employee was a rising star at the station. Strolling into Pete's office one day, Dutch heard him on the phone selling something to someone. The item being sold turned out to be him. With a quick glance over to Reagan to confirm, "You know something about track, right?" Pete had Dutch on his way to Des Moines to cover the Drake Relay Races, the most prestigious amateur track event in the country and, incidentally, to meet the station's owner, Bartlett J. Palmer. A few weeks later, Palmer decided to close up shop in Davenport and merge WOC with WHO. Within four months of getting hired full-time, unexpectedly Reagan was a radio announcer on a fifty-thousand-watt clear channel station,[8] one of only fifteen such stations in the country and NBC's key affiliate in the Midwest. His salary was doubled to two hundred dollars a month.

Pete MacArthur was added to Reagan's long list of mentors along with the Waggoners, Reverend Cleaver, Bernard Fraser, Ralph McKinzie, "Daddy" Gray, and Sid Altschuler.

Many more mentors were added in the years ahead. Some, like Garland Waggoner, were role models; some were mentors from afar—Graham McNamee, Hal Totten, and Grantland Rice—or, like the young woman at WMAQ, someone who flitted through his life like a comet. But many were people he kept in touch with all his life. In the early 1960s, Reagan traveled to Northern Illinois University to speak at the party for Ralph McKinzie's retirement from coaching. He kept up with sportscaster Pat Flanagan and had an ongoing, lifelong correspondence with the Cleavers. He valued and cultivated his friendships. People he hadn't seen in fifty years were astonished that he recognized them at events and called them by name.

Hearing that Bernard Fraser was ill and hospitalized in March 1979, Reagan, who was gearing up for his 1980 run for the presidency, took time to pen a thoughtful note to his longtime mentor. Reagan wrote he was "remembering the many talks you and I had. . . . I don't know whatever led me to this or made it possible; it certainly was nothing I could foresee back in those Dixon days. But one thing I do know, that all of the good things that have happened to me, one B. J. Fraser had a great deal to do with it. You played a very important part in my life, and I shall be forever grateful."[9] When the old man died, shortly after Reagan took office as president, Moon Reagan immediately tracked down his brother through the White House operators to let him know. That same week Garland Waggoner passed away. Reagan wrote notes to his widow and to his daughter, whom he had never met.

In Des Moines, Reagan's life expanded exponentially. He rapidly formed a circle of friends from Drake, a Disciples of

Christ college and sister school to Eureka. For a while he shared an apartment with one of Drake's assistant coaches. The group spent evenings drinking and singing together at a gathering spot called Si's Moonlight Inn. When Reagan moved to Los Angeles in June 1937, some of the Drake group moved along with him. In a letter to a Drake pal, he offered to provide support while he looked for a job in L.A. But the first person he had to take care of was his brother, Moon, who had just graduated from Eureka.

Moon finished college in 1933, a year after Dutch graduated. Not sure what to do next, he toyed with going to law school. His mother, fearing "disintegration could take place if he sat around Dixon, diploma in hand and unemployed,"[10] urged Dutch to help him out. Her timing was perfect. Dutch had just ordered a secondhand brown Nash convertible from an old friend in Dixon. Offering to finance gas and living expenses, he asked Moon to drive the car 250 miles west to Des Moines. Then he added, "Plan to spend two or three days out here and see the station and meet the guys at the station."[11]

Once Dutch got Moon to Des Moines, he got him started on a career by setting him up with Pete for an audition. That fall—a long way from the uncertainty of the year before—Dutch had a show on Friday nights predicting the outcomes of the next day's college football match-ups. One Friday night Moon was in the studio listening to his brother and shook his head as he heard Dutch's predictions. In short order, Dutch introduced Moon to listeners. From there the program evolved into a friendly battle as the two squabbled about which teams would triumph in the Saturday games. A pattern of interlocking careers and mutual support had been set, one that continued throughout their lives.

Despite starting at the same point, the brothers' careers diverged to take different paths. Moon switched from being on the air over to management; he became a program director at the station. In 1939, he followed Dutch to Los Angeles and took a job with CBS radio as a producer; from there he moved into advertising. Always genial, always ready with a quip—"I've got my picture on the Brown Derby wall and Ronald didn't!"[12] Moon signed on with McCann-Erickson, one of the largest ad agencies in the country, and went on to become head of the firm's Los Angeles office.

Their parallel careers put Moon in a good position to assess his brother's strengths. In the 1960s, he told an interviewer that his brother was "probably the best on the staff"[13] at WHO. Asked, from his perspective of years in advertising, "if there was a . . . single quality that Reagan showed in those days that was to make him successful in radio, films and later politics," Moon replied, "I would say in one word. It is what you strive for in directing any dramatic show—credibility. . . . If you have that, you don't have to worry about anything."[14]

Within months of starting out, by faithfully following the advice of Altschuler and the young "angel" in Chicago, Dutch was a star at one of the industry's largest stations or, as he put it, "a sports announcer in the solar plexus of the country."[15] His career had taken off. In the fall of 1933, he picked up some extra income by acting as field announcer for Drake's home football games and emceeing a horse show. Whenever he was asked to take on a new task, he never let a lack of confidence hold him back. His answer was always a wholehearted affirmative. Besieged by invitations to speak to civic organizations in the Des

Moines area, he worked up a speech that centered on sports stories and concluded with a strong Bible-based message. At the suggestion of a fellow WHO announcer, he joined a cavalry unit with the National Reserve primarily to take advantage of the horseback riding, an interest sparked during his days at Lowell Park, perhaps by his admiration for friend and mentor Sid Altschuler. Riding became his passion and kept him in top physical condition. He often quoted Lord Palmerston: "There is nothing so good for the inside of a man as the outside of a horse."

Working in a major radio station, lots of opportunities came his way, but he maintained his focus on his cherished long-term goal. When he interviewed celebrities, he pushed past the formal, on-the-air discussion to learn more about their lives. In Des Moines, he started wearing brown suits—a tribute to his role model from *That Printer of Udell's*. In August 1933, the *Dixon Telegraph* reported that Ronald Reagan was "fast gaining renown as a sports broadcaster." In May 1934, he got another raise, to three hundred dollars a month, and in August the *Des Moines Dispatch* wrote, "The voice of Ronald Reagan is a daily source of baseball dope."

In January 1935, he started writing a column, "Around the World of Sports with Dutch Reagan" for the *Dispatch*. The discipline of finding a story and writing it up for a newspaper column was valuable experience for the future speechwriter.[16] The wheels turning, he came up with the idea of traveling with the Cubs to cover spring training on Catalina Island. It was typical of Reagan to figure out that he couldn't take a vacation during the summer baseball season anyway and flip the situation into a positive. He approached management with the suggestion that if WHO would cover his travel expenses he would magnanimously toss in his vacation time. He pointed out how WHO would benefit: His inside knowledge of the team would pay dividends during the long baseball season. Management snapped up his offer and he got a paid vacation in the depths of the Iowa winter to southern California.

That spring he was hit by some bad news. First Mugs broke off their long-standing engagement. She sent him a note and enclosed the ring he'd given her back at Eureka. The truth was they hadn't seen much of each other since graduation, but ever since his sophomore year in high school, Dutch had expected they would be spending their lives together. He was heartbroken. Nelle asked B. J. Fraser to write to him and encourage him to "look ahead, not behind." Nelle's perspective was always that God had a plan and everything would work out for the best.

The following month, Jack had his first heart attack, and it signaled the end of his working days. He never recovered completely. Nelle's fourteen-dollar-a-week job was now the couple's sole source of income. In her midfifties, she was on her feet ten hours a day, six days a week, clerking at a dress shop in Dixon. She and Jack were forced to rely on Moon and Dutch for support. Fortunately both were now settled in careers.

It was a tough year—dust storms swirled through the Plains, summer temperatures soared to 109 degrees, and the economy continued to struggle. Helping Nelle out was an issue that weighed heavily on Dutch's mind. His relationship with Mugs had kept him tied to the Midwest. Released from the engagement, he could now pursue his career goals more aggressively.

Freeing his mother from the backbreaking toil of earning a living was his central concern and key motivator.

In early 1936, Reagan made his second trip to California with the Cubs to cover spring training. Life in Des Moines had settled into a pattern and the year passed uneventfully as he continued his column for the *Dispatch* and gave more speeches. Late in the year, an interview with Joy Hodges, a young actress and former WHO employee, reawakened his slumbering goal of becoming a movie star. Hodges had successfully transitioned into a career as a cabaret singer in Hollywood. On a trip back to Des Moines to visit her parents, she stopped by the station to say hello and Dutch arranged an on-air interview. Sixty years later she still remembered how he wanted to hear all about her life and career in Hollywood.

Recalibrating

Early in 1937, a country-music orchestra connected with WHO—Al Clauser and his Oklahoma Outlaws—was hired by singing cowboy Gene Autry to appear in his film *Rootin' Tootin' Rhythm.* A savvy entrepreneur, Autry had figured out that using hinterland talent was a great way to generate publicity and keep his core audience engaged. By staying connected with his roots and creating a strong brand for himself, Autry had become very successful. Dutch was impressed by Autry's business model and adapted it as his own in the near term and over the course of his long career. The Outlaws' big opportunity stirred up Dutch's own dreams again: "Suddenly the whole thing awoke. It seemed more possible."[17]

In March 1937, Reagan headed back to California to cover spring training for the third year. But this time he had a hidden agenda—to break into movies. Luck was with him. He arrived in the midst of a torrential downpour that gave him a convenient excuse to postpone continuing on to Catalina. He used his connection with the Outlaws to wrangle an invitation to spend the day watching them film at Republic Pictures. He was fascinated by the firsthand glimpse of the staging, lighting, sound, makeup, and costumes that were all part of making a movie.

Risking the wrath of the Cubs' coach, he booked a room for the night in Los Angeles and looked up his one contact in Hollywood, Joy Hodges. When they first met at the Des Moines radio station Dutch talked her into having lunch with him the next day. By the time he arrived to pick her up, she'd changed her mind. She hid in a closet rather than answer his persistent rings.[18] That didn't stop him from sending a note to her backstage during her show at the Biltmore Bowl. Filled with determination, he wouldn't be put off by a minor issue like being stood up. He wasn't easily deterred from pursuing and achieving his goals.

Over dinner, he told Joy about his interest in acting. Telling him to take off his glasses and warning him to leave them off in the future, she looked at him appraisingly and offered to introduce him to her agent, Bill Meiklejohn. The next day, talking to a blurry image on the other side of a desk, Dutch managed to impress Meiklejohn, who picked up the phone and called casting director Max Arnow at Warner Bros. In short order, Reagan was given a passage from *The Philadelphia Story* to memorize and was scheduled for an audition.

Meiklejohn and Arnow expected the young hopeful would

hang around Hollywood waiting while Warner executives dithered about offering him a contract. Most actors hankering after a studio contract would have done just that. But Dutch wasn't one for taking undue career risks. He headed back to Iowa and the security of his job at WHO. His seemingly nonchalant, take-it-or-leave-it attitude wowed the Hollywood types, but the deciding factor was his well-trained modulated voice. A few weeks later, on April 9, a telegram arrived from Meiklejohn: "WARNER'S OFFER CONTRACT SEVEN YEARS STOP ONE YEAR'S OPTION STOP STARTING AT $200 A WEEK STOP WHAT SHALL I DO?" General Mills, sponsor of Dutch's radio program at WHO, instantly counteroffered with a raise and the promise of a safe, reliable job in Des Moines, but always confident in his own abilities, Dutch jumped at the studio's offer. He raced to the telegraph office to wire back, "SIGN BEFORE THEY CHANGE THEIR MINDS."

His delighted colleagues spontaneously threw a party to celebrate his exciting news. In the midst of the festivities, Pete noticed Dutch was missing and sent someone to look for him. He was found on his knees praying in one of the smaller studios.

"MY FAITH," BY RONALD REAGAN, *MODERN SCREEN*, JUNE 1950 (EXCERPTED)

. . . In school I learned about two basic philosophies: All people are bad until proven good; all people are good until proven bad. I believe the latter. I believe in a force of God behind most people, and so I put my trust in them. . . .

I'm not a fatalist. I don't go along with those who say, "When your number's up, it's up, and there's nothing you can do about it." I think God gave us a certain control over our own destiny. He showed us by rules and by countless examples how to live happily and well. . . .

Even in a minor crisis, faith can help a great deal. When I broke my right thigh during a baseball game, I faced the doctor's verdict without fear. I knew that a broken thigh is difficult to heal. Sometimes the leg becomes deformed or useless. But I was sure that this wouldn't happen to me.

. . . I was flat on my back for several months, but I don't regard that as a real misfortune. I don't think God broke my leg, though it's possible that in the pattern of things I was supposed to slow down and do a little reviewing.

It would be silly to say that those months revolutionized my way of thinking. But when a man is hurt, he can either be very rebellious or else learn patience. I hope I've learned a little patience.

There was a wonderful line in *King's Row*—"Some people grow up and some people just grow older . . ."

Sometimes it takes a tragedy to help us grow up. I don't think we can always analyze why things happen, perhaps it's because we don't see all the results immediately. But there will usually come a day when we can understand the purpose behind some misfortune.

The late Franklin D. Roosevelt, while still a young man, was stricken with polio. There must have been moments when he desperately asked, "Why did this happen to me?"

But today we often wonder: Would he have been as great a man if it hadn't happened? And we consider how the long years of suffering and therapy contributed to his character. The struggle he went through and the patience he learned brought out the greatness which might otherwise have lain dormant within him. For each of us is the sum total, in a way, of everything that happens in our daily lives. . . .

FINDING YOUR MENTORS AND SETTING YOUR GOALS

A goal is a dream with a deadline.

—Napoleon Hill

- Develop a clear vision of what you want to achieve in life. Identify the skills and knowledge you will need to succeed. Resolve to get the education and develop the skills you will need to make your dreams come true.
- Identify people around you whose approach to life you admire. Ask their advice, listen carefully, take notes, and put it into action. After acting on your mentors' advice, you can go back to them to review progress, fine-tune your approach, and set new goals.
- Set aside time to think about and establish goals for your future. Create *A Book about Me*—a brag book in a three-ring binder—in which you can track your successes, write down your goals, and periodically review your progress. Check your goals off as you achieve them and set new ones.
- In your *A Book about Me*, create sections on physical health, career and business life, financial well-being, and relationships. Write down your goals.
- Recognize that in choosing a career goal, you are making an important decision about how you will spend your working life and waking hours. Explore what skills your targeted career requires. Ask people in the field how they spend their time. Ask for pros and cons.

- Despite inevitable setbacks, resolve to stay focused and pursue your goals. Back your goals with determination and commitment. Mentally prepare yourself in advance for challenges and obstacles.
- Recognize that mentor relationships can take a wide variety of forms—from a passing conversation to a lifelong friendship.
- Find a coach you can turn to for advice and for constructive feedback.

Working It In

What is your long-term goal? What do you most want to achieve in life?

____

____

____

____

____

Where is your life heading? Are you happy and comfortable with the path you're on? Do you need to make changes?

____

____

____

____

____

What forms do your mentoring relationships take?

Who can you turn to for constructive advice on your career path?

Cite an example of putting a mentor's advice into practice.

Chapter 3

Evolving into a Brand

Actor and Union Leader—Hollywood, California, 1937–54

Anyone who follows the truth in his heart never makes a mistake.

—Father John Callahan, Notre Dame,
Knute Rockne—All American

The Path to Stardom

On May 21, 1937, Dutch Reagan signed off at WHO Des Moines and headed west on the Lincoln Highway bound for Hollywood. At twenty-six, he was handsome, successful, well paid, and about to be famous. With a contract in hand that promised him two hundred dollars a week, he had achieved, and even exceeded, a goal he had set during his college days: to be earning more than five thousand dollars[1] within five years of graduating.

Unbeknownst to him, two people who were to play significant roles in his life in the coming years were also busy that month. Twenty-one-year-old Jane Wyman was about to marry for the second time. She already had strong roots in the film community. Talent agents and industry staffers concurred—everyone loved Janie.[2] In Chicago, Jules Stein, founder of Music

Corporation of America (MCA), the powerhouse talent agency already established in radio, was getting ready to expand his operations to movies by opening an office in Los Angeles.

Breezing along the highway with the top down on his convertible, Dutch got a close look at the country he came to know so well. He drove across the Plains where vast fields sprouted corn, wheat, and oats, cattle ranches stretched for miles, and lonely farmhouses dotted the landscape. He navigated the twists and turns of mountain roads and passed through canyonlands and sun-baked deserts. On the outskirts of Los Angeles, orange groves lined the highways and filled the air with the fragrance of their blossoms. He long remembered his first days in Hollywood as "painted in a light rosy glow."

Dutch daydreamed about his future as an actor. There was one story that had captured his imagination as an avid fan of college football and eager reader of sports columns, one role he desperately wanted to play: George Gipp, Notre Dame's All-American football player, better known as the Gipper.

Gipp was transformed from star to legend when he died of strep throat in his senior year at Notre Dame. Two weeks earlier he had thrown a record-setting, fifty-five-yard scoring pass in the fourth quarter of a game against Northwestern. As he lay dying, he was voted Notre Dame's first All-American football player. Widely considered the "greatest player in the country," in real life, Gipp was no angel. He was known to skip classes, gamble, and visit the shadier parts of South Bend but, dying at the height of his athletic triumphs, his image was forever preserved in Lord Byron's days of youth, days of glory. In memories, Gipp lived on as a taut-bodied warrior striding into the Colosseum ready for battle. For Dutch and other passionate fans of college football, Gipp was a godlike figure, "one of the all-time great stars."[3]

Dutch picked the perfect time to arrive in Hollywood. Business was booming. As Reagan pulled into town, lyricist Johnny Mercer was penning his hymn to the industry—"Hooray for Hollywood!"—"where you're terrific if you're even good!" The jaunty lyrics captured the exuberance of the era when, in those pretelevision days, 63 percent of Americans went to the movies every week.

He moved into the Montecito Apartments, an Art Deco building with sweeping views of Los Angeles, home to Hollywood stars James Cagney and Mickey Rooney. From the front door it was a short stroll to the restaurants, clubs, and movie theaters of Hollywood Boulevard where he could watch and learn from the work of colleagues and rivals.

But the soon-to-be-star didn't have long to luxuriate in his success. At the studio, he discovered everything about him was wrong. With ruthless honesty, studio experts set about crafting a diamond from the lump of coal standing in front of them. He was put through a blazing furnace of criticism. His hair was terrible, neck too short, shoulders too broad. His name—Dutch Reagan—was a problem. Hal Wallis, Warner's executive producer, took one look at him, dismissed him as a "hick" from the sticks, and shunted him off to the studio's "B movie" track—the sixty-minute films that made up the bottom half of the era's standard double features.

He was ordered to grow his hair longer and part it on the

side. The problem with his neck was solved by sending him to a shirtmaker who had designed a collar that made a neck appear longer. With characteristic pragmatism, once Reagan identified a solution for a problem, he never wasted time rethinking it. For the rest of his life, he ordered his dress shirts from the same shop. In the studio's wardrobe department, a tailor took scissors to his jackets, slashed, altered, and returned them, improved, to their owner.

His name was more of a dilemma. Dutch pointed out, to no avail, that his name was already well known to a large radio audience in the Midwest. The experts were unimpressed. The name "Dutch Reagan" wouldn't work on a theater marquee. Someone suggested Ronald Reagan, as if the idea were brand-new. Everyone agreed it was perfect, or at least not bad. From then on, he was known as Ronald Reagan.

His distinguishing feature—the one trait that set him apart from other Hollywood aspirants—was his voice. Five years after he arrived in Hollywood, his voice was still attracting attention. A brief June 1942 *Los Angeles Times* article on one of his movies was headlined "Voice Won Reagan Chance." The journalist wrote: "His [vocal] ability assured his rise to stardom." That was true, but it would have been even more accurate to say his determination and effort assured his rise to stardom. In Reagan's first days at Warner's, talent scout Max Arnow told him, "You're going to work. You'll have a chance to find out whether you can make it or not if you're willing to work." As at Lowell Park and the radio stations, he approached the job with single-minded tenacity, tempered by a good-natured attitude and a resolve to get along with colleagues.

The studio had an investment in him and was eager, even anxious, to see him succeed. As a contract player at a major studio, he was among Hollywood's elite actors and being groomed for stardom. For his film debut, the studio served up a role that played to his strengths and background. He was cast as a crackerjack crime reporter at a radio station in *Love Is on the Air.* Working on his first movie, he forged a friendship with Bryan (Brynie) Foy, head of Warner Bros. B-movie unit. Later Reagan joked that his pal and mentor Brynie thought up film projects just to keep him around. Over the next eighteen months, under Brynie's watchful gaze on the B lot, Reagan appeared in eleven films and had the opportunity to work with and learn from talented, skilled, and experienced people. By the end of that first summer, with two films under his belt, he felt confident enough of his career prospects to move Nelle and Jack out to Los Angeles.

On his next film, *D-1 Submarine*, Reagan got to know Warner's star Pat O'Brien, who became one of his biggest boosters. Next up was *Hollywood Hotel,* a lighthearted musical. While filming, Reagan, who only had a brief part, met Warner's song-and-dance star Dick Powell who took the new kid under his wing and became another mentor. He had established a pattern. Throughout his life, a strong network of friendships was a key factor in his career success.

In the 1938 film *Boy Meets Girl,* a tale of two lazy screenwriters, Reagan again appeared as a radio announcer but this time he got to work with the studio's stars James Cagney and Pat O'Brien. In these early pictures, he was bedeviled by the same problem that had gotten him fired in his first month at WOC: His reading of the script was flat. Seasoned pros Cagney and O'Brien pleaded with director Lloyd Bacon to talk to Reagan about the problem, but Bacon shied away from the difficult conversation. The unpleasant task of straightening out the novice fell to a tough old character actress who pulled Reagan aside and, in no uncertain terms, laid out exactly how he was ruining the scene and making everyone else's job harder. Then she gave him some pointed advice on how to improve. As he did with the "angel" at WMAQ and with Pete MacArthur's red-hot coaching, he listened. He didn't flinch from the criticism; instead he saw it as the path to improvement. In the next take he put her advice into action, nailed the scene, and never looked back.

With practice, advice, and experience, his acting got better and he developed a comfortable onscreen persona. Cast in indifferent films in ho-hum parts, he wasn't gaining traction with the moviegoing public. His acting career and contract with Warner's was teetering on the brink when he caught a break. He was cast in a surprise hit and box-office bonanza, *Brother Rat,* the story of three cadets at Virginia Military Institute. The film boosted the careers of everyone involved and might have made Reagan a star, but on *Brother Rat* he learned a Hollywood truism—only one star was born per movie. In this instance the lucky guy was costar Eddie Albert.

On the set of *Brother Rat,* he met Jane Wyman, who took an immediate shine to him and quickly set about shedding husband number two. She and Reagan had a lot in common. They had grown up in the Midwest, had difficult childhoods, and were dedicated to their careers. It looked like a perfect match. Wyman was a firm believer in going after what you wanted, and she egged Reagan on, encouraging him to pursue his career objectives aggressively. As a team they supported each other's goals; as a couple they garnered twice the publicity. Movie magazines loved the attractive young couple with parallel careers. With Jane on his arm, Reagan got a second chance at stardom. They married in January 1940 and a year later, their daughter, Maureen, was born. On March 18, 1945, prompted, according to legend, by Maureen, who wanted a brother, they adopted Michael Reagan into their family.

Brother Rat was a blast of oxygen for Reagan's career and led to his being cast opposite Bette Davis in *Dark Victory,* his first A film. It was a huge opportunity and he blew it, turning in a "wooden" performance. At the time it seemed like a disaster. He and the director butted heads over how to play the role. Reagan fancied himself a young stud. He liked to think, "If I stroll through where the girls are short of clothes, there will be great scurrying about and taking cover."[4] The director's vision of the role was a nonthreatening, sympathetic listener to the heroine. The clash in his first high-profile project might have doomed Reagan's career, but Brynie Foy had also moved up to the A's and came to his rescue, sending out a lifeline via a film called *International Squadron.*

Developing an Image

From the moment he arrived in Hollywood, Reagan started talking to anyone who would listen about making a movie based on Knute Rockne, George Gipp, and the Fighting Irish of Notre Dame. He pushed the idea at the studio and asked for advice on how to approach the project. As a sports columnist he was used to looking for stories and filled time on radio programs talking about Gipp's career. Reagan, though warned he might find his pet project hijacked if he talked about it too widely, mused aloud about whether he should write a treatment or a screenplay.

Each Hollywood film studio had a signature style. MGM favored big names. Columbia specialized in screwball comedies. Paramount's slogan was "Famous Players in Famous Plays." Reagan's studio, Warner Bros., made its mark with ripped-from-the-tabloid stories that oozed appeal for Middle America. Warner's was the natural studio for the Rockne/Gipp story, just as wholesome, boy-next-door Ronald Reagan was the perfect fit for the film's idealized version of Gipp. That didn't mean, though, that he would automatically get the part.

In early 1940, leafing through the trade papers one day, Reagan was astounded to see that a film about Rockne was in the works at Warner Bros. and that some of the cast had already been named. Wasting no time, he rushed to Hal Wallis's office to present himself as the logical—the only!—choice for the role of the Gipper. Wallis shrugged his shoulders and shook his head. The role called for someone more robust than Reagan. "But," stammered Reagan, drawing on his encyclopedic knowledge of football, "Gipp weighed five pounds less than I do." Wallis shrugged again.

A studio photographer had once told Reagan that front-office executives only believe what they see in front of their eyes. He "broke all the speed limits" racing home to rummage through a trunk for photographs of himself suited up in football gear at Eureka. He set another speed record returning to the studio. Sprinting into Wallis's office, he slapped the photographs on the desk in front of him. It worked. Wallis was impressed.

Studying the photos, Wallis asked thoughtfully, "Can I hold on to these?" Reagan pal Pat O'Brien, already cast as Rockne, promoted Reagan's cause by pointing out to studio execs that Reagan's in-depth knowledge of football and of Notre Dame history would be an asset on the film set. With O'Brien's enthusiastic backing, Reagan finally got his breakthrough role in an A movie surrounded by an A cast.

On October 3, 1940, *Knute Rockne—All American* premiered in Notre Dame's hometown, South Bend, Indiana. A crowd of twenty thousand turned out to greet the Hollywood celebrities as they arrived by train at midnight. The next day one hundred thousand thronged the parade route to welcome the cast to town. At the Saturday-night banquet, Franklin D. Roosevelt, Jr., read a message from his father saying, "Our need today is for more men strong in body, strong in soul, and strong in faith. In brief, for men who hold to the ideals which Knute Rockne held." Notre Dame's president, Father Hugh O'Donnell, spoke and, after dinner, Ronald Reagan distinguished himself "with his sympathetic and sincere talk which brought a long ovation." It was a major coup for Reagan. His talent and experience as a speaker worked their magic.

Ironically, there wasn't much to the role. Reagan only appeared on the screen as the Gipper for about ten minutes, but the role synced with his innate optimism and All-American persona. He had finally found the role that crystallized who he was and enhanced his natural brand. Reagan's success on the silver screen proved fleeting, but the image of Reagan as Gipp endured in America's collective psyche. "The Gipper" became his lifelong nickname.

In Hollywood, the key to getting to the top was branding. Stars such as John Wayne, Cary Grant, Marilyn Monroe, and Katharine Hepburn developed strong images and found roles they could play time and again. The moviegoing public lined up to buy tickets knowing just what they would be seeing on the screen—the slow-talking westerner, the handsome sophisticate who doesn't take himself too seriously, the vamp, the fast-talking Eastern Establishment type who's forever working on her relationships. The audience wanted to see the actors play those roles over and over in endless variations.

At the film's sneak preview in Pasadena, California, Reagan sensed something special in the audience. In a reprise of his early triumph at Northwestern, as he was dying on screen, he heard sniffles in the crowd. The audience reaction—starting in the theater and followed by a flow of invitations, fan mail, and glowing press reports—was everything the finely tuned antennae of studio executives scanned for: heartfelt feedback that studios couldn't buy no matter how many photos were planted in movie magazines or items in gossip columns, exactly the sort of signals a studio required to push an actor's career to the next level. Early the next morning, Reagan's phone rang with a call telling him to get over to the studio for a fitting. He'd be starring as a youthful General George Custer in *Santa Fe Trail* with Errol Flynn and Olivia de Havilland and supported by the studio's A team. After three years of struggling in lackluster roles, thanks to the help of friends, he was finally on his way. Or so it seemed.

He arrived in the costume department to find a wardrobe staffer tossing finished cavalry uniforms fitted to another actor in a heap and replacing them with uniforms cut for him. The sight made an impression on Reagan. Overnight, his career had leaped forward, but just as suddenly, another actor's career had gone in the opposite direction. In a highly competitive business it was wise not to take success for granted. It might not last.

After three years in Hollywood, Reagan's career was finally on the fast track. Putting his flair for public relations to use to make the most of the opportunity, he accepted an invitation to speak to a Catholic women's club about "some of the problems incident to the making of motion pictures."[5] His topic could have been, and probably was, torn from the pages of Dale Carnegie's enormously influential 1937 best seller *How to Win Friends and Influence People*. Carnegie advised budding public speakers to choose subjects they were passionate about, ideally, something that made them angry. It was the starting point of Reagan's public speaking career.

The Catholic club's event rated a sizable headline in the *Los Angeles Times*. The lesson was obvious: Giving speeches was a sure-fire way to get his name in newspapers. Consciously or not, it was the template he adopted going forward.

After the success of *Knute Rockne—All American*, University of Southern California art students voted Reagan a "20th century Adonis" and invited him to be a model for their sculpture class. He happily posed looking like a Greek statue come to life. His success allowed him to buy his parents the only house they ever owned. He talked the studio into giving Jack a job answering his fan mail.

Warner's now routinely assigned him to A movies, but in a hash of roles. Reagan, ever the clear-eyed realist, called them the "shaky-A's." The studio struggled to define him. Successful screen images have an edge. Reagan's good-guy image lacked the necessary bite to take his career to the next level.

The studio tried him out in a variety of parts. He was teamed up in a western with A-list character actors Wallace Beery and Lionel Barrymore. Next he got third billing in a Warner Bros. comedy/romance that was a studio ensemble piece. The executives seemed to be thinking let's throw them all together and see who bubbles to the top. Apparently they liked what they saw because in his next two films he got top billing with the sort of A-list actors he had worked with on *Santa Fe Trail.* His next big break came with the role that was going to make him a solid star. In *Kings Row* he played Drake McHugh—a cheerful, genial playboy who refuses to let the unnecessary amputation of his legs by an insane doctor ruin his life.

Adapted from a hair-raising novel about life in a small town, it was a precursor to Grace Metalious's best-selling scorcher *Peyton Place.* The story line touched on incest, nymphomania, castration, amputation, insanity, sadism, euthanasia, and death. Experienced screenwriter Casey Robinson toned down the story considerably for the screen. Warner Bros. pulled out all the stops and the cast was full of what *New York Times* film critic Bosley Crowther called "high-priced" talent.

Though Crowther panned the film as "gloomy and ponderous," *Kings Row* received Academy Award nominations for Best Picture, Best Director, and Best Cinematography. The *Los Angeles Times*'s review equivocated with a headline, "Main St. Types of *Kings Row* Human." The public was more enthusiastic, and the film's theater run was extended for weeks. The studio trumpeted, "It has been a long time since a talking picture has elicited the accolades of both the press and the public with the enthusiasm evidenced here." *Kings Row* was Reagan's greatest screen success. The role of Drake McHugh reinforced Reagan's image as the wholesome good guy next door whose sunny disposition would see him through the darkest times.

As Reagan's career was heating up, World War II was raging in Europe and North Africa. That fall of 1941, Reagan, an Army Reserve officer, started to receive notices about being called up for active service. His contract with Warner Bros. was up for renewal and this time he would be represented by cutthroat MCA talent agent Lew Wasserman, who had recently arrived in town with his wife, Edie. Reagan and Jane Wyman had developed a close friendship with the Wassermans. For a while, the two couples got together for dinner every Saturday night. For almost twenty-five years, Wasserman and Reagan spoke on the phone daily.[6] Wasserman was fast becoming a potent force in Hollywood and a major factor in Reagan's success. Studio chief Jack Warner liked what he saw of Reagan's performance in the early rushes of *Kings Row* and was eager to re-sign him. They signed a new contract in November 1941.

Within a month Wasserman, now also armed with enthusiastic reports of Reagan's appealing performance in *Kings Row*, dragged Warner back to the table to renegotiate. This time Wasserman sliced the deal somewhat differently. He wrote a novel contract that called for Reagan to work forty-three weeks a year rather than the Hollywood standard of forty weeks. When Reagan asked him about it, Wasserman's answer was that his goal was to write a million-dollar contract[7] and the three extra weeks put him over the mark. It was a great moment for Reagan's career but an even bigger boost for Wasserman's. Studio trailers, Beverly Hills restaurants, and homes high in the Hollywood hills were soon buzzing with the news of Wasserman's brilliant deal for Reagan, who, when the contract started running, would be earning thirty-five hundred dollars a week. The studio, anxious to put its investment to use, teamed him up again with its charismatic but erratic megastar Errol Flynn in a wartime thriller, *Desperate Journey.*

When *Kings Row* was released in early 1942, Reagan was on top of the world. He was a star in a big-budget movie, with a beautiful, accomplished wife and fifteen-month-old baby, but shortly after the film opened he reported for duty with the army. Along with many other Americans, his career, income, and family were put on hold for the next three and a half years. The press reported that he was the first "prominent actor to leave a wife and child behind" and that he had just been "given star ranking by his Hollywood studio."[8]

Accompanied by Jane and Maureen, Reagan headed to the train station in a crisp, new uniform. Initially, he was posted to Fort Mason in San Francisco as an officer overseeing cargo loading on troop ships headed overseas. Within weeks, he was reassigned to Fort Roach, the Army Air Force's First Motion Picture Unit in Culver City, a few miles from home and family. Jack Warner had lobbied hard for the unit to be housed inside Warner Bros., but Hal Roach's studio, once home to *Our Gang* and *Laurel and Hardy,* got the nod. Roach's entire studio was turned over to the war effort. Officially called Fort Roach, it was soon dubbed Fort Wacky. Reagan was billeted there and saw his family on occasional weekends.

Reagan's 20/200 eyesight meant he was legally blind and precluded any possibility of his being sent overseas. At Fort Roach, his moviemaking skills were put to use for the war effort. He was sorry to give up the "boots and breeches" of the cavalry but agreed that in making training films for the military, he was "a square peg in a square hole." When the "fly-boys" teased him about his five years as a Reserve officer in the horse cavalry, he joked he was "physically unfit for the cavalry, but still plenty good enough for the Air Force."

Like other stars, he was tapped for morale-building efforts among the troops. He showed up in a short film, *Mister Gardenia Jones*—a fund-raiser for the USO—and appeared at a benefit. He narrated an "outstanding short subject" on the heroic exploits of an Air Force pilot following the attack on Pearl Harbor, another on a road built through Burma, and a film on chaplains. He starred in Irving Berlin's fund-raiser for Army Emergency Relief, *This Is the Army*, with MGM star George Murphy. During the filming, Irving Berlin, thinking Reagan was a regular military recruit, pulled him aside to share some advice. "Young fellow," he said, "I just saw some of your work. You've got a few things to correct—for example, a huskiness of the voice—but you really should give this business some serious consideration when the war is over. It's very possible that you could have a career in show business."[9]

The mission of Fort Roach's First Motion Picture Unit could be summed up with a line from *This Is the Army*: "War is a pretty grim business and sometimes a song or a smile is just as vital to an army as food." Fort Wacky was Hollywood's contribution to the war effort.

Speaking at fund-raisers and other morale-bolstering events, Reagan took another step toward his unanticipated future career. In March 1943, he spoke at an American Legion meeting. That fall, he spoke at an enlistment rally. By June 1945, he was selling war bonds to a crowd of a thousand.[10] He served as master of ceremonies at an air show. With each program, he gained experience with audiences and the hard work that goes on behind the scenes to make any event successful.

During his years in service, he fine-tuned his thinking on leadership. He admired the army's tactical approach to getting the job done. He saw what could be achieved by unleashing a small team to accomplish a clear goal but also witnessed the downside of heavy-handed leadership. At Fort Roach, he had a window that looked out on a flagpole. Day after day, an overeager young officer "filled with cadet spirit" pointlessly mustered his men for a drill out to the flagpole—a morale-busting waste of time. Watching the unit march by one day, Reagan pitched his voice to be audible to the men but not to their commander and said, "Splendid body of men—with half this many I could conquer MGM." The soldiers, who should have been inside making pictures, burst into laughter.

In those years at Fort Wacky, he watched people who felt their time was being poorly used squirm and strain under the system and find work-arounds. It was a lesson he never forgot. In the future as a key executive in a small business, as a governor, and as president, he kept his staffs lean, and, for the most part, with clearly delineated responsibilities. In his years in Sacramento and in Washington, D.C., Reagan conspicuously left the office around 5:00 P.M. He would take a stack of material with him and spend much of his evenings reading, but his departure was a signal to his staff that they could go home, get some exercise, and spend time with their families.

Halfway through his military career, Reagan noticed "the first crack in my staunch liberalism."[11] When an order from Washington called for a 35 percent reduction in civilian staff within six months, Reagan was surprised to see bureaucrats shuffle head counts and end up with more employees rather than fewer. He later wrote, "Neither Congress nor the military had figured on the ability of Civil Service to achieve eternal life here on earth."[12] It reminded him of a similar situation when his father had worked for a government agency during the Depression. Jack had noticed his colleagues were more concerned about preserving their jobs and expanding their responsibilities than with doing their jobs or following directives. Containing the growth of government was the first of Reagan's signature issues to bubble to the surface.

When Reagan was discharged from the service in the summer of 1945, Jack Warner told him to relax and take a break while the studio found the right role for him. He headed to Lake Arrowhead, a resort in the San Bernardino Mountains, two hours east of Los Angeles. There he took stock of his successes to date and made plans for the future. Meanwhile, Jane Wyman was racing ahead in her career, on her way to winning her first Oscar nomination. Desperate to break out of light comedies, she had pleaded with Warner executives to loan her to Paramount to play the second lead in a movie about an alcoholic, *The Lost Weekend.*

Released in November 1945, *The Lost Weekend* won Academy Awards for Best Picture, Best Director, Best Actor, and

Best Writing. While Reagan was wiling away hours building models of ships and idly thinking about politics, Wyman was suddenly on a trajectory to superstardom. Soon she was working on *Night and Day,* a big-budget Technicolor project with Cary Grant. For her next project, *The Yearling,* she received her first of four Oscar nominations for Best Actress. In an article headlined "Lauded for Her Dramatic Roles," Wyman commented on the problem with comedies: "It is always a question as to whether the public will be receptive to the picture that aims to make them laugh. . . . Too often these fall flat on their faces, and there's no explanation. . . . [I]t's too much to hope that you'll have success with every light role that you play."[13] Reagan was convinced the problem with his career was that he was cast in too many comedies.

The career Reagan envied and wanted was John Wayne's. Westerns were timeless in their appeal and almost guaranteed money-makers. Reagan's skin didn't photograph well in makeup. Filming outdoors on westerns suited his natural ruddiness and also gave him a chance to ride his beloved horses. In the summer of 1946, he bought his first ranch—eight acres in Northridge, a few miles north of Los Angeles—and started raising horses. Westerns had done wonders for the careers of silent film star Tom Mix, singing cowboy Gene Autry, John Wayne, Gary Cooper, Jimmy Stewart, and even Humphrey Bogart.

Warner Bros. finally presented Reagan with what appeared to be a perfect vehicle for his first postwar film—a western with Alexis Smith and Humphrey Bogart. Though Bogart's career had been scaled back during the war years, it had continued. Reagan thought being teamed up with someone "who hadn't been away" would be "sort of insurance." One week before shooting was scheduled to start, Bogey dropped out of the project. With Bogart gone, the studio decided to film the movie in black and white. The pattern for Reagan's postwar film career had been set. If something could go wrong, it did.

While in the service, Reagan aged out of boy-next-door parts into more mature roles. He liked to think of himself as the easygoing good guy in the white hat—seemingly a perfect fit for westerns—but success eluded him. A June 1942 *Los Angeles Times* article hit on the problem: He "could easily be classified as a typical American young man."[14] "Typical" was not the path to stardom. The roles he was cast in failed to create a sharply identifiable image that motivated moviegoers to buy tickets.

In early June 1947, he started filming *That Hagen Girl* with Shirley Temple in her first adult role. Of the more than fifty films he made, it was far and away Reagan's least favorite. The screenplay hinted that Temple (Mary Hagen) was Reagan's (cast as lawyer Tom Bates) illegitimate daughter. At the movie's end, the two seem to be heading off to get married. At thirty-six, Reagan was horrified to be the love interest of a teenager and appalled by the implication of an incestuous relationship. Problems with his onscreen life mushroomed into problems off-screen. Within weeks of starting work on the film, Reagan was hospitalized with pneumonia and nearly died. Jane Wyman, who was six months pregnant with their second daughter, hovered at his bedside for the first days of his illness. Then she had a miscarriage. The marriage never recovered.

Three months later, Wyman was back at work filming *Johnny Belinda*, the film that won her an Academy Award as

Best Actress. This time her taxing role as a deaf-mute strained the Reagans' marriage to the breaking point. In the fall of 1947, Reagan, now serving as president of the Screen Actors Guild (SAG), was called to Washington, D.C., to testify before the House Un-American Activities Committee. When he arrived home full of news, Wyman snapped. She threw him out of the house, shouting, "You bore me! Get out!" He was devastated. Up to that moment, divorce was something that happened to other people and was so far removed from his thinking and the way he'd been brought up that he "had no resources to call on." He spent a week living with the family of William Holden. He and Holden had struck up a friendship while working together at Fort Wacky. Nelle Reagan, ever unflappable, consoled him with her unfailing advice that "everything happens for a reason." At a New Year's Eve party that year "he wept and wept." Reagan's divorce from Wyman was finalized in June 1948.

As his personal life was falling apart, he was offered two great roles that could have gotten his film career back on track. In the lighthearted comedy *Girl from Jones Beach*, he starred as a magazine illustrator who draws the "perfect" girl, then meets his creation come to life at Jones Beach. In *A Hasty Heart*, Reagan again had the lead role, this time as the goodhearted American, "Yank." From a career management perspective, *A Hasty Heart* was *Brother Rat* all over again. Reagan and costar Pat Neal turned in memorable performances but only one star emerged, Richard Todd, who received a Best Actor nomination for his portrayal of a disgruntled, dying soldier. Both roles offered tantalizing glimpses of success.

Reagan, fueled by the patriotic spirit of a war vet, with plenty of time on his hands and possibly to raise his public profile, started joining organizations and sought out speaking opportunities. As his career and marriage began to fray, he devoted more and more time to volunteer activities, mostly with his union, the Screen Actors Guild (SAG). On October 2, 1946, Reagan took the podium as spokesman for the guild's team of labor negotiators at a membership meeting. Pressed hard by Katharine Hepburn and Edward G. Robinson, Reagan dazzled the crowd with his understanding and clear explanations of the issues involved in the complicated labor negotiations. The evening, though unrecognized at the time, was a life-changing moment.

The guild provided Reagan with an outlet for his considerable energy and political interests. His Air Force pal Bill Holden was now, at Reagan's instigation, also a guild board member. After lengthy board meetings that wrapped up well after midnight, Reagan, Holden, and other board members headed to a diner nearby for a sandwich and to continue their conversation about SAG concerns, careers, family, and sports.

In March 1947, seven of Hollywood's premier actors stepped down from the top spots on the SAG board. The *Los Angeles Times* reported they wanted "to strengthen the guild's position in its approaching contract negotiations with the motion picture producers." The actors "explained that each now has a financial interest in the profits of the pictures in which he stars and that while their primary interest always will be that of actors, they feel they should not hold office in the guild as long as their present status in the industry continues."[15] In other words, they wanted to avoid any appearance of impropriety and self-dealing. They remained on as SAG members. When the dust settled, Ronald Reagan was the newly elected president of SAG. He'd been nominated by the highly regarded Gene Kelly, who was, in turn, nominated for the office. The third candidate in the race was George Murphy. Kelly was elected as first vice president. Bill Holden succeeded Dick Powell as second vice president.

The Screen Actors Guild—staff, members, board of directors—was an exceptionally bright, talented, and able group of people. In the late 1940s, there were about six thousand members,[16] of whom fifty were elected to the board of directors for revolving three-year terms. Executive director Jack Dales had been a track star at Stanford and stayed on for law school. Like Reagan, he graduated in the depths of the Depression and his background was typical of the hard-working, determined people Reagan chose to surround himself with. Hired by the Screen Actors Guild in 1937, Dales expected to spend a year with the organization. He stayed for thirty-five, impressed by the "public spiritedness" of the "fascinating people" who populated the guild's board and membership.

At SAG, Reagan became a skilled negotiator under the tutelage of Laurence (Larry) Beilenson, the guild's ace legal counsel. Born and raised in Helena, Arkansas, Beilenson had degrees from Phillips Andover Academy, Harvard College, and Harvard Law School. Beilenson worked closely with Reagan, mentored him on labor issues and politics, and encouraged his flair for negotiating. Dales remembered Reagan in those days as a "fine negotiator" and as "two men . . . aggressive fighter across the table, then in conference among ourselves . . . more realistic."[17] With an actor's keen sense of timing, Reagan had a talent for defusing discussions that were becoming overheated. Negotiating was a skill Reagan used to great effect during the years he led SAG, from March 1947 to November 1952. A top-notch screen persona eluded him but, through working with his union, he was maturing and growing into a force on the national stage.

Since arriving in Hollywood, he had made extraordinary progress in his career. True stardom had slipped from his grasp, but he had polished his leadership skills during his years in the army and on film sets. By actively volunteering with industry associations, he had made valuable connections and had further developed valuable skills and had emerged as a leader in his industry. Going forward, he would be putting his considerable strengths and skills to use in unexpected ways.

He came to Hollywood with the goal of playing the Gipper. He had fought for the role and won it. The iconic role gave his career a much-needed lift and opened the door to his one brief glimpse of true stardom. While his image as the All-American star lacked the grit to make for a stellar movie career, in a larger sense the role of the Gipper captured him, and the nickname stayed with him for the rest of his life. He had taken the essence of the role—the wholesome good guy with the positive attitude—and made it his own. In the years ahead, he modified the movie role into his own persona—the Gipper on horseback—ruggedly handsome, quintessentially American, the man in the white Stetson riding across the purple-sage hills of the West. Through determination, he had transcended the weak vehicles that Hollywood offered him.

At Lake Arrowhead after leaving the service, as at Lowell Park after graduation, he took time to think about his strengths—what had worked well and what hadn't—and set goals to recharge his career. While working at Fort Wacky, he'd overheard conversations among young women, and he, the consummate realist, had no illusions that anyone was holding his breath waiting for him to return to the screen. Once again, he squarely faced the question, what did he want to do? What did he want to achieve? What goals could he set? Then he started putting his plan into action. His first step forward was to join as many groups as possible.

As his Hollywood career stalled, he wasn't sure what was ahead. He toyed with the idea of pursuing a career as a football coach. He tried on the role. One morning, he visited a local high school football team with a neighbor who was the team's coach. It wasn't quite the right fit. His old hero Dick Falkner from *That Printer of Udell's* provided a more accurate glimpse of what lay ahead. In the book's final scene, Falkner was on his way to Washington, presumably bound for a career in politics. Though Reagan was adamant that he wasn't interested in a political career, somehow that was the path that kept pulling him forward.

A Clear Vision of the Goal

In looking to enduring role models, Reagan had intuited the core principle of branding. He started by deciding he wanted to be a sports star, like his heroes Frank Merriwell, Garland Waggoner, and George Gipp. At Eureka, to the best of his abilities, he made his dream happen. Then, faced with the daunting challenges of finding a career and making a living, he got clear on his real strengths. He tweaked his goal and put his knowledge and passion for sports to use as a broadcaster. In Hollywood, he stayed focused and relentlessly pursued his goal of aligning his image with Gipp's. Ultimately, through identifying the attributes he admired in his heroes, he moved past them and superseded them in his own accomplishments.

Grant Schneider, chief marketing officer at Time, Inc., sums up the steps involved in establishing a brand: "Identify the unique set of principles that guide your behavior. Then consistently align and deliver those principles in every experience with you."[18]

Reagan branded himself as an optimist who believed in America. That's who he was at his core. A 1956 *Los Angeles Times* profile said, "He's the epitome of a happy, contented man. A man with brains and heart who knows how to exercise both."

In the decade ahead, Reagan remained convinced Hollywood was where he would find success. Instead it turned out to be a way station on a much longer journey. In radio he learned how to talk to a wide audience of listeners. In movies he learned to project himself through a screen to an audience. By following his instincts, he had gained lots of experience speaking to live audiences. He was about to get a lot more.

"HOW TO MAKE YOURSELF IMPORTANT," BY RONALD REAGAN AS TOLD TO GLADYS HALL, *PHOTOPLAY* MAGAZINE, AUGUST 1942 (EXCERPTED)

A fine and fancy storyteller holds his punch for the story's end, I'm sure. But as I'm a plain guy with a set of homespun features and no frills, I may as well write accordingly.

So then, the whole deal on how to make yourself important is, as I see it, to (a) love what you are doing with all your heart and soul and (b) believe what you are doing is important, even if you are only grubbing for worms in the back yard.

I am enormously in earnest about this. In fact, I believe I may say with some pride that I think I have something here. I hold that all of this business about making yourself important by means of externals is no good. Clothes, being seen in the Right Places, show, swank—NO! They may make you seem important, but that is not what I am talking about. . . .

Look, you must love what you're doing. You must think what you are doing is important because, if it's important to you, you can bet your last ducat that other people will think so, too. It may take time, but they'll get around to it. And one thing more, one really important thing: If, when you get a job, you don't believe you can get to the top in it, it's the wrong job.

Now, of course, I don't mean that just believing you can get to the top will always get you there. But I do say that you'll never get there unless you believe that you can.

I'm not writing anything I don't believe myself, you know. Nor anything that doesn't come right out of my own experience. For me, the one job in the world I want to do is acting. Offer me ten times the money for something else, and I wouldn't do it. And right from the start, down there in "B" pictures where I began, through four years of "bit" parts (the "Poor Man's Errol Flynn," they called me), I was sure that I was in the right business for me, I knew I'd get to the top, if I kept on working and learning. That's not brash self-confidence, either. Put me in any other job and I'd eat humble pies by the dozen. I'd lack self-confidence because I'd be in the wrong job.

Of course, doing what I wanted to do didn't put me always in a favorable light. For example in college I majored in sociology and economics. Not because I liked the subjects, but because they gave me the most time for the things I really liked, namely, college dramatics, football and a dive into campus politics. . . .

Point being that success, for me, is where the heart is.

BRANDING YOURSELF

Bring me my Bow of burning gold,
Bring me my Arrows of desire:
Bring me my Spear: O clouds unfold!
Bring me my Chariot of fire!

—William Blake, "Jerusalem"

- To develop a strong brand or image, start by getting clear on your goal. How do you want to be seen? Then set about becoming the person you want to be.
- Tap into the expertise of others. Actively seek out advice from experts and implement it.
- Look for opportunities to learn from those around you.
- Resolve to absorb and learn from constructive feedback and to value coaching; as any athlete knows, coaching is the path to improvement and success.
- Proactively take charge of and manage your career. Don't wait for things to happen; make things happen. That doesn't mean being pushy or arrogant. Be prepared to take advantage of opportunities that come your way.
- Be pragmatic. Life and careers take unexpected twists and turns. It will not always be clear where the path is leading.
- Periodically take time to take stock of successes and plan for the future.
- Once you find a solution to a problem, don't waste time and energy rethinking the issue. Solve the problem and move on.

Working It In

Who do you want to be?

____

____

____

____

____

What do you want to achieve in life?

____

____

____

____

____

How do you want to be seen by others?

____

____

____

____

____

What steps do you need to take to develop into that person?

____

____

____

____

____

List three ways to polish your image.

____

____

____

____

____

Chapter 4

Creating a Network of Contacts and Support

Television Star and Corporate Ambassador with General Electric, 1954–62

> I have found Ronald Reagan to be a kind man. He is a gentle man. To the discomfiture of those who have misread this, he also is a strong man.
>
> In defense of the values he believes in, he can be indomitable.
>
> —Earl Dunckel, General Electric

On a peaceful Sunday in December 1941, a stealth attack was unleashed on the U.S. naval station at Pearl Harbor, Hawaii. Coming in waves, 353 planes systematically bombed the base and ships docked in the harbor. Two thousand four hundred and fifty-nine Americans were killed, almost thirteen hundred were wounded. Japan's strategy of "deceptive diplomacy" had worked. America was shocked.

Within days, President Roosevelt issued an urgent plea to America's business leaders. They were needed in Washington, D.C., to ramp up manufacturing for the war effort. Senior executives responded. They cleaned out their offices and headed to the capital. For the next four years, talented managers at the hastily organized War Production Board (WPB) steered the U.S. economy through World War II. Industrial production doubled, outproducing the combined output of America's allies and enemies. Yet the war effort was never allowed to exceed 40 percent of the nation's gross domestic product.[1] In 1945, as fighting in Europe and the Far East drew to a close, the WPB throttled back and returned the country to peacetime production levels without undue disruption to the nation's economy.

Three men recruited to the War Production Board had an impact—directly and indirectly—on the career of Ronald Reagan. As role models and mentors, Charles E. Wilson, Ralph Cordiner, and Lemuel Boulware influenced Reagan, opened doors for him, and guided his evolution into politics.

Wilson, president of General Electric before and after the war, was known as "Electric Charlie" to distinguish him from another Charles E. Wilson—"Engine Charlie," CEO of General Motors. *Time* magazine dubbed Wilson "the strong man of WPB." The *New York Times* described him as "a big man by any standard, physical, moral, or mental." Even his chief adversary, Jim Carey, head of GE's largest union, the CIO Electrical Workers, admired Wilson. Electric Charlie cast a big shadow. Born in the rough-and-tumble world of Manhattan's West Side, Wilson left school in seventh grade to help support himself and his widowed mother.[2] In his sixties he still looked liked the stocky club heavyweight fighter he once had been—Superman in Clark Kent guise, complete with horn-rimmed glasses. Working at WPB, Wilson enlisted Ralph Cordiner, a "small, high-domed spark plug"[3] production manager from GE, and Lemuel

Boulware, a manager who, by design, had accumulated a varied business background. After the war, the three executives headed back to General Electric, Boulware lured to the company by Wilson.

Ronald Reagan once described his years with General Electric as a "postgraduate education in political science" that "wasn't a bad apprenticeship for someone who'd someday enter public life." During the eight years he was associated with the company, he was surrounded by some of the best minds in American business. He admired GE's executives and learned from them. While traveling around the country meeting GE employees, Reagan's career slowly pivoted from entertainment to politics. Senior managers at GE were the people who nurtured his new persona.

The origin of Reagan's connection with General Electric lay in a series of paralyzing strikes unleashed by labor unions against American business after the war. In the 1940s, one-third of the labor force were union members. Labor leaders felt they had been patient in not asking for increases during the war years. In 1946 they struck.

General Electric was hit hard. A strike against the company lasted seventeen weeks. Only two business units, both led by the recently hired Boulware, continued running. Faced with a contentious labor environment, Wilson decided the best long-term solution for the company, its employees, shareholders, and customers, was to tackle the problem head-on. He wanted employees to understand how business works, how a company makes a profit, and how each job fits into a complicated big picture.

Working with Cordiner, Wilson came up with a plan. He asked Boulware to head a department charged with developing a strategy to communicate with GE employees and the broader world. Boulware hesitated; he didn't know anything about employee and community relations programs. Wilson and Cordiner saw his inexperience as a plus. They wanted something new, something different, something that hadn't been done before. The something they wanted was Ronald Reagan. But it took a few years to figure that out.

A Trusted Confidante

For Ronald Reagan in the early 1950s, still hurting from his painful divorce from Jane Wyman, the only bright spot in an otherwise dreary landscape was a young actress named Nancy Davis. After graduating from Smith and working in summer stock, she followed in her mother's footsteps and headed to New York to try her luck on Broadway. Her mother's many friends—Zasu Pitts, Spencer Tracy, Walter Huston, and Clark Gable among them—tried to help her out, but success on Broadway proved elusive. It was television that gave her a big break.

In television's early days, New York City was the epicenter of the industry. Madison Avenue advertising agencies were the industry's matchmakers. Agencies introduced deep-pocketed corporations to television executives who had programs on which to showcase, advertise, and promote corporate wares. Initially the business model worked perfectly. Like radio, television was designed to sell products. Programming was almost a secondary consideration. Television thrived on corporate sponsorships. America's premier companies—Firestone, Goodyear, Colgate, Texaco, and Kraft—jumped at opportunities to sponsor programs. Mike Dann, programming chief at CBS, said television "could turn an unknown product into a goldmine."[4] He cited how "*Kraft Television Theater* transformed lackluster sales of McLaren's Imperial Cheese into a national favorite."

But producers soon found having one major sponsor per program was problematic. Corporate sponsors felt they owned "their" programs and proved to be bossy and demanding clients. It was hard for a producer to relax and enjoy a three-martini lunch at Le Pavilion or "21" while increasingly irate messages on bright pink slips of paper piled up back at the office. Networks tweaked their business model and moved on to using the magazine arrangement of multiple advertisers.

In the late 1940s, television shows—many of them plays acted out live in front of a camera—were a fertile source of employment for young, would-be Broadway actors such as Nancy Davis. A movie producer spotted her on a show and issued an invitation to Hollywood for a screen test. Off she went in pursuit of fame and fortune in the West.

Accounts vary, but it appears that Ronald Reagan and Nancy Davis first met at a dinner party in the early fall of 1949. He, distracted by a broken leg, career troubles, his recent divorce, and SAG issues, failed to take notice. She refused to give up. She got a friend, MGM director Dore Schary, to call his pal SAG president Ronald Reagan on her behalf. This time she wasn't running the risk of getting lost in a crowd. The pretense was that she was concerned her name was showing up on a list of communist sympathizers. He checked it out. It was clear there were multiple Nancy Davises in Hollywood. She had nothing to worry about. With a quick good-bye, he was ready to hang up the phone. Not so fast. Dore's friend Nancy would be greatly reassured if his pal Ronnie would take her out to dinner and explain that in person. This time it worked. In Ronald Reagan, Nancy Davis found someone who had interests beyond his acting career and with whom she had a lot in common. Over dinners at Chasen's, the preferred hangout of Hollywood elite, they talked about the Screen Actors Guild—a close friend of her mother's had been a founder—labor unions, horses, the Civil War, and wine. They had both grown up in Illinois. Her adoptive father was from Galesburg. They had both suffered difficult childhoods.

Nancy's birth certificate read Anne Frances Robbins, but shortly after she was born her father deserted her mother, leaving Edith Prescott Luckett Robbins to raise Nancy on her own. Caring for a small child was not easily combined with earning a living as an actress on Broadway and traveling around the country with touring companies. Edith's solution was to park Nancy in Bethesda, Maryland, with her sister and brother-in-law, who had a daughter close to Nancy's age.

When Nancy was seven, her mother appeared with the news that there was a new man in her life—a neurosurgeon from Chicago named Loyal Davis. If it was all right with Nancy, Edith would marry Dr. Loyal and they would all live together in Chicago. For Nancy, it was a Cinderella moment—whisked out of the drab existence of a paid boarder to a glamorous new life with her exuberant mother and impressively credentialed stepfather on Chicago's Gold Coast.

Spurred on by a particularly unsatisfactory visit with her birth father—he'd locked her in a bathroom for hours over some infraction—at fourteen, she boarded a train, got herself to New Jersey, and pressed him to sign a document that waived his parental rights. She then talked Loyal Davis into adopting her officially. On her first date with Ronald Reagan, when the conversation briefly touched on the problem they were ostensibly together to discuss, Reagan suggested she change her name—a not uncommon practice in Hollywood. She was shocked. Looking at him with enormous eyes, she responded, "But it's my name." Indeed, she had worked hard for it and it meant a lot to her.

Over the next few years, Reagan, by his own account, did everything wrong. He traveled on SAG business and casually dated other women. He was preoccupied by career challenges, SAG duties, and speaking engagements. Then one day, faced with driving to San Diego to speak at a Junior League convention, he realized there was only one person he wanted in the seat beside him on the long ride. Years later he said Nancy Davis came along and "saved him from a soulless existence."

They married on March 4, 1952, in the Little Brown Church on Coldwater Canyon. Bill and Ardis Holden, the only guests, acted as witnesses and hosted the newlyweds for lunch at their Toluca Lake home after the ceremony. Nancy became Reagan's sounding board. Before speeches, he fine-tuned his thinking and tried out his phrasing on Nancy. She was integral to his success; a trusted confidante. They were a team, their bond forged in a hurricane of hardships.

In early 1952, his film career was crumbling beneath his feet. When the accounting department at MCA paid his estimated taxes based on his income level in prior years, the situation turned into a full-blown crisis. Nancy went to work. Though already pregnant, she appeared on *Ford Theater, The Schlitz Playhouse of Stars,* and *Climax Mystery Theater.* Five months after their daughter Patricia was born in October 1952, Nancy costarred with Lew Ayres in a sci-fi thriller, *Donovan's Brain.* She was paid eighteen thousand dollars and later said, with a shrug, "It wasn't a classy picture but it did pay some bills."[5] She kept her hand in—popping up on the occasional *General Electric Theater* episode and with Reagan on radio programs. When *General Electric Theater* was canceled on short notice in 1962, Nancy again helped out with the family finances by going back to work. She showed up on *The Dick Powell Show, 87th Precinct*, and *Wagon Train.*

Working His Network

Through the difficult years of the early 1950s, as his film career was collapsing, Reagan refused to give up. He aggressively worked his network, spending hours on the phone every day promoting his career by staying in touch with contacts and checking in with his agent. With dogged determination, he pushed through the hard times. In later years, he loved to tell a story about a little boy who, confronted with a barn filled with manure, picks up a shovel and starts digging, saying, "There's got to be a pony in here somewhere!" Ronald Reagan strongly identified with that apocryphal child, whose approach to life mirrored his own. When times were tough, he worked harder than ever.

Reagan wasn't the only actor dealing with nerve-racking career problems. In 1952, nobody in Hollywood was working. At least that's how it felt. In January, Universal slashed Reagan's five-picture contract to three films after he rejected two roles he considered beneath him. Under pressure from union strikes, a 1948 Supreme Court ruling that forced the studios to divest themselves of their distribution outlets—the movie theaters—and from television, production at Hollywood's once-booming studios had slowed to a crawl. In 1951, cities with television reception reported drops in movie attendance of 20 to 40 percent. Once-packed movie theaters were being converted to bowling alleys.

The television tsunami crushed other businesses as well. Attendance at sporting events plummeted as formerly reliable fans stayed home to watch televised games from the comfort of living-room sofas. Radio was another casualty. Ratings and listenership plunged. As always with major changes in technology, some clung to the past; others, with more vision, made fortunes in the new medium.

Hollywood stars were certain television was a passing phenomenon. Gazing down their noses at the new medium from their carefully crafted perches, they occasionally deigned to appear on a program as a "guest star." The problem with television, as Hollywood stars saw it, was that series didn't last long and when the program was canceled, the actor—strongly branded by the role—found it difficult, if not impossible, to move on to a new assignment.

But for Reagan's talent agency, MCA, television was a goldmine. Spotting an opening as television blossomed, they developed a new line of business, Revue Productions, to produce television programs.

MCA's stable of stars gave Revue an enormous pool of talent to tap. Producing television shows was the perfect complement to their agency business. There was only one snag. The Screen Actors Guild had a rule unique to their union that was designed to prevent producers from double-dipping with clients and favoring a chosen few. The rule prohibited producers from acting as agents. MCA needed a waiver.

As the film industry contracted under pressure from television, Stein and Wasserman approached SAG in early 1952 with a proposal. They pointed out that the center of the television business was New York City and likely to remain so. At a meeting with SAG representatives, the pair hammered home their point: "Your guys here are not going to get a whiff of it."[6] Their proposal was that MCA's subsidiary Revue Productions would guarantee to make lots of television programs in Los Angeles and keep lots of SAG actors busy earning a living "*if* you can work it out with us as an agent."[7] The idea was shocking.

SAG's board of directors was faced with a stark choice: Find a way to work with MCA or lose the television business to the East Coast. Recently hired SAG lawyer Chester (Chet) Migden was the new kid in the room the night MCA's proposal was put before the thirty-five members of the SAG board. The debate raged for hours. In a 1989 interview, Migden summed up the heated issue: "It's conflict of interest, that while you represent talent as their agent, you are . . . representing the talent and you should at all times represent talent and not be someone who sits on the other side of the table as producer. You can't sit on both sides of the table at once. How do you employ people you represent?"[8] Migden recalled: "Reagan didn't say anything, he was in the chair." It was a management strategy that Reagan had picked up from watching leaders he admired at SAG. Listening carefully was the signature attribute of his leadership style. He wanted to hear the views of others and refrained from cutting off forthright discussion by stating his own views. Finally Walter Pidgeon spoke up. His situation was typical. He'd been a major contract player for twenty years at MGM, twice nominated for Academy Awards. He'd recently been let go.

Looking around the table at his fellow actors, Pidgeon clarified the issue, defined the argument, and made an impassioned plea. Migden remembered Pidgeon as saying, "Now, now wait a minute. . . . We're dying [in Hollywood]. What's the alternative? To go to New York and work in live television for a couple of hundred dollars? We're starving to death. We're going down in flames. What have we got to lose? Let 'em try it. I mean the worst thing that can happen is it'll work."

Suddenly it seemed obvious. By putting in place a highly detailed agreement with MCA to ensure fair treatment of the actors—for example, MCA could not "double-dip" by charging their own clients a commission—Hollywood actors had nothing to lose and possibly a lot to gain by granting the waiver to MCA. The issue was put to a vote. On July 14, 1952, SAG's board of directors voted overwhelmingly in favor of the waiver.

The decision triggered a shift in the tectonic plates underlying the television industry. Soon the production side of the business was sliding toward the Pacific. Exactly as Stein and Wasserman had predicted, the waiver was a boon to Hollywood actors and the local economy, but the decision haunted Reagan and MCA. The waiver was hotly declared "unprecedented." It was. But that was hardly surprising. SAG as an institution was less than twenty years old. It had been founded in 1933 by established stars to protect all actors from the grueling demands of studios. The emergence of television as a competitor for entertainment dollars was the first time screen actors had been confronted with a threat to their livelihood.

Surely, some suggested, there was a sweetheart deal between Reagan and his agent, Lew Wasserman, at MCA. According to Chet Migden, that "was one bum rap."[9] Migden had "never voted for Ronald Reagan to be president of the United States, but I have a conscience about telling it the way it really was."[10] The entertainment industry was in a transition phase and people made mistakes. Faced with a similar decision, CBS management granted Lucille Ball and Desi Arnaz all residual rights to *I Love Lucy.* In the case of the waiver for MCA and *I Love Lucy* residuals, nobody foresaw that with the stroke of a pen, they were giving away fortunes.

Ten years later, under pressure from the Justice Department, MCA was forced to make a choice between the company's two lines of business. Stein and Wasserman tossed the talent agency aside and focused on production. Eventually, Revue acquired record companies, publishing firms, a radio station, and Universal Pictures, but in 1952 the company was focused on putting together shows for the burgeoning television industry. Once they secured the waiver agreement with SAG, the next big challenge was to get reluctant stars enthusiastic about appearing on television.

In June 1952, Reagan was juggling an imploding career, the complicated waiver issue at SAG, a new marriage, a new home, young children from his first marriage, and a baby on the way, but he took time to deliver a commencement address. The venue was a small Disciples of Christ–affiliated women's school, William Woods College in Fulton, Missouri. A contact from college days had recommended him. Nancy Reagan remembered watching him write the speech on the eastbound train. The talk was a shift from his at-the-time-standard Hollywood-centric speech toward a broader perspective and an almost imperceptible step toward his next, as yet unseen, career.

Delivered on June 2, 1952, the address, titled "America the Beautiful," became part of history as Ronald Reagan's first fully recorded speech. Set against newspaper headlines of eight million refugees fleeing communist regimes in eastern Europe and war raging on the Korean peninsula, Reagan talked about "the inherent love of freedom in each one of us" and said "the great ideological struggle that we find ourselves engaged in today is not a new struggle." He explained the basis for democracy is "that no group can decide for the people what is good for the people so well as they can decide for themselves." He concluded by quoting Abraham Lincoln: "And with your help I am sure we can come much closer to realizing that this land of ours is 'the last best hope' of man on earth."

That fall, Reagan headed Democrats for Eisenhower and stepped down as president of SAG after five and a half terms but remained on the board of directors. He was justifiably concerned his role as head of the Screen Actors Guild was having an adverse effect on his career. Jack Dales, SAG's executive director, thought he had a point. "When you see a fellow across the table all the time, and you're arguing cold facts and dollars, you're not thinking of him in terms of how would he look opposite Bette Davis in something."[11]

As head of the Screen Actors Guild, Reagan dealt with competing voices within the industry; he balanced the interests of corporations with those of individual contributors; and he visited the White House to talk to President Truman about the economic impact of making movies in other countries. During his years as president of SAG, he shepherded the industry through cataclysmic changes—the mandated shedding of the theater chains and the onslaught of a new medium. In contract negotiations, he fought hard for SAG members' fair share of the bounty in residual payments from the flourishing new television industry.

Meanwhile, the Reagans' financial situation was disintegrating. There was a mortgage on the ranch Reagan had bought near Malibu Lake in 1951 after selling his ranch in Northridge, and two mortgages on the home he bought with Nancy on Amalfi Drive in Pacific Palisades. Their living room remained empty for two years. They didn't have the money to buy furniture.

The Path to a New Career

They appeared in print advertisements. She, the "winsome socialite," endorsed Blue Bonnet margarine—"tastes sunny-sweet."

He showed up in ads for a "greaseless, good grooming" hair product, Chesterfield cigarettes, Union Pacific's Domeliner, and Van Heusen shirts that "won't wrinkle ever!" Just when things looked hopeless—"at the lowest point of all"—they were saved by the unexpected offer of a role in a film called *Law and Order*. Coming at Christmastime, Reagan joked he could hear "the sound of sleigh bells and tiny hoofs on the roof."

Still, he refused to do Broadway or a television series. Broadway didn't pay enough. Reagan once commented at a SAG meeting that one's earnings as an actor are based on how many people will pay to see you perform. The core economic issue was that movies reached a broader audience than Broadway or television. He was sure a role in a television series would destroy any chance of rekindling his movie career. In early 1954, his agent called to ask if he would work with a stripper in Las Vegas. The answer was a firm no. No matter how much money they waved in front of him. The agent tweaked the deal and called back. How about opening for a nightclub act in Las Vegas? Reagan hesitated. Normally he kept in close contact with his agent by phone, but this time he arranged a meeting in person at the MCA office. What would he be expected to do? They replied with a question of their own: "How many benefits have you done?" He replied, "Hundreds." His after-hours hobby was about to provide him with a way to climb out of a very deep hole.

The money—fifteen thousand dollars a week for two weeks—was irresistible. The Reagans packed their bags—including a suitcase full of books—and headed to Vegas. The shows were sellouts. With strong support from a team of

Hollywood gag writers, he did a credible job as the emcee for a group called the Continentals who sang and did comedy routines. Nancy sat through every performance sipping a glass of water. Reagan was a hit, and offers were soon flowing in from New York's Waldorf-Astoria and nightclubs from Chicago to Miami. But it didn't feel like the right fit. After two weeks, the Reagans were relieved to be heading home. But home to what?

Another movie offer came along. *Cattle Queen of Montana*, starring Hollywood pro Barbara Stanwyck in the title role. Reagan was still hoping for a breakthrough role in a western. Filmed in Technicolor in Montana's breathtaking Glacier National Park, the project looked like a winner. Like too many of Reagan's postwar films, it was a disappointment. He put a good face on it, characterizing the film as "solid" but not "earthshattering." *Variety*'s review was closer to the truth: "listless and ordinary," and "short on imagination and long on cliché." Just when it looked as if his career couldn't withstand any more disasters, he caught a break.

On the Road with General Electric

General Electric, under Electric Charlie's leadership, developed an outreach program to its 750,000 employees. Headed by Lemuel Boulware, the effort came to be known as "Boulwarism." The term was also used more narrowly to describe a management negotiating strategy. The view from the GE executive suite was that management didn't want to be seen as at odds with the best interests of employees. Instead of letting union negotiators wrestle concessions during prolonged and painful negotiating sessions, management put their "fair and final" offer on the table at the start of the process.

To educate employees on how business, industry, and capitalism work, Boulware's team, the Employee and Community Relations Program, had developed a multipronged approach. Radio programs, television shows, newsletters, and book clubs were all part of the effort. The team developed *College Bowl*—"The Varsity Sport for the Mind"—exactly the sort of high-minded programming GE liked to sponsor. *College Bowl* donated scholarship money to the schools that participated. Their tag line was "General Electric Cares."

Nineteen forty-eight was the year sales of television sets took off, and General Electric was in the forefront of communicating with customers through the new medium. The company's first attempt at developing a signature program had the earmarks of a committee at work. It was a flop and was dropped after one performance. Next was a quiz show that lasted for twelve weeks. Then, in April 1949, they tried an adaptation of a big band radio program—the *Fred Waring Show*. An improvement on its predecessors, the show survived for a couple of seasons.

In the early days of television, corporations looked to their advertising agencies, in General Electric's case BBD&O, for programming suggestions. In a few smoke-filled meetings, BBD&O execs came up with what sounded like just another familiar format—the anthology—but their version had an edge. They would lure movie stars to the program by giving the actors the opportunity to choose their roles and play against type. GE sweetened the pot with one other significant benefit: Ownership of the program was turned over to the star after the program was aired a few times. Thirty years later those early black-and-white programs were still showing in remote corners of the world, and the stars were still receiving their residual checks. Actors loved that. Major stars of the era—Jimmy Stewart, Joan Crawford, Fred Astaire, Joan Fontaine—made their television debuts on the program. On February 1, 1953, Boulware's Department of Public Relations Services launched *General Electric Theater*. It was declared an "all company project."

In its first two seasons, *General Electric Theater* made a name for itself with ground-breaking projects. The goal was "outstanding entertainment" in a wide variety of formats. That presented a challenge. With no link or consistency from week to week, the show lacked a cohesive brand. Searching for a way to provide continuity between episodes, BBD&O hit on the idea of having a host introduce the show each week. GE was "very definite" about the kind of person they wanted: "good moral character, intelligent." They considered a number of actors. When Taft Schreiber at MCA suggested Ronald Reagan, it went through almost immediately. In August 1954, the Reagans took the train to New York to meet with GE executives.

Reagan's meeting in person with the MCA team about the gig in Las Vegas seemed to trigger a new line of thinking about his career. The spark may have been the conversation about the many speeches he'd given. Perhaps it was his success as master of ceremonies for the Continentals. Or his new look. In his five and a half terms as SAG president, he'd gone from wearing open-neck shirts and sports jackets to dressing in suits and ties. The guild, populated by smart, talented, highly capable people, had served as an incubator for him. He'd developed a dignity that gave weight to his words, conferred on him a certain status, and made him automatically the center of a group. His new persona, or brand, synced with what a corporate sponsor was looking for. He projected mature, solid, and dependable.

Taking On a New Challenge

If GE had approached Reagan in 1946, he would have turned the offer down flat, still harboring the dream that there was a promising career ahead for him in films. After eight frustrating years, he had few remaining illusions about his movie career. In the summer of 1954, when the most respected company in America offered him the best time slot on the busiest, most prestigious television night of the week, on the so-called "Tiffany network,"[12] it was a solid-gold opportunity. He would be host-narrator and occasional star of the showcase program of America's premier corporation on Sunday evenings at nine o'clock on CBS. The program would have a strong lead-in from Ed Sullivan's top-rated program—first known as *Toast of the Town*, after his newspaper column, and later as the *Ed Sullivan Show*.

And he was interested. Since his deal with Universal had imploded fourteen months earlier, he had been floundering, and now he was ready for a steady job. The opportunity with GE offered the benefit of a predictable income stream without the usual typecasting problem associated with a television series. Taft Schreiber brokered the deal and crafted the contract to give him the flexibility to choose his own roles—catnip to an actor—and how often he appeared on the show in an acting role. Nancy wasn't an official part of the deal, but she appeared on *General Electric Theater* from time to time. There was one other component to GE's offer. The company wanted him to act as an in-house cheerleader for the program. As a strong extrovert, son of a salesman and would-be actress, he loved the idea of being in front of a live audience.

The deal came together rapidly. In short order he was signed to a three-year contract at $125,000 a year. That December, three months after Reagan took the helm as host, the show broke into the top ten programs as ranked by Nielsen. The program's success was largely due to the visits Reagan made to GE facilities to meet employees. Representing the thinking of GE management, his core message "was that the only way wages could be increased was for the corporation to be successful. He explained how the private enterprise system works, how it is to the advantage of the worker to make good products so that they will sell well. This is the only way a company earns the money to pay higher wages."[13] The message seemed self-evident, but it wasn't popular. Reagan faced "a lot of heckling"[14] at first.

Earl Dunckel was recruited in the late 1940s to join the company as a "communicator." It took some coaxing to get him to give up his newspaper job, but once he was onboard he was rapidly promoted to advertising account supervisor. From there he was bumped up to be one of two executives in charge of *General Electric Theater*. His colleague handled the overall management of the project and the show itself. Dunckel, tasked with handling "what we call audience promotion,"[15] was Reagan's primary contact and traveling companion for the first year on the road with GE.

Dunckel recalled meeting Reagan for the first time on a sound stage in New York City. "It was affection at first sight for us both, I think. . . . My reading and my previous limited first-hand experience with Hollywood types had not prepared me for the smiling, affable, and obviously sincere man who shook hands with me that afternoon. No arrogance. No preoccupation with self. No posturing. No visible vanity. Just a tall, slim, good-looking man with twinkling eyes and a firm handshake." Dunckel thought Reagan was a perfect fit for what GE had been looking for: someone who had "intelligence and depth who would, we hoped, reflect the dignity and enterprise and credibility of the company."

Dunckel said, "The tours were something new." As a way to communicate with employees, the tours were unique to General Electric and Reagan. The principal objective was "to have Ron meet and charm these GE vice presidents all over the country." After all, Dunckel said, "If you try something new, your biggest obstacle is your own people. . . . The old not-invented-here syndrome." The goal of the tours was to generate positive word of mouth about the program among GE's thought leaders. The thinking was that once employees met Reagan, they couldn't help but like him and would want to support the program. Secondary goals were to leverage Reagan "as an audience promotion device" and "as an employee communications device" beyond the program. Over the next eight years, by Reagan's estimate, he spoke with 250,000 GE employees at 139 plants scattered across forty states.[16]

The first stop was GE's sprawling headquarters on six hundred acres in Schenectady, New York. The pace was grueling. In the smoke-filled factories of the era, Reagan couldn't wear his contact lenses, and he was, as always, reluctant to wear his eyeglasses. At times he functioned almost blind. He walked miles on concrete plant floors—stopping constantly to greet and chat with assembly-line employees. The turbine plant alone covered thirty-one acres. At the end of the first day, his feet were so swollen he had to cut his shoelaces to get his shoes off. Ever the actor, despite the physical demands, Reagan managed to come across as easygoing and happy. On that first, eight-week swing, Dunckel had planned visits to GE's largest and most important plants—Cleveland, Cincinnati, Boston, and Philadelphia. Since the schedule had already been announced, they had to stick to it. Dunckel remembered the tour as "almost beyond the limits of human endurance."[17] Going forward, they made adjustments.

One of their early trips was to the GE plant in Erie, Pennsylvania. At the time, Reagan refused to fly, so he and Dunckel traveled everywhere by train. To get to Erie, they boarded an overnight train in New York's Grand Central Terminal, arrived in Erie at 6:30 A.M., and were whisked into a waiting car. They put in a full day walking the plant floors, talking to employees, and meeting with GE execs and fell into bed at the hotel after midnight. As they toured the plants, women pressed "mash notes" on Reagan and occasionally bared a breast for an autograph. Men huddled on the sidelines, muttering dark thoughts about the actor. Reagan cheerfully chatted with the women, then excused himself, walked over, and introduced himself to the men. By the time he left, the hostile crowd was laughing, slapping him on the back, and giving him the 1950s equivalent of high fives.

Listening to formal presentations and casual conversations, Reagan got to know GE's executives and came to understand the challenges they faced in running a business. By coincidence, Boulware's team had commissioned a shortened version of Reagan's Eureka economics textbook by Lewis Haney and distributed copies throughout the company to serve as a basis for discussions. On long train rides between plants and from coast to coast, Reagan pored over GE's internal newsletters targeted at different levels of the staff, briefing documents put together by Dunckel's team, and local newspapers, and squabbled about politics.

Reagan's politics were shifting in the 1950s, spurred by the expansion of the federal government under the Roosevelt administration, sky-high tax rates of up to 90 percent, and his experience with communism in Hollywood. Yet, despite supporting Republican candidates, Reagan still saw himself as a committed Democrat. Dunckel was a self-avowed "staunch conservative."

Self-Confidence Through Experience

Early in their travels, on a three-day swing through Schenectady, Reagan was presented with what turned out to be a life-changing opportunity. Thousands of teachers had gathered at the city's armory for a conference. On short notice, their keynote speaker canceled. A representative from the group, knowing Reagan was in town, contacted GE to ask if he would fill in. Dunckel's immediate reaction was no. The idea made him "scared stiff" and "nervous." If the event went badly it would be "a real black mark" on his career. Reagan was still giving his "standard talk about Hollywood," and this event called for something different: a speech that would connect directly with the concerns of the teachers. Heavily scheduled with GE commitments, Dunckel didn't have time to write a new speech. Reagan, with more faith in himself, felt different: "Dunk, let's give it a try." He delivered. The teachers gave him "a good ten-minute standing applause afterward." Word of the success rippled through the GE grapevine. From then on, wherever he went, local offices arranged to have him speak to their community organizations.

Over the next eight years, he gave an estimated nine thousand[18] speeches to GE employees and their communities. He spoke to "Elks, Moose, LIONS, at American Legion Halls and soapbox derby contestants."[19] He spoke to auditoriums filled with executives and to small groups of workers who had turned off their machines and briefly stepped away from assembly lines. He learned to listen and adapt. A 1956 *Los Angeles Times* article titled "Reagan Chides Producers for Losing Touch With the Public" said he had "met more people in one year on this job than our moviemakers encounter in a lifetime" and that he had a "good idea" of what people were thinking.

By 1957, *General Electric Theater* had settled into comfortable success as the number-three program on television, beaten in the ratings only by its lead-in program, Ed Sullivan's show, and *I Love Lucy*. Reagan signed a new contract that doubled his salary to $250,000, and the family moved up the hill to a new home in Pacific Palisades. Built by GE as "the home of the future," it was packed with General Electric appliances and gadgets. Suddenly, Reagan's Hollywood peers were clamoring for their own television shows. MCA's Revue Productions was happy to oblige. It arranged shows for, among others, Jane Wyman, Loretta Young, and Reagan's old friend from his days at Warner's, Dick Powell.

The years rolled on with more speeches, more train rides, and more walks through GE plants. In 1958, the Reagans welcomed a new cast member—Ronald Prescott Reagan—nicknamed "Skipper." That year Reagan told the Executives' Club in Chicago, "This superstructure of government imposed on our original form is composed of bureaus and departments and is unchanged by any election. This hierarchy threatens to reverse the relationship of citizen and civil servant." Ralph Cordiner, Electric Charlie's highly regarded successor, nudged his thinking along with the advice, "You'd better get yourself a philosophy, something you can stand for and something you think this country stands for." Reagan took the advice to heart. Cordiner said, "I think this is when he really started to change."[20]

Criss-crossing America on trip after trip, Reagan spoke out against government regulation and for free enterprise. His thinking on the issues he cared about—taxes, bureaucracy, and freedom—began to take shape and appear in his speeches. With Cordiner's endorsement, Reagan waded further into politics. Though still formally a Democrat, in 1960 he gave about two hundred speeches on behalf of GOP presidential candidate Richard Nixon. Taft Schreiber, senior executive at MCA, said, "I think he sharpened his wits and saw what it might be like to be a politician—to be confronted with issues he had no total involvement in. He began to speak out, and I think this is what made him a politician."

Moon Reagan attributed his brother's change of heart to two things: "number one, his activities with General Electric—because a major point of his activity was not the show; it was the trips he made to General Electric plants to talk to the employees out in the shops—that, plus the beating that he took mentally during the Screen Actors Guild strike with two of the unions. . . . This was the first time he ever saw any bunch of pickets swinging three-foot lengths of log chain at people's heads who were just trying to go in and go to work. . . . It finally brought him around to the place where he thought maybe the country needed some changes."[21]

In November 1959, Reagan reluctantly agreed to serve again as president of SAG to guide the organization through a contract strike and try to reverse agreements already made about residual payments. Or, as he put it, "one, the end of the stop-gap clause and the establishment of the principle of repayment for re-use; two, the setting up of a pension and welfare fund."[22] In the end, SAG's negotiating team realized they couldn't fight a battle that had already been lost and settled for a pension plan as a tradeoff for residuals.

The years with General Electric executives had an impact on him. Jack Dales noted a "distinct growth. I saw him really assume a tremendous leadership and leap in the 1960 negotiations. . . . I think that he became much more adroit and much stronger in '60." On April 18, 1960, at a mass meeting of SAG members, Reagan outlined the strike-settlement agreement he and his team had reached with studio heads. He was rewarded with a standing ovation. Members overwhelmingly approved the deal. The lopsided vote was 6,399 to 259. In June, Reagan resigned as president, and a month later he resigned from the board.

Less by design than by chance, in his years with GE he created a vast network of contacts and an army of supporters. In 1961, he spoke to, among others, the Phoenix Chamber of Commerce, Illinois Manufacturers' Costs Association, and employees of Forest Lawn Cemetery. His speech constantly evolved. He tweaked it and renamed it "Losing Freedom by Installments," "No Place to Escape To," "Encroaching Control," and "A Time for Choosing." His speech was used as an article in business publications and distributed within organizations. Talking to fellow citizens, he found they reminded him of the solid, feet-planted-firmly-on-the-ground neighbors he'd grown up with in Dixon. In his years with GE, his perspective had changed. "By 1960, I realized the real enemy wasn't big business, it was big government."

Warning signs were flashing that *General Electric Theater* was nearing the end of its run. The public had lost its enthusiasm for anthology-style programs. Interest had shifted to stories that centered on a family. In 1959, *Bonanza*—a program about a widower with three sons living on a huge ranch called the Ponderosa—had debuted on NBC. For two years the series languished in a Saturday night time slot opposite *Perry Mason*. Scheduled for cancellation, *Bonanza* was given one last shot because it was filmed in color and RCA, the network's parent corporation, was in the business of selling color television sets. In 1961, the show was moved to the high-profile 9:00 P.M. Sunday slot against *General Electric Theater.* Competing with GE's creaking black-and-white program, *Bonanza* took off, rocketing to the top of the Nielsen ratings where it remained for ten years.

In 1961, sixteen GE executives were convicted in a price-fixing scandal. Suddenly Reagan's contacts had retired, moved on to new roles, or were scrambling to protect their own jobs. The company's antagonists spotted an opening. At a shareholder's meeting, "an inveterate needler" demanded Cordiner resign. Jim Carey, head of GE's largest union, denounced management in a sixteen-page speech. In the tumult, Reagan's pleas to film *General Electric Theater* in color went unheeded. The era of the dignified host-narrator, far removed from hawking GE's wares, was over. He turned down a last-minute offer to stay with the company. Three years later Reagan wrote Dunckel, "off the record . . . the last call I had twelve hours before the show was cancelled was a query as to whether I would continue on the speaking tours, but confine my remarks to selling G.E. products."[23] The last episode of *General Electric Theater* aired in May 1962.

Taking Time to Think and Plan

For Reagan, the program's cancellation was a blow. At fifty-one, he still had young children to support and put through school. He pleaded with Wasserman to find him a new project. But Wasserman had his hands full at MCA and little time for a fading actor. That spring, Reagan was on his own. Just as he had when deciding on a career path at Lowell Park and after the war at Lake Arrowhead, Reagan took the time to think, plan, and establish goals for his future—this time at a resort in Arizona where he did a lot of horseback riding—and talked things over with a friend. He set to work on an autobiography and got involved in Richard Nixon's 1962 losing gubernatorial campaign.

He was still a registered Democrat. He had considered switching his registration during the 1960 campaign but candidate Richard Nixon told him he would be more effective as a spokesman if he remained a registered Democrat. Finally in 1962, while he was onstage speaking at a campaign event, a registrar, waving the paperwork in her hand, demanded to know if he had changed his party affiliation yet. She walked up the aisle and handed him the document. He signed and gave it back to her. At fifty-one, he had finally switched his party registration to Republican. He later joked, "I didn't leave the party. The party left me."

Mulling over his options, Reagan wasn't sure what was next. In 1963, he showed up on a few television shows as a guest star and worked on his book. He wrote, "One does what he feels he can do best and serves where he feels he can make the greatest contribution."[24] He said he was trying on a number of different hats. There was one he was sure didn't fit. That was politics.

On January 1, 1964, he emceed the Tournament of Roses Parade in Pasadena with one-time Miss America and television personality Bess Myerson. He seemed to have come full circle, back to describing for the audience exactly what he was seeing in front of him. He appeared in his last film, *The Killers*, based on an Ernest Hemingway short story, and signed on to host another TV show, *Death Valley Days.* With plenty of time on his hands, he got involved with one other project, his friend Barry Goldwater's campaign for president.

LETTER TO HUGH HEFNER, JULY 4, 1960

Dear Mr. Hefner,

I've been a long time answering your letter of May 13 and my selection of the "The 4th" as an answering date is coincidence plus the fact that Holidays are "free time" days around our house:

Your letter has been very much on my mind and I question whether I can answer in a way that will make sense to you. First because I once thought exactly as you think and second because no one could have changed my thinking (and some tried). It took seven months of meeting communists and communist influenced people across a table in almost daily sessions while pickets rioted in front of studio gates, homes were bombed and a great industry almost ground to a halt.

You expressed lack of knowledge about my views, political background, etc. Because so much doubt has been cast on "anti-communists," inspired by the radicalism of extremists who saw "Reds" under every "cause." I feel I should reveal where I have stood and now stand.

My first four votes were cast for F.D.R. my fifth for Harry Truman. Following World War II my interest in liberalism and my fear of "neo-fascism" led to my serving on the board of directors of an organization later exposed as a "Communist Front" namely the Hollywood Independent Citizens Committee of the Arts, Sciences & Professions. Incidentally Mr. Trumbo was also on that board.

Now you might ask who exposed this organization as a "Front"? It was no crusading committee of Congress, or the D.A.R. or the American Legion. A small group of board members disturbed by the things being done in the organization's name introduced to their fellow board members a mild statement approving our Dem. system and free enterprise economy and repudiating communism as a desirable form of govt. for this country. The suggestion was that by adopting such a policy statement the board would reassure our membership we were liberal but not a "front". The small group who introduced this measure were such "switch hitters" as James Roosevelt, Dore Schary, Don Hartman, Olivia De Havilland, Johnny Green & myself.

Leaders of the opposition to our statement included Dalton Trumbo, John Howard Lawson, and a number of others who have since attained some fame for their refusal to answer questions. I remember one of their group reciting the Soviet constitution to prove "Russia was more Democratic than the U.S." Another said if America continued her imperialist policy & as a result wound up in a war with Russia he would be on the side of Russia against the U.S. We suggested the "policy statement" was perhaps a matter for the whole organization to decide—not just the board. We were told the membership was "not politically sophisticated enough to make such a decision."

When we resigned the organization went out of existence only to reappear later (minus us) as "Independent Citizens Committee of the Arts, Sciences & Prof." in support of Henry Wallace & the Progressive Party.

The "seven months" of meetings I mentioned in the first paragraph or two refers to the jurisdictional strike in the Motion Pic. business. There are volumes of documentary evidence, testimony of former Communists, etc. that this whole affair was under the leadership of Harry Bridges and was aimed at an ultimate organizing of everyone in the picture business within Mr. Bridges longshoreman's union.

Now none of what I've said answers your argument that freedom of speech means freedom to disagree, does it? Here begins my difficulty. How can I put down in less than book form the countless hours of meetings, the honest attempts at compromise, the trying to meet dishonesty, lies and cheating with conduct bound by rules of fair play? How can I make you understand that my feeling now is not prejudice born of this struggle but is realization supported by incontrovertible evidence that the American Communist is in truth a member of a "Russian American Bund" owing his first allegiance to a foreign power?

I, like you, will defend the right of any American to openly practice & preach any political philosophy from monarchy to anarchy. But this is not the case with regard to the communist. He is bound by party discipline to deny he is a communist so that he can by subversion & stealth impose on an unwilling people the rule of the International Communist Party which is in fact the govt. of Soviet Russia. I say to you that any man still or now a member of the "party" was a man who looked upon the death of American soldiers in Korea as a victory for his side. For proof of this I refer you to some of the ex-communists who fled the party at that time & for that reason, including some of Mr. Trumbo's companions of the "Unfriendly 10".

Hollywood has no blacklist. Hollywood does have a list handed to it by millions of "movie goers" who have said "we don't want and will not pay to see pictures made by or with these people we consider traitors". On this list were many names of people we in Hollywood felt were wrongly suspect. I personally served on a committee that succeeded in clearing these people. Today any person who feels he is a victim of discrimination because of his political beliefs can avail himself of machinery to solve this problem.

I must ask you as a publisher, aside from questions of political philosophy, should a film producer be accused of bigotry for not hiring an artist when the customers for his product have labeled the artist "poor box office," regardless of the cause?

I realize I've presented my case poorly due to the limitations of pen & paper so may I ask one favor? Will you call the F.B.I. there in Chi. ask for the anti-communist detail, then tell him our correspondence (show him my letter if you like) and ask his views on this subject of communism as a political belief or a fifth column device of Russia.

Now my apologies for having taken so long in answering your letter and my appreciation for your having taken the time & trouble to write in the first place.

Sincerely,
Ronald Reagan

CREATING YOUR NETWORK OF CONTACTS AND SUPPORTERS

Not knowing when the dawn will come,
I open every door.

—Emily Dickinson

- Volunteer with industry, nonprofit, or alumni associations. These organizations provide you with opportunities to develop contacts in your field and learn new skills. The more you put into it, the more you will get out of it.
- Keep in touch with your network of friends and supporters.
- Maintain good relationships with opponents and rivals. You never know when you will need their help and cooperation.
- Find a life partner or trusted confidant who is supportive of your goals and dreams. That person will be integral to your success.
- Forge strategic alliances. Seek out business partners whose strengths and talents complement your abilities.
- Surround yourself with positive, upbeat people who support your success.
- Value and cultivate friendships. A strong network of friendships and connections will be a key factor in your career success.

Working It In

Identify three to five organizations that you can benefit from joining, supporting, or getting involved with.

Which will strengthen your network?

Which will allow you to develop new skills and learn from others?

How can you stay in touch with your connections? Find a way that works for you.

Chapter 5

Turning Point

Transition into Politics—Los Angeles, California, 1964

Instead of reading a speech, Reagan read his audience.

—Kurt Ritter, Professor of Communication,
Texas A&M University

In the summer of 1964, GOP senator Barry Goldwater's presidential campaign was struggling. There was little enthusiasm for Goldwater among the Eastern Establishment wing of the GOP. He'd been bloodied by a bruising primary battle with New York governor Nelson Rockefeller. Discouraging poll results further eroded support. But campaign heavyweights in southern California were not easily daunted. They saw themselves as "champions of lost causes."[1] In a brainstorming session, businessmen Holmes Tuttle, Henry Salvatori, A. C. "Cy" Rubel, and Ed Mills came up with a novel solution to their fund-raising problem. They would throw an unprecedented thousand-dollar-a-plate dinner. Asked to run the event, Holmes Tuttle replied, "Sure." Working with his team, he lined up the Ambassador Hotel's Cocoanut Grove, invited Ronald Reagan to be the speaker, sold tickets, and raised more than four hundred thousand dollars. That evening the group chalked up an even more significant accomplishment, though it took a while to become evident. The dinner launched Ronald Reagan's political career.

Reagan's instinct was to keep his after-dinner comments brief. But since he was the only speaker on the program, aside from a few comments by Tuttle and a quick introduction by Mills, Tuttle encouraged him to deliver his standard speech, a version of the speech he had been giving for General Electric and for GOP candidates Nixon and Goldwater. That evening, as he had countless times before, Reagan talked about skyrocketing national debt, excessive taxes, burgeoning bureaucracy, and America as a beacon of liberty for the rest of the world. As waiters cleared the tables, guests besieged Tuttle and his associates with pleas to bring Reagan's speech to a wider audience. Like a rapid-response team, Tuttle's group sprang into action.

Talent and Experience Fuse to Produce Opportunity

Within weeks, on a late October evening, Reagan appeared on prime-time television to give an address on behalf of Goldwater. That night, his well-honed talent fused with his extensive experience to produce an enormous opportunity. Suddenly he was catapulted to the forefront of a political movement.

He spoke with the zeal of an Old Testament prophet, rocking back and forth on his heels. In a torrent of words, he poured out his "own ideas" on the matters he cared about most: freedom, democracy, government's role in society, and America's role in the world. He based his thinking on the principles of the

Founding Fathers and backed his arguments with compelling statistics. He spiced the text with anecdotes about Cuban refugees, farmers, and ordinary citizens and used stories to illustrate his points about rampant growth of government, out-of-control spending, compulsory health care "regardless of need," and "subordinating American interests" at the United Nations. He concluded with Lincoln's description of America as " 'the last best hope' of man on earth." It was a speech meant to inspire and inform. It was the speech that changed his life.

The formal title of Reagan's address was "A Time for Choosing," but in political lore, it came to be known simply as "The Speech." Woven seamlessly into the fabric of his life, no records exist of exactly where or when it was delivered. A senior advisor recalled it as being in San Francisco. A family member thought the venue was Phoenix. In his 1990 autobiography, Reagan vaguely described the location as a "big NBC studio." Most likely the program was taped on a sound stage in Burbank where Reagan and his brother Moon had contacts stretching back to the earliest days of the television industry, Reagan as a guest star on variety shows and host of *General Electric Theater* and Moon in the course of his thirty-year career with advertising giant McCann-Erickson.

On Tuesday, October 27, 1964, the *Chicago Tribune* ran an article about Reagan's speech that was scheduled to be shown that evening. Hinting at the time and place of the taping, the reporter mistakenly described the program as "a sequel to one Reagan delivered Friday night over NBC." The fingerprints of Reagan's energetic and well-connected mother-in-law, Edith Davis—who, in the words of a friend, "was always behind everything"[2] were all over the article, which concluded with a local angle: "Reagan, 53, is married to actress Nancy Davis, daughter of Dr. and Mrs. Loyal Davis of Chicago." The *Tribune* noted that Reagan, as California cochairman of Barry Goldwater's presidential campaign, had been speaking "at least three times a day, six or seven days a week," throughout the state.

Officially, Reagan's speech was a fund-raiser for Goldwater. Unofficially, it was a rallying cry for conservative principles. The broadcast was arranged and sponsored by the "TV for Goldwater Committee," a group of supporters spearheaded by self-made businessmen and long-term Republican activists Holmes Tuttle, owner of four Ford dealerships, and oil magnate Henry Salvatori. Both had known Reagan socially for years. Tuttle first met Reagan in the 1940s through Reagan's first wife, Jane Wyman. Reagan had left a lasting impression. Tuttle remembered the Reagan of the 1940s as "quite outspoken in his beliefs, and several times when we were together we had—I'll put it this way—some spirited discussions."[3] Tuttle's involvement in politics was spurred by his concern about ballooning social welfare programs. As he saw it, "Our federal government is taking a position that the Constitution never intended for it to do." Salvatori, on the other hand, only cared about "the preservation of this nation from the threat of subversion and Communist control." For him, "everything else was secondary."

At Reagan's suggestion, a friendly audience of Goldwater supporters—"the kind of audience I'd been talking to for years"—had been invited to the taping. Some young women were decked out in cowboy boots and Stetsons as a tribute to Senator Goldwater's western heritage. He was born in Phoenix in 1909 when Arizona was still a territory. Most of the audience were the sort of sober citizens found at any evening lecture. After a few words of introduction, Reagan spoke for just under thirty minutes.

There was laughter and applause as he spoke. The crowd loved his pithy one-liners on current events. It was a technique he had perfected during years of public speaking. Before each speech he scoured local newspapers in search of material. References to hometown issues or headline news brought his speeches to life and engaged the audience. That night when he finished speaking, people jumped to their feet in a rousing ovation. Some had tears in their eyes. Reagan had articulated the distinctly American passion for freedom and liberty that slices through political affiliation. His words went straight to the hearts of many listeners and sparked an enduring love affair between Ronald Reagan and a large swath of America.

The broadcast ran in place of David Frost's weekly program—a spoof on people and places in the news, *That Was the Week That Was,* which aired on NBC channels from 9:30 to 10:00 P.M. on Tuesday. Reagan faced stiff competition for viewers from a new soap opera, *Peyton Place,* the sitcom *Petticoat Junction*, and in some markets, a PBS special, *Man's First Winter at the South Pole at 102 Degrees Below Zero.* But the program was masterfully scheduled and promoted by advertising wizard Moon Reagan. The time slot had a strong lead-in from the network's hugely popular James Bond–style spy show *The Man from U.N.C.L.E.* Plenty of publicity was generated by prominent display ads and listings among the weekly specials on television pages in newspapers around the country.

Concerned that the Goldwater campaign would end up heavily in debt, Tuttle and Salvatori had "a little rider"[4]—some called it a "beggar"—added to the tape. As Reagan spoke, a message scrolled across the bottom of the television screen asking viewers to send in a check or call Goldwater headquarters to make a pledge of support. As the credits rolled, the reaction was immediate. In homes all over America, viewers stood up, reached for their telephones, their checkbooks, and their pens.

On October 27, the Reagans watched the broadcast of the program with friends in Los Angeles. As the credits rolled, everyone congratulated Reagan on doing a great job, but he wasn't so sure. He went to bed that night worried he "might have let Barry down." Meanwhile, Goldwater campaign headquarters in Washington, D.C., was being flooded with phone calls.

Response to The Speech was overwhelming. An elated Goldwater aide couldn't wait for morning to tell the Reagans. Calling from Washington, D.C., at 3:00 A.M. eastern time, he woke them with the news that Goldwater headquarters had been deluged with calls from people wanting to make donations. Nine days later, the *New York Times* reported Reagan's speech had raised $750,000. The funds arrived mostly in contributions of less than ten dollars. Thanks in large part to The Speech and the campaign's tight-fisted treasurer, Ralph Cordiner, retired as president and chairman of General Electric, the Goldwater campaign ended with an unprecedented and somewhat controversial surplus of $1.2 million. Some campaign operatives felt every penny available should have been spent. Others, seeing a rout looming on the horizon, preferred to husband the funds for a future battle. The Goldwater campaign was termed "a glorious disaster," but it put the conservative cause on the map and The Speech established Reagan as a Republican star.

Thousands of letters poured in from all over the country; people wrote to the Republican National Committee, to the Goldwater campaign, and to Reagan. With little administrative support to help—a secretary came in once a week—Reagan tried to answer the stacks of mail himself, or at least open all the envelopes, just as he, or one of his parents, had responded to his fan mail in his early days in Hollywood. He'd never seen anything like the torrent of mail that streamed in after The Speech. Letters beseeching him to run for office were piling up in boxes in his garage. In her 1989 autobiography, *My Turn,* Nancy Reagan recalled, "By the end of 1964, Ronnie was receiving dozens of letters every day urging him to run for governor in 1966. Some of the people who wrote to him were Democrats, and they said that if Ronnie ran, they would switch parties in order to support him." A letter from Mrs. Fred E. Eberlin of Tampa, Florida, to the Goldwater campaign captured the feelings of many:

> We've always been Republicans but have been seriously considering voting for Johnson. After watching Ronald Regan's [*sic*] speech last night we have returned to the fold. His speech was excellent—just packed with facts . . . We've come to the conclusion that Goldwater has the right ideas but doesn't

> know how to express himself. What's the matter with his speech writers? . . . After some of Goldwater's speeches my husband and I have looked at each other and said, "So what—he really didn't say anything."[5]

The demand for copies of the speech was huge. On October 31, the *Chicago Tribune* reported "more than 5,000 requests for copies" had been received and three thousand reels were already in the mail. Salvatori, watching the Reagan broadcast from his Los Angeles home, fielded a barrage of calls "from Bangor, Maine to Salem, Oregon." He quickly alerted the owner of the small company he had hired to tape Reagan's speech in front of the live audience. For the next few days the videographer worked around the clock to fill orders for copies at about fifty dollars each. The profits created another substantial revenue stream for the campaign's coffers.

According to Goldwater spokesmen, the reaction had been "enthusiastic throughout the nation." The Speech was rerun in prime time in Chicago, followed by a thirty-minute talk by Reagan's fellow Republican John Wayne, and broadcast again the following night. Across the country, grassroots GOP organizations sponsored broadcasts of The Speech on local channels and showed the tape at campaign rallies.

On November 1, the *New York Times* reported from Columbus, Ohio, that Reagan's speech had "so impressed some Republicans that they bombarded the state Central Committee with demands that it be reused and put up the necessary money." The Buckeye GOP made The Speech the centerpiece of a get-out-the-vote effort aimed at "undecided voters and

Republican defectors." They had Reagan's speech rebroadcast in twenty television markets around the state.

From Florida, a Goldwater campaign worker telegraphed:

> You have the film so use it. Show it day and night on every spot you can beg, borrow or steal, if no spots available then put it on CBS tonight [Thursday, October 29] instead of Goldwater . . . since he is not going to change any votes at this late date but the Reagan film will.[6]

Ironically, Goldwater's top advisors, Denison Kitchel and William J. Baroody, Sr., had been dead set against airing Reagan's speech. In the days between the Friday night taping of the speech and its scheduled broadcast on Tuesday, October 27, they coaxed Goldwater into calling Reagan to ask him to pull the film. Reagan and Goldwater were close personal friends. They had first met in March 1952 when the newly married Reagans visited Nancy's parents at their winter home in Phoenix. In 1964, Reagan was an early supporter of Goldwater's presidential bid and had delivered scores of speeches on behalf of his candidacy. It was an embarrassing and painful call on both ends of the phone line. Reagan responded that he'd "been making the speech all over the state for quite a while . . . and it's been very well received."[7] He pointed out that the decision to replace the program wasn't his to make and had the presence of mind to ask if Goldwater had seen the tape or read the speech. He had not.

Baroody and Kitchel may have been influenced by economics. If the media buy for the time slot had been placed through the campaign's ad agency, a twenty-three-thousand-dollar commission would have gone to them. With the Californians calling the shots, the media placement was handled by Moon Reagan and the hefty commission was going to his shop. Up to three hours before the broadcast, Baroody and Kitchel were suggesting alternatives—such as a rerun of a Goldwater program. They even managed to talk Goldwater into calling Grace Salvatori, the official holder of the purse strings, who had raised most of the funds for the Reagan program. When Goldwater inquired about using the time slot for another campaign program, she sweetly asked, "Well, do you have the money?" The Californians were adamant; if Reagan didn't get the time, nobody would.

The strongest argument Baroody and Kitchel could come up with for pulling Reagan's speech was that his views on Social Security would terrorize senior citizens. A key part of Reagan's speech was his illustration of how citizens saving for retirement could get a better return on their investments in the "open market." He explained how an insurance policy purchased at the age of twenty-one by a young man "would guarantee $220 a month at age sixty-five. The government promises $127." Reagan added that the hypothetical young man, "could live it up until he is thirty-one and then take out a policy that would pay more than Social Security." It was exactly the sort of illustration that Reagan and his audiences loved—a vivid example of government waste and inefficiency. When Goldwater finally watched a tape of the program, according to Moon Reagan, who was in the room, he turned to Baroody and Kitchel and demanded, "What the hell's wrong with that?"[8]

Despite Reagan's effort, the election's outcome was inevitable. The country, still grieving over the shocking death of President Kennedy less than a year earlier, elected his vice president, Lyndon Johnson. During the campaign, Johnson, with some help from Goldwater, had painted the senator as a right-wing extremist. The result was a landslide. Johnson won with 61.1 percent of the popular vote and 486 electoral votes. Goldwater racked up an anemic 52 electoral votes capturing just five states across the South and his home state of Arizona.

Speaking to die-hard Goldwater supporters on election night at the Ambassador Hotel, Reagan, ever the optimist, betrayed a hint of wishful thinking as he declared, "It's a shame there isn't some place in a campaign for quality to pay off. Sure we're disappointed. Sure, we didn't expect this . . . but take a look at the figure on our side and remember every one [vote] represents a conservative we didn't have when we started out."[9]

Despite the disappointment, Reagan didn't miss a beat. A week later he was back at the Ambassador telling enthusiastic young Republicans, "This is not a post mortem nor an autopsy." Goldwater, he said, had been the target of the "worst campaign of vilification and the worst betrayal of those who should have given us their trust."[10] That month he met with William F. Buckley, Jr., author of *God and Man at Yale,* and founder of *National Review*, and novelist John Dos Passos, among others, to form the American Conservative Union. Major media outlets, including *Time* magazine, the *Washington Post,* and the *Wall Street Journal*, closely monitored his activities. Like a helium balloon, his name kept popping up in the press as a potential candidate.

All residual rancor among Republicans was saved for moderates whom conservatives saw as "traitors" for failing to support the national ticket—the legacy of the bitter primary campaign. Within days of the broadcast, Reagan was being touted as a candidate for governor of California, the nation's largest state. On November 15, the *Los Angeles Times* reported Reagan consistently vetoed the suggestion, saying, "Running for office has never appealed to me," and, if asked to run, "I hope I could turn it down." By 1964, he had a lot of experience doing just that.

In 1954, Holmes Tuttle first approached Reagan about running for a U.S. Senate seat on the Republican ticket. Reagan "turned down the offer with thanks," saying, "I'm a ham—always was and always will be."[11] That same year, Reagan was also approached by a group of Democrats on the same mission with the same results. In 1962, Reagan refused another plea from California Republicans to run for a Senate seat, saying he couldn't afford the pay cut.

The steady stream of acclamation that poured in after the broadcast began to change Reagan's thinking about running for office. In the weeks following The Speech, a relentless drumbeat reverberated up and down California calling for Reagan to run for governor. Soon an undeclared rival felt it necessary to come out and dismiss Reagan as " 'intelligent, articulate and handsome' but not a moderate."[12] By the end of November, the *Los Angeles Times* was calling Reagan "the hottest—and newest—prospect" in the 1966 race for governor.

Reagan still saw himself as being in "entertainment." That was the career path he'd set for himself thirty years earlier and he was making a good living at it. That August, at the urging of his brother, he had signed a contract with Moon's client, U.S. Borax, to be "host-narrator and occasional star" of the company's television series, *Death Valley Days.* It was a reprise of his role with *General Electric Theater* from 1954 to 1962 but without the back-breaking travel commitment of touring company plants and facilities.

And yet, another path was tugging at him. Over many years, many miles, and many conversations in his years with General Electric and on the campaign trail for Richard Nixon and Barry Goldwater, Reagan's thinking had coalesced into a coherent political philosophy. He knew what he thought, why he thought it, what he stood for, and what he believed in. Unexpectedly, his experiences had led him to a life-changing moment on an otherwise unremarkable October night. Everything that happened afterward—his years in Sacramento and in the White House—flowed from that transformational evening. His journey had been launched by a love of being in the limelight, powered by years spent polishing his communication skills, and driven by countless conversations with fellow citizens in tiny hamlets and big cities across America. Along the way his thinking crystallized into The Speech.

In speech after speech, he talked about the issues he cared about most: freedom, democracy, unleashing the innate creativity and resourcefulness of human beings from excessive taxes and government regulations—in his words, "The freedoms that were intended for us by the Founding Fathers." On March 16, 1964, the *Los Angeles Times* reported he was giving a speech called "A Time for Choosing" for the "annual membership tea of the San

Marino Republican Women's Club" at the Huntington-Sheraton in Pasadena. He had given countless speeches for similar audiences. By October 29, 1964, political insiders Rowland Evans and Robert Novak were already referring to him in the *Washington Post* as "that old Republican warhorse from Hollywood."[13]

The Washington hotshots little expected that in coming years the old warhorse would be elected governor of California with a plurality of one million votes and would be handily re-elected four years later, or that he would challenge a president from his own party to a primary contest, and despite losing the first six races and almost running out of money, he would fight back hard to arrive at the party's convention with 1,070 delegates versus the incumbent's 1,187. Four years after that, with many of his schoolmates retired to rocking chairs, he once again strode onto the political stage, this time to take on a first-term president. The old warhorse won that election with 91 percent of the electoral votes and swept twelve newly elected senators and thirty-four freshmen House members into office with him. In 1984, he breezed to victory, winning forty-nine states. His opponent won only his home state.

But all that was ahead, in the unknowable future, in the fall of 1964.

"A TIME FOR CHOOSING," THE SPEECH AS DELIVERED OCTOBER 27, 1964 (EXCERPTS)

I am going to talk of controversial things. I make no apology for this. I have been talking on this subject for ten years, obviously under the administration of both parties. I mention this only because it seems impossible to legitimately debate the issues of the day without being subjected to name-calling and the application of labels. Those who deplore use of the terms "pink" and "leftist" are themselves guilty of branding all who oppose their liberalism as right wing extremists. How long can we afford the luxury of this family fight when we are at war with the most dangerous enemy ever known to man?

If we lose that war, and in so doing lose our freedom, it has been said history will record with the greatest astonishment that those who had the most to lose did the least to prevent its happening. The guns are silent in this war but frontiers fall while those who should be warriors prefer neutrality. Not too long ago two friends of mine were talking to a Cuban refugee. He was a businessman who had escaped from Castro. In the midst of his tale of horrible experiences, one of my friends turned to the other and said, "We don't know how lucky we are." The Cuban stopped and said, "How lucky you are? I had some place to escape to." And in that sentence he told the entire story. If freedom is lost here there is no place to escape to.

It's time we asked ourselves if we still know the freedoms intended for us by the Founding Fathers. James Madison said, "We base all our experiments on the capacity of mankind for self-government." This idea that government was beholden to the people, that it had no other source of power except the sovereign people, is still the newest, most unique idea in all the long history of man's relation to man. For almost two centuries we have proved man's capacity for self-government, but today we are told we must choose between a left and right or, as others suggest, a third alternative, a kind of safe middle ground. I suggest to you there is no left or right, only an up or down. Up to the maximum of individual freedom consistent with law and order, or down to the ant heap of totalitarianism; and regardless of their humanitarian purpose those who would sacrifice freedom for security have, whether they know it or not, chosen this downward path. Plutarch warned, "The real destroyer of the liberties of the people is he who spreads among them bounties, donations, and benefits. . . .

The specter our well-meaning liberal friends refuse to face is that their policy of accommodation is appeasement, and appeasement does not give you a choice between peace and war, only between fight and surrender. We are told that the problem is too complex for a simple answer. They are wrong. There is no easy answer, but there is a simple answer. We must have the courage to do what we know is morally right, and this policy of accommodation asks us to accept the greatest possible immorality. We are being asked to buy our safety from the threat of "the bomb" by selling into permanent slavery our fellow human beings enslaved behind the Iron Curtain, to tell them to give up their hope of freedom because we are ready to make a deal with their slave masters.

Alexander Hamilton warned us that a nation which can prefer disgrace to danger is prepared for a master and deserves one. Admittedly there is a risk in any course we follow. Choosing the high road cannot eliminate that risk. Already some of the architects of accommodation have hinted what their decision will be if their plan fails and we are faced with the final ultimatum. The English commentator [Kenneth] Tynan has put it this way: he would rather live on his knees than die on his feet. Some of our own have said "Better Red than dead." If we are to believe that nothing is worth the dying, when did this begin? Should Moses have told the children of Israel to live in slavery rather than dare the wilderness? Should Christ have refused the Cross? Should the patriots at Concord Bridge have refused to fire the shot heard 'round the world? Are we to believe that all the martyrs of history died in vain?

You and I have a rendezvous with destiny. We can preserve for our children this, the last best hope of man on earth, or we can sentence them to take the first step into a thousand years of darkness. If we fail, at least let our children and our children's children say of us we justified our brief moment here. We did all that could be done.

TURNING POINTS AND TRANSITIONS IN YOUR LIFE

An aim in life is the only fortune worth the finding; and it is not to be found in foreign lands, but in the heart itself.

—Robert Louis Stevenson

- As your career progresses, continue to tap your raw talents and seek ways to use and develop your innate gifts. Unanticipated opportunities appear when natural talent fuses with extensive experience.
- Pursue your interests. Success will follow.
- Become an expert in your field by reading and studying widely on your subject. Know what you think and why you think it. Be prepared to back up your thinking with facts.
- Resolve to work hard to achieve your goals. Success is the natural outgrowth of small decisions and habits. Develop a mental attitude of working hard and completing every task you set yourself.
- As the saying goes, opportunities come "in work clothes." They may not appear attractive at first and it's impossible to know in advance how they will develop. Take advantage of opportunities that come your way.

Working It In

What sources can you tap for inspiration? Literature, music, nature, hobbies, supportive groups or relationships?

What steps can you take to cultivate a positive attitude?

What can you do to become a recognized expert in your field? Publish articles? Offer your services as a speaker or panelist? Volunteer your time with organizations in your field?

Think of an example of an opportunity that came your way that mushroomed into more than you expected. What did you learn from the experience?

Chapter 6

Unleashing the Power of a Team

Campaigning for Governor of California, 1964–66

> Ronald Reagan, to my way of thinking, was about as near as perfect a candidate as you can get, because he let people handle the mechanics of the campaign. He didn't interfere. He let people do what they did best.
>
> —Lyn Nofziger, Communications Director, 1966–80

From the 1964 postelection gloom, Holmes Tuttle emerged as the moving force behind Reagan's rise in politics. The cheers of Johnson supporters and wails of recrimination among Republicans were still floating in the air when Tuttle approached Reagan about running for governor of California in 1966. To Tuttle's way of thinking, "We couldn't give up."

In Reagan, Tuttle and his associates saw a leader who had a clear, logical, well-thought-out political philosophy. Reagan was encyclopedic in his knowledge and understanding of the American Revolution and the history of the U.S. Constitution. In almost every speech he referred to the Founders and Declaration of Independence. Traveling with GE, he filled lonely hours in hotel rooms reading books on the Founders' thoughts on government and democracy. He had thought through complicated issues. Mike Deaver, who joined Reagan's staff in Sacramento and traveled extensively with him, remembered how, after settling in his seat on a plane, Reagan would get out his briefcase, work on speeches, read briefing papers, and then relax by reading books and articles about economics.[1] In conversations with fellow citizens Reagan fine-tuned his thinking and polished his arguments. Over the years he worked out his beliefs, his values, and his core principles, giving a consistency and internal harmony to his positions and speeches.

Not only did Reagan know exactly what he thought and why he thought it, he articulated his thinking exceptionally well. He couched his arguments in clear, lucid, simple-to-understand words. As a practiced speaker, he developed an ability to connect with an audience. Listeners could easily follow his logic and found themselves paying close attention as he spoke.

Unsparing in his own efforts and intensely goal-driven, he was an inspiration to others. His upbeat, can-do, let's-figure-it-out-together attitude was contagious. People enjoyed working with him. But most important, he listened, and he placed considerable value on the opinions and efforts of others.

Like a born salesman, Tuttle rounded up the support of his associates. Tuttle, Rubel, Salvatori, and Mills had known each other for years. Rubel and Mills had met as frat brothers at the University of Southern California. Tuttle and Salvatori had crossed paths in Oklahoma in their twenties. Mills had worked his way up from stock boy to president of a baking company. Rubel had retired as chairman of the board and chief executive of Union Oil. Like Reagan, they were self-made men and active in civic organizations. Their bond had been forged while working on prior campaigns. In the mid-1950s, they had rallied around the Right to Work campaign, which held that "all Americans must have the right to join a union if they choose to, but none should ever be forced to affiliate with a union in order to get or keep a job."

Tuttle put it to the others, "Why shouldn't we see if we can convince Ronald Reagan to give up his career and run for the office of governor of California."[2] Then he set about convincing Reagan. Refusing to take no for an answer, Tuttle persevered, going back to Reagan again and again, even bringing his wife along for support.

Tuttle and Mills evolved into Reagan's most reliable supporters—the only two who were with him from the evening at the Cocoanut Grove through to the White House. Rubel died shortly after Reagan became governor in 1967. Salvatori—idealistic, stubborn, and opinionated—came and went. In the 1976 primaries, he backed President Gerald Ford; in the 1980 GOP primary, he supported Governor John Connolly of Texas. But in 1964, the group was united in purpose and a potent force. Mills served as finance chairman and paid the bills. Cy Rubel raised money, worked on strategy, reached out to contacts across the state, and provided the group with a place to meet when they got together. Salvatori backed up the fund-raising effort and enlisted support. "Holmes was over all."[3]

In 1962, Tuttle and Mills had been among the group that asked Reagan to run for a Senate seat. Reagan had considered the idea for a week before turning it down. This time he thought harder. Reagan's heart was in his acting career, but the steady stream of people knocking on his door, plus casual conversations with gas station attendants and hotel clerks, gave him pause. They all urged him to run for office.

Compliments and off-handed conversations were easy to shrug off. In his garage, though, there was mounting evidence that there truly was a nationwide clamor for his candidacy. Boxes of mail had piled up—four or five thousand letters just from California residents. In his years as a movie star and as a television personality, he had never seen anything like it. Even with that, according to Salvatori, "Reagan had to be convinced that people really wanted him." Reagan strongly believed that it was up to the voters to choose who should run for office. He was willing to serve if called.

Listening and Exploring

He agreed to test the waters with a few appearances at events within driving distance of home, but Reagan was adamant he wasn't doing it alone. In March 1965, he struck an agreement with Tuttle's group that they would "arrange it and make it possible so that I can go around this state."[4] Reagan suggested they start with a low-profile, exploratory campaign to test out wider voter reaction to a potential run. For months Reagan's attitude remained, "I can't believe I'm doing this."[5]

From the beginning, Reagan said he would make a final decision about running in December 1965. As soon as he declared his candidacy, his income would stop. To comply with the Federal Election Commission's Equal Time Rule for political candidates, he would have to step down from his role on *Death Valley Days.* The FEC regulation, first established in

1927, meant Reagan's old movies—often rerun on weekends and late nights—and television programs would be taken off the air. That would be the end of residual income from the films and programs, not only for him but also for the rest of the cast.[6] He was concerned other people's income would be hurt by his decision to enter politics. Therefore, he refused to make an official announcement until early 1966, but once he committed to the trial run, Tuttle's group rapidly expanded.

By May 1965, the team was ready to formalize the exploratory effort by announcing the formation of the Friends of Ronald Reagan. Tuttle, Salvatori, Rubel, and Mills chipped in the funds to send out "a little letter."[7] They hoped to raise ten thousand dollars. They got back more than one hundred thousand dollars, enough to finance the initial phase of the campaign.

They snapped up supporters in northern California. Influential businessman Jaquelin Hume was a key recruit in San Francisco. Reagan made a trip to San Francisco to meet with him one-on-one. Other Goldwater contacts signed on. Looking ahead, the Reagan team kept spaces open on the campaign's organizational chart for supporters of other candidates after the primary. Running against four rivals, Reagan handily won the GOP primary with 65 percent of the votes in June 1966. His main rival, San Francisco mayor George Christopher, captured 31 percent. As votes were tallied, Tuttle called, wooed, and recruited Christopher's supporters—most notably, Leonard Firestone, heir to the tire business, and Arch Monson, owner of the largest theatrical supply company in the western states. Another valuable recruit from the Christopher campaign was Nancy Clark Reynolds, who became a formidable asset for both Reagans. Reynolds initially signed on as assistant press secretary for radio and television in Sacramento and stayed on in various roles for twenty years, "ten years paid and ten years unpaid."[8]

In early 1967, after Reagan took office, *Los Angeles Times* political reporter Carl Greenberg dubbed his early supporters the "kitchen cabinet,"[9] a term coined in 1829 to ridicule newly inaugurated Andrew Jackson's klatch of informal advisors. The Reagan nucleus eschewed the description as absurd. For one thing, the cast changed constantly. But latecomers desperately wanted in and went to great lengths to claim membership in the exclusive club. The lucky ten named in the Greenberg article were: Leonard Firestone, Jaquelin Hume, Leland M. Kaiser, Edward Mills, Arch Monson, Jr., A. C. "Cy" Rubel, Henry Salvatori, Taft Schreiber, William French Smith, and Holmes P. Tuttle.

Harnessing the Strengths of Others

In 1965, Reagan already had extensive experience as a campaigner at the presidential level, but state-level politics was new to him. Even as a tentative candidate, he rapidly recognized the need to get up to top speed on the key issues facing California and also to tap the expertise of seasoned pros who understood the mechanics of running a campaign. He needed people who understood California politics from the precinct level up. On a spring visit to his in-laws in Phoenix he discussed the problem with Goldwater, who recommended political consultants Stuart Spencer and Bill Roberts. Their firm, Spencer-Roberts, was riding high after bringing Rockefeller from forty-five points down to within a few points of beating Goldwater in the 1964 California primary. Reagan put in a call. Spencer and Roberts were already talking to George Christopher, who was mulling a run for governor.

In the course of this fledgling effort, Reagan's management style emerged. Whenever possible he liked to get another perspective. One morning he called his brother and asked him to join him for lunch; he was meeting with Spencer and Roberts for the first time. Over the next few weeks, he gathered key supporters, in addition to Roberts, Spencer, and Nancy Reagan, for lengthy strategy sessions at the Reagans' home. Reagan called these meetings "roundtables." They started at 8:00 P.M. and, like the meetings at SAG, extended into the early hours of the morning—finally breaking up at 3:00 or 4:00 A.M.

Dithering over whose campaign to support, Spencer and Roberts found the meetings helpful. They were "interested in where [Reagan] was philosophically, what kind of a person he was. He satisfied our questions in our minds."[10] What they found, according to Spencer, was a man who was "almost a libertarian in beliefs. He thinks we should be able to work these things out without the government encroaching on the individual choice."[11] In Spencer's view, Reagan's thinking was in line with Goldwater's; Reagan just had a more effective way of stating and explaining his positions.

Pressed for a decision by Reagan, the pair decided "time had passed George [Christopher] by"[12] and signed on with Reagan to handle scheduling and make introductions. They added value to the team by knowing, in Reagan's words, "Who the people are in the state, that if they endorse you it has a significance; if they agree to work for you, it's more significant."[13] It didn't take long for Reagan to figure out that some proffered endorsements could hurt his candidacy.

In marketing terms, Ronald Reagan in 1965 was already a multimillion-dollar brand thanks to the name recognition he had developed as a sportscaster, as a movie and television star, traveling with GE, and campaigning for Richard Nixon and Barry Goldwater. The public, used to seeing Reagan on television and in movies, naturally thought of him as an actor. The first challenge Spencer-Roberts faced was how to rebrand him to capture his broader experience as a union leader, corporate ambassador, and emerging politician. They came up with a defining phrase—"A Citizen Politician." "It came somewhere out of our long brainstorming sessions," Spencer said. "It was a strength. . . . That's what people wanted for a change, somebody that wasn't a bureaucrat or in the present system, so to speak." Spencer worked on outreach and making introductions; Roberts worked directly with the candidate.

They commissioned a poll to test the strength of possible GOP candidates. Former U.S. senator Tom Kuchel was leading, George Christopher, who had jumped into the race, was in second place, and Ronald Reagan was in third. But the poll also showed that any of the Republicans could defeat incumbent Edmund G. "Pat" Brown, who was running for a third term.[14] Reagan was considered a long shot. In the general campaign, he was seen as the underdog. Throughout his career he benefited from being underestimated. In the 1980 presidential election, he was called "Jimmy Carter's Favorite Candidate," a reprise of the

1966 campaign, when he was referred to as Pat Brown's "Favorite Candidate."

The summer of 1965 and into the fall, Reagan and Roberts traveled the state attending "all the parades and gatherings and everything we could find in the way of schedules."[15] Spencer-Roberts set up the necessary structure for a successful campaign and scoured Republican groups for community and county chairmen. They started a direct mail campaign. "We'd just pick an assembly district and mail the whole district and see if we couldn't get enough returns out of it to mail to the next one. We would get more than enough, maybe five or six or seven thousand dollars over the cost to mail the next one."[16]

Spencer-Roberts worked closely with Reagan to figure out how he most efficiently absorbed information. They found a former actor turned California assemblyman to coach him on the workings of state government and put together briefing books, recruited experts on topics of greatest concern to Californians, and presented Reagan with both sides of an issue so he could come to his own conclusions—a practice that stayed with him in years ahead. By early fall, they had worked out the kinks in the effort, and people close to Reagan sensed he had made the mental commitment to move forward.

During the 1964 presidential campaign, Goldwater's opponents had successfully labeled him an "extremist." Startling statements such as, "I could have ended the war in a month. I could have made North Vietnam look like a mud puddle," made it easy for them. Given Reagan's high-profile association with Goldwater, the media painted him with the same broad brush—in Reagan's words, "as a kook with horns." The "extremist" meme sank deep into the minds of journalists and proved impossible to dislodge. From the beginning, dealing with the press was a challenge for the Reagan campaign.

To handle relations with the press, the team recruited Lyn Nofziger, an unconventional blend of newspaperman, Californian, Republican, and eccentric. Nofziger was happily working in Washington, D.C., for the Los Angeles–based Copley newspapers. Strenuous coaxing and a shove from his boss got him to take what he thought would be a temporary assignment. He worked as Reagan's press liaison, on and off, for the next twenty years. Traveling with the candidate, working on press handouts and speeches while rushing between events, Nofziger soon spotted Reagan's ability to connect with voters. He commented to Bill Roberts, "I can't put a finger on it, but there's something between him and the people, and I think he can be elected governor . . . even president some day." Roberts's response was, "You're out of your mind!"[17]

Surrounded by seasoned associates, Reagan quickly learned that "a hostile press or audience was won over more easily with a joke than with counter-hostility."[18] At Occidental College he encountered protesters waving signs that said "Down with Reagan," "Down with Nancy," "Who Wants Boraxo in Sacramento?" He waited for a pause in the racket and said, "That may be only soap to you, but it was bread and butter to me."[19] That took the wind out of the protesters and impressed everyone else.

Reagan wasn't a backslapper and had no interest in swapping jokes and war stories in bars after hours with the press. He talked issues, not politics. Happy to put in a full day's work, he only asked that schedulers get him home to have dinner and spend evenings with Nancy. Backers and advisors agreed he had an inner strength. Ed Mills summed up the perspective of many: "Reagan has always been his own man. He's not a gullible person, and he's not the kind of an individual who's influenced against his principles. He's a man of principle."

On the campaign trail, Reagan surpassed even the expectations of his supporters. His exceptionally strong memory was impressive. From childhood on, observers described his memory as "photographic." Now that he was fully engaged in the effort, they found he anticipated suggestions and recommendations. They urged him to set up a task force to develop position papers. He had already ordered back issues of annual reports put out by the municipal departments of the government and was reading them to come "to his own conclusions about what his position should be on issues. This was typical of Ron."[20] Reagan impressed Jack Hume as "an extremely able individual. . . . Most people had no comprehension that he had such an excellent mind." His easygoing management and communication style was deceptive. As president, he was known to ask someone to translate for him. It might sound as if he was making a suggestion; it was, in fact, an order. When he settled on a clear goal, he drove the outcome. Once he made his mind up about pursuing the governorship, there was no stopping him.

Jack Wrather, who first met Reagan in the 1940s, knew a rarely seen side of him. He was "a very good businessman, a good business brain. He understands economics, and he understands fiscal problems and policies. He understands that one great, basic rule . . . you can't spend more money than you've got very long without going broke."[21] Gaylord Parkinson, head of the California GOP in the 1960s, firmly believed that no one got to the top by being an easy target. In his opinion, "Nobody could influence Ronald Reagan to do anything in my book. He's his own man and he should be." Eleanor Ring Storrs, a Republican activist from San Diego and early Reagan supporter, described him as "one of these guys that gets up in the crack of dawn and does his study work. . . . He has a very brilliant mind which people don't realize."[22]

With a solid team in place, the campaign gained traction. Reagan was pleased that Californians—particularly young, suburban, middle-income, and entrepreneurial—were enthusiastically supporting his candidacy. The average campaign contribution was less than twenty dollars. Small donations indicated grassroots interest, which, in turn, generated positive word of mouth. Reagan proved to be a popular draw at events. Volunteers pitched in to distribute pledge cards and encourage neighbors to help out or make a donation. Seasoned campaigners were amazed by how many people showed up to hear him speak. In 1979, Stu Spencer told an interviewer, "You've got to remember, Ronald Reagan had charisma."

By hiring the right people and getting out of their way, he unleashed the talents of his team and empowered and motivated them to do their best. Stu Spencer thought this particular skill came out of Reagan's experience making movies; he was used to working with a team on a project. Reagan recognized he didn't have the know-how to tell the experts how to run the campaign. He was comfortable delegating and trusting others to do their best. He acknowledged that the organizational part of politics was something that "even as cochairman for Goldwater, I only saw dimly. I realized that it was there and I didn't know anything about it,"[23] Spencer said. "He just totally left that up to us." Harvard Business School grad Jack Hume simply saw it as good management. "Ron functioned by turning a matter over to someone and expecting him to take care of the matter properly. I do not think he tries to tell people how to handle the details of what they are doing."[24]

In early 1966, two college professors were added to the team: Stanley Plog of UCLA and business partner Kenneth Holden of San Fernando Valley State College. Both held doctorates in psychology, Holden from Ohio State and Plog from Harvard. With Nofziger and Roberts, they took turns traveling with Reagan, but their main task was to develop position papers and expand the briefing books. They found it was important to be "for things," so they worked on coming up with a "positive program, with conservative underpinnings." Taking the lead from Kennedy's "New Frontier" and Johnson's "Great Society," Reagan's team settled on "the Creative Society" and developed a new speech that was lighter in tone and broader in appeal than "A Time for Choosing."

Transformation

This phase of Reagan's life was a crucible for him. He was taking lessons learned while traveling with GE and broadening them to the larger world. Focused on the concerns of Californians, he displayed a talent for getting to the heart of a matter and articulating "its elemental simplicity."[25] He had an extraordinary ability to explain complex issues in terms that were understandable to the average voter. As he talked to audiences about his ideas, he no longer had to think out, in Jack Hume's view, "the answer to most questions when they are presented to him. The question just fits into a slot in his philosophy so the answer is obvious to him. This makes it easier for him to answer questions because he has already thought so many problems through to a logical conclusion."[26] A 1981 interviewer summed up Plog's impressions that "Reagan had the innate capacity to assimilate information quickly and to transform that information into an effectively communicated message suggesting to the voting public that he would make a good governor."[27]

Reagan had developed a surefire formula for a speech: bedrock beliefs based on the Founders' principles, updated to current issues, backed by statistics, and leavened with quotations from impressive historical figures. He usually started with a few jokes or an allusion to something local—a poem or historical reference—that encouraged his audience to relax. He had a flair for turns of phrase like "cut, squeeze, and trim." William French Smith described the "catchy cadence" of that phrase as "just a classic example of the kind of thing he'd come up with. He's good at that. He's really good at that."[28]

Smith, trying to be helpful in the heat of a political convention, once offered Reagan "an absolutely superb conclusion to an acceptance speech" written by a couple of English professors. Smith recalled it as "extremely well done, the kind of thing I would have latched on to." He took it to Reagan, who read it over and agreed it was very good, "but it's not I." He came up with his own lines. He always seemed to know just what he wanted to say and preferred to put it into his own words. In Sacramento and at the White House, he delegated the task of speechwriting but still "meticulously"[29] reviewed his speeches.

On the 1966 campaign trail, rivals snarled that Reagan was just an actor used to reading a script. Reagan responded by shortening his presentations and highlighting the question and answer sections of his presentations. Calling it a "dialogue instead of a monologue,"[30] he pared back his formal remarks to "a brief opening statement of principles"[31] and then asked for "hostile and unfriendly"[32] questions. Beyond stilling the criticism of opponents and the press, the format worked in his favor by forcing him to further fine-tune his thinking and polish his interactions with audiences. When first hired, Mike Deaver came up with what he thought was a brilliant idea. They would stage-manage the question-and-answer period by coming up with the questions in advance. Reagan patiently heard out Deaver's great idea and turned it down, saying, "You can't hit a home run on a soft ball."

Starting out, he overanswered questions but soon learned to trim back his comments. The subliminal message conveyed by the new format that emphasized spontaneous interaction was, "Hey this guy's got a brain. He just gave you a speech, but he also can do these things . . . people would walk out of the room saying, 'The man had some smarts.'"[33]

With experience, he got increasingly adept. At an event in San Diego, he was asked about California's chronic water problems. It was a tough question by a rival's plant, intended to put him on the spot. He turned it into a joke: "You know, Brown thinks he invented water." In Los Angeles at a Rotary Club event packed with a thousand attendees, the first question asked was, "Mr. Reagan, I'd like to have you give three of your weakest points and three of Governor Brown's strongest points." Reagan paused, gathered his thoughts, and said, "Now, this is a two part question. I'll answer the second part first. Number one, Brown has a beautiful family, a beautiful wife, and is very devoted to his family. We know this to be a fact because he has every one of his relatives on the state payroll."[34] The audience roared with laughter and he left it at that.

During the run-up to the 1966 general election, Reagan displayed a flair for resolving conflicts within his team. One day he buzzed Henry Salvatori and asked that he and Holmes Tuttle come upstairs to discuss running ads ahead of an anticipated smear campaign to blunt the impact. Bill Roberts felt strongly that they had to move forward. Reagan knew the opinionated Salvatori and Tuttle were just as strongly opposed. Reagan, "in his usual affable and friendly manner,"[35] heard out Salvatori and Tuttle. Then he suggested a compromise. The ad could be reworded so that it would be satisfactory to them. Heading back to their office, Tuttle commented, "Well, we certainly won our point." Everyone ended up happy. Roberts had achieved his goal and Salvatori and Tuttle were satisfied with the changes. Years later Salvatori told the story to illustrate Reagan's "acute understanding of human relationships."[36] Reagan's skill at smoothing over conflicts among colleagues was another weapon in his leadership arsenal.

Keeping Information Flowing

Through one-on-one meetings and "roundtables" Reagan kept the lines of communication open with his team. Information and opinions flowed freely back and forth. He wanted to hear not just the opinions of the people present but also what they were hearing from their sources and the scuttlebutt they had picked up. As he put it, "Hearing their input which came from what they were hearing."[37] In the months leading up to the gubernatorial election, every couple of weeks he gathered his aides and supporters together to review progress, take a look at the current situation, and establish short- and long-term goals. Reagan listened as everyone else talked. He didn't criticize or make suggestions or comments—even if provoked. He just heard people out. Nofziger noticed, "He's a very good listener. After he's heard everything he may ask some questions, or he may decide that a decision should be made differently from what looks like is going to be made. He was there and he participated and he agreed. When he didn't agree, he said so."[38] The important thing was that he heard everything that people had to say and that participants felt heard.

Life on the campaign trail wasn't always smooth, but in his years giving speeches, Reagan had gained plenty of experience with the endless array of things that can go wrong at a speaking event. He was unflappable in the face of hiccups and only grumbled about unjust attacks and scheduling glitches. But in March 1966, Reagan ran into a situation that almost changed his mind about going into politics. At a state convention of black Republicans held in Santa Monica, rival candidates George

Christopher and William P. Patrick goaded him into losing his customary cool by implying he was a bigot. The issue that provided the opening was Goldwater's vote on the 1964 Civil Rights Act.

Asked by a delegate why he would not have voted for the bill, Reagan responded that he liked what the bill was trying to accomplish but that he had not yet read all of it and thought it was "a bad piece of legislation." He added, "If I didn't know that Barry Goldwater was not the very opposite of a racist I could not have supported him."[39] Christopher and Patrick jumped at the opening. Patrick said, "It's very difficult to defend an indefensible position." Christopher said, "Contrary to my opponent, I would have voted for the bill . . . the position taken by Goldwater did more harm than any other thing to the Republican Party." Reagan, incensed, stormed out, muttering "I'll get that SOB." Later he chalked up his reaction to being a "novice in politics." Christopher, who had achieved his desired result, exploited the situation by telling the press, "I extend my sympathy in this moment of his emotional disturbance."

Goldwater had voted in favor of civil rights legislation in 1957 and 1960. In 1964, along with Senators Al Gore, Sr., and J. William Fulbright, among others, he voted against the act, saying, "You can't legislate morality." A key concern of the dissenters was that the act, as written, would lead to busing schoolchildren to achieve racial quotas in schools. Over the next decade, forced busing became an explosive issue. White families fled to suburbia or sent their children to parochial or private schools rather than subject them to lengthy bus rides. The result was that inner-city schools ended up more segregated rather than less. Running for re-election as governor in 1970, Reagan told parents at a racially mixed school in an inner suburb of Los Angeles that busing "was unfair to the kids." He was quoted as saying, "It would deny them the opportunity to engage in such extracurricular activities as organized sports."[40] He was "intrigued" by the concept of vouchers and explained, "The state would then be subsidizing the education of the individual, rather than subsidizing the institution."[41]

Nothing upset Reagan more than being accused of bigotry. That afternoon in 1966, a flurry of phone calls rocketed around among consultants and candidate. Reagan was persuaded to return for the event's dinner that evening. He made it clear to the organizers his anger was aimed at his Republican opponents. Going forward, his campaign team helped Reagan look past attacks in the heat of the moment and search for the motive and the goal. Plog said, "The more we could intellectualize with him, so that he could see it was a strategy on their part and that we had counter moves planned, the more he could handle it."[42] The press leaped on the opportunity to label Reagan an extremist and hothead. Like the controversial SAG waiver, the incident haunted him.

In the wake of the contentious Goldwater–Rockefeller battle, Gaylord Parkinson, popular head of the California GOP, decreed that there was an Eleventh Commandment, "Thou shalt not speak ill of another Republican." It was meant to protect Reagan, who was known to be thin-skinned,[43] particularly on race issues. He got better at ignoring personal attacks, but Spencer and Roberts, who worked for Ford in the 1976 campaign, knew it was Reagan's weak point and used it to needle him.

The pressure-cooker atmosphere of a campaign can lead to "a star complex focused on the candidate."[44] Aides, fans, and supporters rally around after an event to sing the candidate's praises. In Reagan's case the situation was exacerbated because he actually was a star. Campaign advisor Stanley Plog said, "So there's a tendency for straight information not to get through. It gets changed into a constant rosy picture. You can't be negative in a situation like that; you have to work with him and tell him here's what it is, here's what went well, here's what could be changed the next time. And he was quite capable of that."[45] Reagan was used to having his performances critiqued from his days as an actor. Nancy Reagan became an invaluable support on the campaign trail, absorbing the audience's reaction, taking in the fine points of his speech, and debriefing afterward.

Reagan, as he had done throughout his career, continued to network and make connections within the Republican Party despite lukewarm support from easterners. For the next fourteen years, he traveled around the country, doing favors for candidates by speaking at events and fund-raising. Sometimes a portion of the funds raised would be allocated to his campaign, sometimes there was no immediate payoff for him, but he created a vast network of goodwill. Gordon Luce, party activist, San Diego businessman, and Reagan's secretary of business and transportation in Sacramento, commented in 1986, "Ronald Reagan was the best, and still is, in party support. He always was available to do the speaking at various fund-raising events for various candidates. He would sign many a letter for fund-raising work. He was a party builder."[46]

Running on a platform of "Integrity and Common Sense," Reagan was positioned "as almost a nonpolitical candidate."[47] Nofziger's old employer, the Copley newspapers, endorsed Reagan, saying, "Mr. Reagan has moved up through a creative public life to become a national voice in the challenge of our times—the question of how far should government go in the control of our lives."[48] Anyone hoping for an exciting neck-and-neck race on election night was disappointed. The results came in fast. Reagan won by almost a million votes.

FRANKLIN D. ROOSEVELT'S FIRST INAUGURAL ADDRESS, DELIVERED MARCH 4, 1933

(Ronald Reagan often said, if you want to know what I really believe, read Franklin D. Roosevelt's first Inaugural Address.)

I am certain that my fellow Americans expect that on my induction into the Presidency I will address them with a candor and a decision which the present situation of our Nation impels. This is preeminently the time to speak the truth, the whole truth, frankly and boldly. Nor need we shrink from honestly facing conditions in our country today. This great Nation will endure as it has endured, will revive and will prosper. So, first of all, let me assert my firm belief that the only thing we have to fear is fear itself—nameless, unreasoning, unjustified terror which paralyzes needed efforts to convert retreat into advance. In every dark hour of our national life a leadership of frankness and vigor has met with that understanding and support of the people themselves which is essential to victory. I am convinced that you will again give that support to leadership in these critical days.

In such a spirit on my part and on yours we face our common difficulties. They concern, thank God, only material things. Values have shrunken to fantastic levels; taxes have risen; our ability to pay has fallen; government of all kinds is faced by serious curtailment of income; the means of exchange are frozen in the currents of trade; the withered leaves of industrial enterprise lie on every side; farmers find no markets for their produce; the savings of many years in thousands of families are gone.

More important, a host of unemployed citizens face the grim problem of existence, and an equally great number toil with little return. Only a foolish optimist can deny the dark realities of the moment.

Yet our distress comes from no failure of substance. We are stricken by no plague of locusts. Compared with the perils which our forefathers conquered because they believed and were not afraid, we have still much to be thankful for. Nature still offers her bounty and human efforts have multiplied it. Plenty is at our doorstep, but a generous use of it languishes in the very sight of the supply. Primarily this is because the rulers of the exchange of mankind's goods have failed, through their own stubbornness and their own incompetence, have admitted their failure, and abdicated. Practices of the unscrupulous money changers stand indicted in the court of public opinion, rejected by the hearts and minds of men.

True they have tried, but their efforts have been cast in the pattern of an outworn tradition. Faced by failure of credit they have proposed only the lending of more money. Stripped of the lure of profit by which to induce our people to follow their false leadership, they have resorted to exhortations, pleading tearfully for restored confidence. They know only the rules of a generation of self-seekers. They have no vision, and when there is no vision the people perish.

The money changers have fled from their high seats in the temple of our civilization. We may now restore that temple to the ancient truths. The measure of the restoration lies in the extent to which we apply social values more noble than mere monetary profit.

Happiness lies not in the mere possession of money; it lies in the joy of achievement, in the thrill of creative effort. The joy and moral stimulation of work no longer must be forgotten in the mad chase of evanescent profits. These dark days will be worth all they cost us if they teach us that our true destiny is not to be ministered unto but to minister to ourselves and to our fellow men. Recognition of the falsity of material wealth as the standard of success goes hand in hand with the abandonment of the false belief that public office and high political position are to be valued only by the standards of pride of place and personal profit; and there must be an end to a conduct in banking and in business which too often has given to a sacred trust the likeness of callous and selfish wrongdoing. Small wonder that confidence languishes, for it thrives only on honesty, on honor, on the sacredness of obligations, on faithful protection, on unselfish performance; without them it cannot live.

Restoration calls, however, not for changes in ethics alone. This Nation asks for action, and action now.

Our greatest primary task is to put people to work. This is no unsolvable problem if we face it wisely and courageously. It can be accomplished in part by direct recruiting by the Government itself, treating the task as we would treat the emergency of a war, but at the same time, through this employment, accomplishing greatly needed projects to stimulate and reorganize the use of our natural resources.

Hand in hand with this we must frankly recognize the overbalance of population in our industrial centers and, by engaging on a national scale in a redistribution, endeavor to provide a better use of the land for those best fitted for the land. The task can be helped by definite efforts to raise the values of agricultural products and with this the power to purchase the output of our cities. It can be helped by preventing realistically the tragedy of the growing loss through foreclosure of our small homes and our farms. It can be helped by insistence that the Federal, State, and local governments act forthwith on the demand that their cost be drastically reduced. It can be helped by the unifying of relief activities which today are often scattered, uneconomical, and unequal. It can be helped by national planning for and supervision of all forms of transportation and of communications and other utilities which have a definitely public character. There are many ways in which it can be helped, but it can never be helped merely by talking about it. We must act and act quickly.

Finally, in our progress toward a resumption of work we require two safeguards against a return of the evils of the old order; there must be a strict supervision of all banking and credits and investments; there must be an end to speculation with other people's money, and there must be provision for an adequate but sound currency.

There are the lines of attack. I shall presently urge upon a new Congress in special session detailed measures for their fulfillment, and I shall seek the immediate assistance of the several States.

Through this program of action we address ourselves to putting our own national house in order and making income balance outgo. Our international trade relations, though vastly important, are in point of time and necessity secondary to the establishment of a sound national economy. I favor as a practical policy the putting of first things first. I shall spare no effort to restore world trade by international economic readjustment, but the emergency at home cannot wait on that accomplishment.

The basic thought that guides these specific means of national recovery is not narrowly nationalistic. It is the insistence, as a first consideration, upon the interdependence of the various elements in all parts of the United States—a recognition of the old and permanently important manifestation of the American spirit of the pioneer. It is the way to recovery. It is the immediate way. It is the strongest assurance that the recovery will endure.

In the field of world policy I would dedicate this Nation to the policy of the good neighbor—the neighbor who resolutely respects himself and, because he does so, respects the rights of others—the neighbor who respects his obligations and respects the sanctity of his agreements in and with a world of neighbors.

If I read the temper of our people correctly, we now realize as we have never realized before our interdependence on each other; that we can not merely take but we must give as well; that if we are to go forward, we must move as a trained and loyal army willing to sacrifice for the good of a common discipline, because without such discipline no progress is made, no leadership becomes effective. We are, I know, ready and willing to submit our lives and property to such discipline, because it makes possible a leadership which aims at a larger good. This I propose to offer, pledging that the larger purposes will bind upon us all as a sacred obligation with a unity of duty hitherto evoked only in time of armed strife.

With this pledge taken, I assume unhesitatingly the leadership of this great army of our people dedicated to a disciplined attack upon our common problems.

Action in this image and to this end is feasible under the form of government which we have inherited from our ancestors. Our Constitution is so simple and practical that it is possible always to meet extraordinary needs by changes in emphasis and arrangement without loss of essential form. That is why our constitutional system has proved itself the most superbly enduring political mechanism the modern world has produced. It has met every stress of vast expansion of territory, of foreign wars, of bitter internal strife, of world relations.

It is to be hoped that the normal balance of executive and legislative authority may be wholly adequate to meet the unprecedented task before us. But it may be that an unprecedented demand and need for undelayed action may call for temporary departure from that normal balance of public procedure.

I am prepared under my constitutional duty to recommend the measures that a stricken nation in the midst of a stricken world may require. These measures, or such other measures as the Congress may build out of its experience and wisdom, I shall seek, within my constitutional authority, to bring to speedy adoption.

But in the event that the Congress shall fail to take one of these two courses, and in the event that the national emergency is still critical, I shall not evade the clear course of duty that will then confront me. I shall ask the Congress for the one remaining instrument to meet the crisis—broad Executive power to wage a war against the emergency, as great as the power that would be given to me if we were in fact invaded by a foreign foe.

For the trust reposed in me I will return the courage and the devotion that befit the time. I can do no less.

We face the arduous days that lie before us in the warm courage of the national unity; with the clear consciousness of seeking old and precious moral values; with the clean satisfaction that comes from the stern performance of duty by old and young alike. We aim at the assurance of a rounded and permanent national life.

We do not distrust the future of essential democracy. The people of the United States have not failed. In their need they have registered a mandate that they want direct, vigorous action. They have asked for discipline and direction under leadership. They have made me the present instrument of their wishes. In the spirit of the gift I take it.

In this dedication of a Nation we humbly ask the blessing of God. May He protect each and every one of us. May He guide me in the days to come.

UNLEASHING THE POWER OF YOUR TEAM

There is more hunger for love and appreciation in this world than for bread.

—Mother Teresa

- Surround yourself with bright, energetic, upbeat people. You will benefit from tapping their strengths. Success comes from gathering the best team possible.
- Give your team members plenty of room to use their talents. There is no greater morale-buster than micromanaging another person's efforts.
- Continue to reach out and expand your network and build relationships. Connecting with people is a top priority.
- Employ a "board of directors approach" to get the best out of your team.
- To achieve a goal, develop a practical strategy, test the waters, request support as needed.
- Resolve conflicts head-on. Actively listen to opinions, synthesize points of view, and offer solutions.
- When working on a major project, bring your team together periodically to hear their suggestions, comments and feedback.
- Make an effort to get to know new team members on a personal level. Establishing personal relationships with colleagues will pay rich rewards.
- Identify how you prefer to take in and absorb information. It will allow you to learn and to manage your time

efficiently. Take advantage of down time during the day to read or listen.

- Find a trusted advisor that you can turn to for feedback and critiques of your performance. Throughout your career you will benefit from fine-tuning and polishing your strengths.

Working It In

Think of a leader who brought out the best in you. What did that person do? How did it make you feel? What were the results?

____

____

____

____

____

To balance your own strengths, what qualities do you need to tap in your team members?

____

____

____

____

____

Form a mastermind group with two partners. Focus on a common challenge and meet once a month to share different approaches and for mutual support.

____

____

____

____

____

Chapter 7

Leadership

Governor of California, 1967–75

> Reagan starts with the position that the federal government was put in to provide for public safety of certain kinds—war, floods, famine, disease, and so on. . . . [H]e sees a free society as constantly in tension between keeping enough away from government so the government doesn't possess you and supporting government enough for the public safety. Also when you think of how many people are employed by government—it certainly is a swing vote in winning elections.
>
> —Alex Sherriffs, Education Advisor to Ronald Reagan and State University Administrator, 1969–82

In January 1967, Reagan was the new governor of California and about to turn fifty-six. For thirty-five years he had been a star in radio, movies, and television. Seven times he had been elected president of the Screen Actors Guild. A much-in-demand public speaker, he had traveled all over America and developed an enormous network of contacts. Taking on the responsibility of governing the nation's largest state, Reagan was in the forefront of dealing with tough economic and social issues as the baby boomer bulge began to move through the economy like a rodent through a snake—swelling demand for schoolrooms, jobs, and homes. In his first month in office, Reagan set about dealing with California's out-of-control budget and implementing necessary but unpopular changes in the state's college system.

Leading by Example

Reagan's January 5, 1967, inaugural address provides a window into his thinking and links his 1964 speech with his farewell from the Oval Office in 1989. Written, as he put it, "on his lonesome," he started by connecting the Sacramento ceremony to the U.S. Constitution and called democracy a "miracle." He said "freedom is a fragile thing and is never more than one generation away from extinction," and "the most meaningful words" in the Constitution "are the first three, 'We the People.'"

He quoted eighteenth-century French social commentator Montesquieu: "The deterioration of every government begins with the decay of the principle upon which it was founded." He talked about government's role in society, about crime, education, taxes, and welfare. He called for a shift from "relief check to paycheck" and said, "Only private industry in the last analysis can provide jobs with a future." He took aim at bloated government and high taxes, saying, "The cost of California's government is too high; it adversely affects our business climate." He promised to "squeeze and cut and trim until we reduce the cost of government." Acknowledging it wouldn't be easy, he announced he would set an example by starting with budget cuts in his own office. He finished with a story about a soldier wounded in Vietnam who had carried a small flag into battle. As Reagan spoke, the soldier's flag was flying above the Sacramento capitol.

Before taking office, Reagan unleashed the energy, resources, and talents of his team to recruit staff from outside the normal channels of state government. Jack Hume recalled, "We wanted individuals who were dedicated to a philosophy of having as efficient and effective a government as possible. We did not want individuals to be employed because of political support but rather have them chosen for their quality."[1] Reagan also wanted "people who were philosophically dedicated to a private enterprise, conservative, profit-oriented society."[2]

Sensing an opportunity to ferret out waste and run the state more efficiently, Reagan appointed the Business Task Force—a "realization" of themes he had been talking about on the campaign trail. He said, "After years of preaching about what government should be, I had a chance to practice what I preached." Hume spearheaded the effort. He asked his business peers to loan out "top quality executives," and 250 were unleashed throughout the state's bureaus and agencies. They spent six months seeking out ways to streamline systems and update antiquated business practices. The result was close to sixteen hundred suggestions. Many of the best ideas were from state employees who knew where there was room for improvement.

While Reagan was on the 1966 campaign trail, one issue emerged as the biggest concern of voters. At every campaign stop, the first question was about Berkeley—the crown jewel of the California university system. Californians were outraged by the violence and disruptions at the state's premier university.

Buildings were vandalized, lives threatened, and professors driven from classrooms. Reagan said it was "the number one thing on the people's minds."[3] Voters had a "very, very deep and great pride in the university system. Because of that, they were very emotionally involved and disturbed with what was happening to what they thought was the great pride of California. My own position was born of the answers that I gave to those questions."[4]

Shortly after assuming office, Reagan was handed an opportunity to tackle the problem with Berkeley's "articulate agitators"[5] head-on. As governor, he was a member of the state's Board of Regents. Prior governors had stayed at arm's length from the board. On January 20, Reagan showed up for a board meeting. Clark Kerr was the longtime chancellor of the university system and president of University of California, Berkeley. At the first hint of budget cuts and suggestion of charging tuition, Kerr called a halt to all admissions "until the financial crisis is clarified."[6] Then he set the stage for a showdown with Reagan and the Board of Regents.[7]

Ironically, given Reagan's own days as a student activist egged on by a professor, Berkeley's faculty was behind the campus problems. Berkeley's vice chancellor, Alex Sherriffs, said, "As far as I'm concerned, the phenomenon of the sixties was basically a 'young Turk,' young faculty production. . . . It grew out of a whole lot of things, like oversupply of jobs. The young faculty were in a position to demand fewer teaching units. They could demand more research assistants. They could come and soon leave for a better offer. Their loyalty was not to the institution. If ever the guy on the make in business had a parallel, it was the young faculty in those days."[8] Faculty members made duplicating machines available to campus radicals but not "to the Students for a Responsible Society and the various defense groups that formed at the same time."[9] In 1999, Berkeley professor Leon Wofsy recalled "with a smile" that a 1965 report characterized him as "the most successful Communist youth organizer in history."[10]

The campus violence peaked at 3:42 A.M. on August 24, 1970, when self-styled radicals set off a bomb at the University of Wisconsin's Madison campus. Their target was the Army Mathematics Research Center housed in Sterling Hall. A warning call less than two minutes in advance gave police no time to locate and alert people in the building. The blast ripped through the physics and astronomy departments and math center and destroyed the lifework of five professors and the research of twenty-four Ph.D. candidates. Four men were injured and a thirty-three-year-old graduate student named Robert E. Fassnacht was killed. He left behind a young widow, a three-year-old son, and one-year-old twin daughters.

Reagan's position on dealing with campus troublemakers, who weren't always students, was well known. During the campaign he was quoted as saying, "There should be a rule that nothing could take place on campus which would interfere with educating students."[11] Demonstrators, he said, had "distorted the meaning of free speech." In his view, the disruptions were inconveniencing people who wanted to finish their programs, get their degrees, and move on with their lives.

Since the violence had first erupted, Kerr had routinely submitted his resignation only to have it turned down. Nobody wanted the responsibility for dealing with the problem. Coming into the January 20 Regents meeting, Kerr asked for a vote of confidence and expected the usual response. He didn't think the new governor would risk taking him up on his offers to resign.[12] He was wrong.

Reagan assured the Regents they should not be concerned that the press would use the issue to embarrass him. He was prepared to take any criticism that came his way. After a private meeting, the regents asked Kerr to consider resigning. He refused. Theodore R. Meyer, chairman of the UC Board of Regents, wrote an account of the incident for the *Los Angeles Times.* Before an announcement was made public, the board asked Kerr to "reconsider his refusal to resign. He said that he would not do so and that the board must take the responsibility."[13] Kerr's tenure was a matter between him and the Board of Regents but, as the issue played out in the press, Reagan got the blame or credit, depending on one's perspective. In his first month in office as governor, Reagan's image was set: a no-nonsense man of principle.

Installed as governor, Reagan soon discovered the state's finances were more precarious than he had known. The state was losing $1 million a day and the deficit was ballooning. By statute, the governor was required to submit a balanced budget before the start of the state's fiscal year on July 1. He had campaigned on providing tax relief to property owners. Raising taxes was out of the question. He proposed a hiring freeze and a 10 percent cut across the board in the budgets of state agencies, and suggested the state's colleges and university start charging tuition—four hundred dollars for the university, two hundred dollars for state colleges. Faculty and students were aghast at the idea of charging tuition at the state's free schools. They immediately organized protest marches and hung Reagan in effigy. The public, though, was on Reagan's side. Incoming mail ran three to one in favor of charging tuition.[14]

He soon found himself locked in combat with the state's legislature. Everyone agreed, even he conceded, that as a novice, he made mistakes, but he learned from the experience. Going forward, he worked at building bridges with political opponents, and the strategy evolved into a hallmark of his leadership style.

He learned that governing, particularly when faced with a rancorous legislature, meant he had to be more flexible and pragmatic than his rhetoric—or reputation—implied. During the campaign for governor, he had repeatedly and memorably said his "feet were set in cement" on the issue of tax withholding. The concept of tax withholding through payroll deductions was a novel idea. Reagan was adamant that citizens should feel the pain of writing out a check for their state taxes. He wanted voters to hold their representatives responsible for how tax dollars were spent. But to cover revenue shortfalls, it came down to a choice between withholding or raising taxes. He opted for withholding.

Despite the challenge of being chief executive of, as he put it, "the seventh largest economy in the world," he thrived in the role. Cabinet official Gordon Luce observed, "The more he learned, the more he enjoyed the job."[15] Though Reagan's calendar was crammed with staff meetings, press conferences, television appearances, cabinet meetings, interviews, dinners, celebrations—such as the fortieth anniversary of the Port of

Oakland—and cultural events, whenever Luce needed him, Reagan was available to meet with the team.

With his team, he worked at setting policies and goals. Selecting "the best people"[16] was critically important to his success. In his postpresidential autobiography, he acknowledged criticism of his "hands-off" management style but stated, "I don't believe a chief executive should supervise every detail of what goes on in his organization."[17] He said, "I think that's the cornerstone of good management: set clear goals and appoint good people to help you achieve them."[18]

Communicating Effectively

The most important part of his job, as he saw it, was communicating with California's citizens. He looked for ways to stay connected with voters and served as chief spokesman for the administration. He kept the lines of communication open with constituents through informal meetings. Meeting with business leaders from the Young Presidents' Organization, he engaged the group by setting a relaxed tone for the gathering in his office. Rather than making a formal presentation, he leaned against his desk with legs outstretched and casually crossed in front of him. From time to time, he helped himself to a large jar of jelly beans on his desk. He told the group he only intended to speak briefly and would answer any questions they had. He wanted to know what was on the mind of his constituents and to address their concerns directly. The dialogue continued for an hour. If he didn't know the answer to a question, he summoned the person who did. The executives were invited to lunch in the governor's private dining room. Spouses grumbled as they were escorted onto a waiting bus until the driver turned around and said, "I'm taking you to the governor's home for lunch with Mrs. Reagan."[19]

After three weeks in office, Reagan was asked by a *Los Angeles Times* reporter about the possibility of his running for president as a "favorite son" candidate in 1968.[20] Reagan clearly had given the matter some thought. Major media outlets were soon buzzing with rumors. Associates dismissed the talk as idle chatter, huffing that it was part and parcel of being governor of New York or California. But once in the air, the idea took hold. Reagan was reluctant to jump into the race, but Holmes Tuttle and other supporters urged him to run. Their primary goal was to prevent Rockefeller from capturing California's rich trove of convention delegates. The embers of old enmities from the 1964 campaign were still smoldering. A secondary goal was to launch Reagan on the national stage for a future run—a strategy used to great effect by Senator John F. Kennedy at the 1956 Democratic convention.

The Reagan trial run took off. William French Smith recalled that "everywhere he went, he evoked such enthusiasm that it sort of became contagious."[21] A novelty on the national political scene, Reagan was a magnet for publicity. Smith thought it was because "he had a glamour about him that created an interest far broader than any normal politician. . . . [H]is background as an actor alone was an extremely appealing thing to a lot of people. So there was no question about the fact that he was different. When he moved to Sacramento I can remember reading that all the news services were sending twice as many people to cover him in Sacramento as covered any other governor up there before."[22]

Crafting a Speech

In Sacramento, Reagan continued to write his own speeches until his schedule became overwhelming. In 1969, former newspaperman Jerry Martin was added to the senior policy team and worked with Reagan as a speechwriter. Speeches were Reagan's most effective tool for connecting with the public. Calling it "a lobbying technique," Martin described Reagan's speeches as a way of "reaching out to the people to tell them about things."[23]

When Reagan committed to giving a speech, Martin was notified of the date to give him as much lead time as possible. Reagan met with Martin to get down the key points of what he wanted to say. For efficiency's sake, they sometimes discussed a couple of upcoming speeches at a time. A major address, such as a state of the state or announcement of a major initiative, was a collective effort. The text was circulated among cabinet officers for input. As a member of the senior policy-making staff, Martin sat in on cabinet meetings, so he was familiar with Reagan's thinking on important issues.

Reagan came to meetings with Martin with "a full briefcase" prepared to focus and work. They'd start out by chatting—Martin remembered him as "a natural, Irish, gregarious conversationalist"—then they'd get down to business. Reagan knew what he wanted to say, what he wanted to focus on, and what he thought the audience would be interested in hearing about. In the case of one of the administration's programs, they worked on what they were trying to present, the challenges the initiative faced, and the hoped-for outcomes.

Martin was adamant the final product was Reagan's. The speechwriter's job, in his view, was to capture the personality and reflect the thinking of the person giving the speech. Martin thought it helped if the speechwriter had "a similar philosophy." Like Reagan, Martin had grown up as a Democrat—"We didn't even know what a Republican was"—and his thinking on politics had gradually shifted. Martin's speechwriting style synced with Reagan's—like "newspaper editorials, they get to the point."[24] He noted newspapers use analogies, Reagan liked to use stories and to throw in a few jokes. He had "a million" of them warehoused in his mind. Sacramento press aide Nancy Clark Reynolds, who saw Reagan deliver hundreds of speeches, noticed Reagan "never used big gestures. He convinced with his voice and with his ideals."[25] Reagan repeatedly told Mike Deaver, "Don't ever turn the lights down in the room when I'm speaking, because I want to see their eyes."[26]

In his first year as governor, Reagan was forced to request a hike in taxes to cover the state's looming budget deficit, but he pledged that when the state returned to fiscal solvency, any surplus in the treasury would be returned to taxpayers. At the end of his two terms he was pleased that four times his administration was able to return funds—totaling $5 billion—to taxpayers. He was proud that during his years in Sacramento, the administration had been able to reverse the expansion of welfare. When he came into office, welfare recipients were increasing in California at the rate of "40,000 a month in good times and bad."[27]

The era's resources were unequal to tracking the welfare recipients and there was a suspicion that some were "paper people." His team reversed the upward trend, but just as important, his administration gave the "truly needy"[28] the first increase they had seen since 1958. In Nofziger's estimation, Reagan was "as good a governor as we've had in this state." As he left office, a poll "showed he had a higher job approval rating now than at any other time during his eight years as governor."[29]

Over the years, the once-reluctant candidate of 1965 had vanished. In early 1973, he was perfectly positioned to be the anointed Republican presidential candidate in 1976, taking over from Richard Nixon. He began to put the pieces in place for a serious run.[30] Then Watergate happened and changed everything. Gerald Ford, appointed in 1973 to replace disgraced former vice president Spiro Agnew, announced he would not be a candidate for president in 1976. Reagan took him at his word and continued laying the groundwork for a campaign. Within weeks of assuming the presidency in August 1974, Ford changed his mind and announced he "probably" would run. In November, attempting to forestall Reagan, Ford made it official by declaring his candidacy. But Reagan couldn't wait; he would be too old, at sixty-nine, in 1980, much less 1984. From his vantage point, it was now or never.

Leaving office in January 1975, his goal was to stay in the news and keep up his connections. He signed on to do a radio program and syndicated newspaper column. Before the term "viral networking" was coined, Reagan understood the concept. As he saw it, one person who heard him on the radio, read his column, or heard him speak at an event might tell friends about it over a cup of coffee at a diner. He knew it worked. As he traveled around the country, people told him, "Oh, Governor, I heard your program today, and it was terrific. You were right on target."[31] Person by person, he built a "whole complex matrix of volunteers."[32]

Sacramento aides Mike Deaver and Peter Hannaford established a public relations firm with Ronald Reagan as their premier client. Deaver put to use his political acumen and Hannaford used his strengths in crafting and developing messages. The idea had bubbled up from conversations with a radio producer and newspaper chain that were eager to partner with Reagan.[33] Longtime staffers Helene von Damm and Nancy Clark Reynolds rounded out the team. Building a campaign organization, von Damm meticulously managed administrative tasks, typing up file cards on anyone who contributed one dollar or more, and wrote a book titled *Ronald Reagan* that explained his policy positions in easy-to-understand terms. Reynolds reached out to press contacts and did advance work on speaking events.

His campaign war chest of $1 million was used to rekindle his political action committee and renamed "Citizens for the Republic." Lyn Nofziger took charge and developed workshops for GOP candidates. Reagan now had his eye fixed firmly on the White House. He created an atmosphere of "we're all in this together" and gave his staff plenty of room to use their strengths. Reynolds says, "He just expected that you would do your best."[34] At the end of long days, as he had in Sacramento, he encouraged staffers to go home, get some rest, and spend time with their families. They nodded, kept working, and couldn't wait to get back to work the next day.[35]

The 1976 Campaign: Keeping Up Morale

Out of office, Reagan spent time at his beloved mountaintop ranch near Santa Barbara, riding horses, clearing brush, building fences, and thinking. He thought "about the lost vision of our Founding Fathers and the importance of recapturing it." As in 1964, supporters across the country urged him to run for president. This time, though, it wasn't sufficient to answer the call. Running against a sitting president from his own party wasn't a popular decision with the Republican establishment. He hurt his candidacy by abiding by Parkinson's "Eleventh Commandment" and refusing to criticize Ford directly. Reluctant to make a strong argument against Ford, he appeared hesitant about making the case for his own run. The press and voters sensed he was not fully committed to winning.

On November 20, 1975, he declared his candidacy for president of the United States in a splashy debut at the National Press Club in Washington, D.C. The event was designed to make a favorable impression on the eastern press, who remained resolutely unimpressed. As always, the Washington and New York journalists were contemptuous of Reagan and his candidacy. The day after his announcement, *New York Times* senior columnist James Reston wrote it was "astonishing . . . that this amusing but frivolous Reagan fantasy is taken so seriously by the media and particularly by the President. It makes a lot of news, but it doesn't make much sense." Nancy Reagan remembered the '76 campaign, as "so exciting, so dramatic, and so emotional—especially at the convention—that in my mind it almost overshadows Ronnie's four victories."[36] Operating out of a "dinky little headquarters"[37] in a storefront building in Los Angeles, Reagan barnstormed the country. For Nancy Clark Reynolds it was a blur of planes, hotels, and auditoriums—"travel, travel, speech, speech."[38]

Reagan hired John Sears, wizard of Richard Nixon's against-all-odds comeback in 1968, as his campaign manager. Being a little too clever, the weekend before the crucial New Hampshire primary, Sears pulled Reagan out of the state. His rationale was that the high-profile candidate was a distraction from the get-out-the-vote effort. It was a bad call. Reagan lost to Ford by 1,317 votes. In rapid succession, Reagan lost elections in Massachusetts, Vermont, Florida, and Illinois. The press, egged on by Reagan's former advisors Spencer and Roberts, who were working with Ford, had only one question: "When are you going to drop out?"

The turning point occurred in North Carolina on March 23, 1976. If Reagan hadn't stopped the hemorrhaging, it would have been the end of his political career. He was saved by a fluke. At a campaign event in February, someone in the crowd asked what he thought of Ford's plan to transfer ownership of the Panama Canal to Panama. The topic had never come up before. Like the simmering resentment toward campus radicals in 1966, the issue hadn't been picked up in polling or by the press. But American tempers flared at the suggestion of the "giveaway" of the Panama Canal. Put on the spot, Reagan came up with one of his clever, catchy phrases. The crowd stirred. Peter Hannaford took the phrase and developed a speech that called for a more aggressive stance on U.S. foreign policy. Reagan had found his hot-button issue. At a rally in Florida in early March, Reagan thundered, "We built it, we paid for it, it's ours and we're going to keep it!" The crowd roared their approval.

On the heels of the losses, Reagan's campaign coffers were depleted. One morning his campaign plane sat on the tarmac at LAX while staffers at campaign headquarters hurriedly tore open envelopes to see if they had enough money to take off. Then a donor stepped forward and offered to loan the campaign one hundred thousand dollars to broadcast the new foreign policy speech on television in North Carolina. In almost a reprise of the 1964 program for Goldwater, Reagan headed back to Los Angeles to tape the speech. Worn out by long days and late nights, he looked terrible. Deaver overheard the director gushing to Reagan about his great performance. He knew Reagan could do better. A lot better. He made a pot of strong coffee and they went back for take two. This time the old warhorse nailed it. In Deaver's opinion, North Carolina "may have been the most important political victory of Ronald Reagan's life."[39] His unexpected win transformed and re-energized the campaign. By the time they arrived at the GOP convention in Kansas City, Reagan had almost caught up. The delegate count stood at 1,187 for Gerald Ford, 1,070 for Ronald Reagan.

In a Hail Mary attempt to pick off wavering Ford delegates, Reagan announced his running mate, Senator Richard Schweiker of Pennsylvania. His startling departure from tradition caught some attention, but Ford managed to keep his delegates in line and won the bid. Ford, after giving his own acceptance speech, invited Reagan, sitting half a football field away, to come to the podium and say a few words. With little time to catch his breath and gather his thoughts, Reagan talked to the crowd about the future, not the past, and focused on America, rather than himself. He placed the evening in the context of history and set the stage for another run in 1980.

A few weeks later Reagan wrote to his old friend Earl Dunckel: "As the campaign has gone on, I've come to realize we could have been on the way to winning a convention and losing an election. The Northeast states were sitting out on the Republican side, ready to concede to Carter." Then he added, "Ford can't win in November and Carter must not." With hardly a pause, he went back to taping radio addresses, writing newspaper columns, and speaking at events around the country. The Panama Canal became his signature issue, keeping his name in the news through 1977 and 1978.

The 1980 Campaign: Maintaining a Positive Attitude

On November 13, 1979, at the New York Hilton, he once again announced he was running for president. This time there was no mistaking his commitment to the all-out effort. He said for him "our country is a living, breathing presence, unimpressed by what others say is impossible, proud of its own success, generous—yes and naive—sometimes wrong, never mean and always impatient to provide a better life for its people in a framework of a basic fairness and freedom." A few weeks later he again wrote to his old GE traveling companion, Earl Dunckel: "There wouldn't be any point in my looking for that job if I were willing to change those things that I believe in order to get it. I am still preaching the same old message—hoping now and then to change the wording a bit—so I can continue to sing the song."

That year his old political consultant Bill Roberts was backing a rival candidate, former Texas governor John Connolly, and was sure he was with a winner. Bursting with confidence, Roberts admitted to "needling" his old Reagan associates by pointing out that "the only time he's ever won was when we were with him, and he hasn't won since. This rankles some of them." For a while, it looked like Roberts might be right, at least in part. His own candidate never caught fire, but a dark horse, George H. W. Bush, at 2 percent in the polls in November 1979, suddenly came roaring from behind to score a major coup with a win in Iowa. Once again, Reagan campaign manager John Sears had made a bad call. This time he kept his candidate out of the crowded field. Bush blew into New Hampshire on the wings of his triumph in Iowa crowing about his momentum—"the Big Mo"—he called it. Like many before and after, Roberts and Bush had fallen into the trap of underestimating the determination and grit of Ronald Reagan.

Before 7:00 A.M. the day after the Iowa disaster, Reagan was on the phone with Jerry Carmen, head of the Republican Party in New Hampshire. They had known each other since Reagan first got involved in national politics in the early 1960s. Once or twice a year, Carmen invited Reagan to speak at a GOP event in the electorally important state. At a fund-raiser for a congressional candidate, Carmen had witnessed Reagan's impact on a crowd. After introducing the candidate, Reagan, as had been arranged beforehand, left the room so the crowd could focus their attention on the candidate. The entire audience followed Reagan out of the room. Carmen, spry, wiry, with an infectious can-do attitude and a steel core of determination that matched Reagan's own, was the ideal person for Reagan to be talking to the morning after the Iowa caucuses.

Carmen went into action, saying, "Here's what we're going to do. . . . By the way, where are the kids? Can they help us out?"[40] Michael, Patti, and Ron Reagan had other commitments, but Maureen was there the next day. Claiming the state's college campuses as her turf, she'd tell audiences, "I don't always agree with my father but let me tell you why he thinks what he thinks." Blessed with Jane Wyman's sparkle and Reagan's unflappable temperament, Maureen was a hit. Some considered her an even more talented speaker than her father. With a handful of scribbled words as inspiration, she spoke with "a unique sense of timing and style."[41] Students warmed to her friendly and engaging personality and listened.

The *Nashua Telegraph* had arranged a debate between GOP frontrunners Bush, who had the newspaper's endorsement, and Reagan. With only days to go before the event, the Federal Election Commission ruled the *Telegraph* was making an illegal contribution to the Bush and Reagan campaigns. The *Telegraph* withdrew its backing. Reagan badly needed the one-on-one confrontation with Bush. Carmen, staring into an empty campaign account, said, "We'll fund it."[42] As New Hampshire went to the polls on election day, Reagan replaced John Sears with New York power broker Bill Casey, who had been a highly effective fund-raiser for the campaign. From there on, it was a steady march to the convention for Reagan.

By early September, internal campaign polls showed Reagan with a comfortable lead. Network polls indicated a landslide in the offing. But Reagan wanted more. He wanted to capture the hearts and minds of Americans. He decided he had to debate. Two events were arranged, the first with Congressman John Anderson, who was running as a third-party candidate and the second in late October with President Jimmy Carter. Reagan didn't have a lot of experience debating. He set aside ten valuable campaign days to rehearse in a garage in Middleburg, Virginia. His team pulled together a roster of experts. Congressman David Stockman, formerly Anderson's top aide, stood in as the opponent. Communications guru Myles Martel was recruited as an advisor on the fine points of political debating.

Carter came into the debate full of confidence. Even afterward he and his supporters were pleased with his performance. They were sure he had won, because he had worked in mentions of each of his key constituencies. But in focusing on details, the Carter team missed the big picture. In Reagan's closing summation, he looked America straight in the eye and asked, "Are you better off than you were four years ago?"

It was Reagan in a landslide. Carter conceded two hours before the polls closed in California.

ON REAGAN'S LEADERSHIP

Character matters and Ronald Reagan had character behind his eloquence.

—Aram Bakshian, Director of Speechwriting, Reagan White House

But he wasn't a guy to dominate a meeting. . . . I think he always felt that he was there to learn, not to tell everybody how smart he was. . . . He didn't hesitate to say no. I never had the feeling that any of us were dominating him.

—Lyn Nofziger, Press Aide

Charismatic personality. Knows his position and the position of others. . . . He is not a map reader, he is not a reactor. Reagan knows who he is and what he stands for. His library is stacked with books on political philosophy. He can take information and he can assimilate it and use it appropriately in his own words.

Kenneth Holden, Ph.D., Campaign Consultant, 1966

He had a unique speaking capability, and that was, he could talk to an audience of three or four, or he could talk to an audience of ten thousand people. Yet you always felt that he was talking right at you, that you were the one he wanted to talk to. It was amazing, because even in those huge auditoriums, you had this feeling that he was talking to you.

—Caspar Weinberger, Secretary of Defense, Reagan White House

[He] had a philosophy that the best government is the least government, that you should not have government trying to solve the problems of society. After all there is no such thing as "government" which exists apart from people. It is entirely made up of people. There is no body of government money that exists apart from taxpayers. All the money spent by the government comes from the people.

I think the experience he had working for General Electric was very important for him. He was employed by General Electric when its labor force was among the most radically dominated labor forces in the industry. For years he traveled around the country to the 130 plants of General Electric. He would go down the production line talking to small groups, sometimes as many as fifteen or twenty different groups in a day, I understand.

—Jaquelin Hume, Kitchen Cabinet

The President learned that you work hard in your life and you can get places. I don't think he set out to be President of the United States. I think he set out to get a job in an era where there weren't a whole lot of jobs, in the Depression. He's a self-made man. He believes everything that he said. That was really the key to Ronald Reagan. He wanted to make the best he could out of what he had and he wanted that for everyone else. He knew America offers anything that you want to anybody in the world. If you come here and you work hard and you're willing to sacrifice at times, then you can get that.

—Joanne Drake, Reagan's Chief of Staff

Anyone can be optimistic when times are good, but Ronnie remains hopeful even in the worst of times. When the space shuttle *Challenger* was destroyed, he could reassure the nation that the seven astronauts had not died in vain, and that this tragedy would not mark the end of our scientific progress. When his meetings in Reykjavik in 1986 with Mikhail Gorbachev ended without an agreement, Ronnie was able to set aside his anger and continue talking to the Soviets. After his disastrous first debate with Walter Mondale in 1984, he recovered in time for the second debate. When he was shot in 1981, and again when he had surgery for cancer four years later, Ronnie's positive attitude helped him make a fast recovery.

—Nancy Reagan, *My Turn*

HONING YOUR LEADERSHIP SKILLS

> Example is not the main thing in influencing others. It is the only thing.
>
> —Albert Schweitzer

- Lead by example. You will inspire others by setting high goals and working hard to achieve them.
- Be clear on your goals and objectives and share them with your team.
- To run effective team meetings, prepare a well-thought-out agenda and set a clear goal.
- As the leader, use strategy sessions to listen to varying viewpoints. Voicing your opinion will shut down the flow of communication.
- Use team meetings and one-on-one conversations to keep information flowing in both directions.
- Bond with team members by taking the time to talk to them on an individual basis. They will be strengthened by the personal connection with you.
- In negotiating, be clear on your agenda, stick to your prepared points, and know where you can make some compromises.
- Hire people whose skills and abilities you have confidence in. Understanding their strengths allows you to capitalize on them. Your success will come from delegating responsibilities to team members.
- Cultivate a positive outlook. Listen to books and programs that inspire you to be your best.

- Highly productive teams not only work together, they play together. Celebrate achievements, reward outstanding efforts, recognize milestones.

Working It In

Think of someone you know personally whom you consider to be a great leader. What is it about that person that you admire?

____

____

____

____

____

How, in actions, not words, do you set an example for your team?

____

____

____

____

____

How can you keep the lines of communication open with your team?

____

____

____

____

____

What strategies can you use to keep up the morale of your team?

____

____

____

____

____

What are you reading, or listening to, that helps you maintain a positive attitude in good times and through challenges?

____

____

____

____

____

Chapter 8

The Great Communicator

The White House Years, the First Administration, 1981–85

> Reagan was not believable because he was the Great Communicator; he was the Great Communicator because he was believable.
>
> —Lou Cannon, Washington Journalist

Setting Clear Priorities

Reagan's campaign slogan—"A New Beginning"—struck the right note with Americans who were ready to leave behind a grim decade of gas shortages, an ill-defined war, political turmoil at home, and terrorism abroad. When the votes were tallied, Reagan had swept to victory with forty-three states and 489 electoral votes—almost a mirror image of the 1964 Johnson–Goldwater election results. Republican candidates rode into office on Reagan's coattails. Winning twelve Senate seats, the GOP captured the U.S. Senate for the first time since Eisenhower was elected in 1952. Republicans picked up thirty-four seats in the House of Representatives and governorships in Arkansas, Missouri, North Dakota, and Washington. The country was so eager for change that as the breadth of Reagan's victory became evident, people flooded to campaign celebrations. Streets around the Washington Hilton were clogged with cars.

From the stage of the Century Plaza Hotel in Los Angeles, before an adrenaline-fueled crowd, Reagan gave a brief but characteristic speech. He quoted Abraham Lincoln's quip to journalists the day after his election, "Well boys, your troubles are over now, mine have just begun." He thanked campaign supporters from "our national headquarters in Arlington, Virginia," to the "literally hundreds of thousands of volunteers" all over the country. "Together," he said, "we're going to do what has to be done. We're going to put America back to work again." He would "tap that great American spirit that opened up this completely undeveloped continent from coast to coast and made it a great nation." As he had at the end of his speech at the GOP convention, he asked for the nation's prayers and closed by thanking his "two hometowns," Tampico and Dixon, Illinois.

Back in his hotel suite, President-elect Reagan barely paused to savor the victory. He got down to work pulling together his team. Within hours, Sacramento aide Ed Hickey was on his way back from a State Department assignment in London to handle security.[1] Wizard-of-stagecraft Mike Deaver was put to work designing the inaugural ceremonies. Helene von Damm was already in D.C., as Reagan's liaison at the soon-to-be-established Transition Team headquarters, and assigned to filling the administration's top jobs. Nancy Clark Reynolds took on staffing the East Wing. Speechwriters Peter Hannaford and Ken Khachigian went to work on drafts of the Inaugural Address.

A few weeks after the election, Khachigian arrived at the Reagans' home in Pacific Palisades to work on the speech with the president-elect. They roamed through rooms stacked with moving boxes, in search of a place to sit. Khachigian took notes on a yellow pad while Reagan talked. Reagan "knew what he wanted to say."[2] He zeroed in on the themes he had been talking about for more than thirty years: unleashing the economy, containing bureaucracy, and defeating communism. He had one other goal: to revive the country's slumbering patriotism. He remembered how FDR had used the American flag to rally the spirits of citizens at a difficult time. The flag conveyed a sense of being on a team, that we're all in this together. Reagan's vision of America as "a shining city on a hill" was a leitmotif that ran like a ribbon through his presidency, tying speeches and events together and giving his presidency an overarching thematic harmony.

Reagan realized that to achieve his goals, he needed the support of the American people and the cooperation of Democrats in Congress. His Inaugural Address was designed to state the key issues clearly, lay out a blueprint for solving the most pressing problems, and ask for support. His 1967 address in Sacramento served as a model.

Historically, the east side of the U.S. Capitol had been used for the president's swearing-in. Under Deaver's direction the ceremony was shifted to the west facade facing out toward the Washington, Lincoln, and Jefferson monuments and across the river to Arlington National Cemetery. The Capitol's dome was undergoing renovation work at the time, so to mask the scaffolding and construction efforts, American flags were hung between the columns of the rotunda. Always impressive, the stars-and-stripes-adorned Capitol was a magnificent backdrop for the inauguration.

As in his 1967 speech in Sacramento, Reagan began his January 20, 1981, Inaugural Address by linking democracy's orderly transition of power to the Constitution, calling it "nothing less than a miracle." Then he set out his agenda. Signaling his intention to run a business-friendly administration, he started by saying, "The business of our nation goes forward. These United States are confronted with an economic affliction of great proportions." Taking a stand against "a tax system which penalizes successful achievement and keeps us from maintaining full productivity," he continued "we are a nation that has a government—not the other way around." Lastly he spoke of concerns beyond America's shore: "We will again be the exemplar of freedom and a beacon of hope for those who do not now have freedom."

Challenges lay ahead—especially for the economy, which had just slipped into a recession that lasted for almost two years—but the new administration got off to a promising start when, during the traditional lunch with congressional leaders following the inauguration, Reagan was notified that the fifty-two American hostages held captive for 444 days by Iranian militants had been released and were on their way home. Americans heaved a collective sigh of relief and rejoiced.

Building Bridges

Reagan began his presidency surrounded by Californians who knew him well from Sacramento and who supported his long-held policies. Seeds were sown, though, for trouble ahead by placing an unwieldy troika at the top of the organizational chart. More pragmatic than was generally recognized, Reagan liked having issues, information, and opinions filtered through the perspective of pragmatists and idealists. He was cautious about being pulled too far to the right. As he joked in the early days of the administration, sometimes "our right hand does not always know what our far-right hand is doing." Long-time advisors Ed Meese and Mike Deaver were joined by newcomer James A. Baker III. The efficient Baker, who knew the ways of Washington, complemented Meese's gifts for synthesizing complex policy issues and focusing on long-term goals. Deaver was master of the visual image and Nancy Reagan's conduit to the West Wing.

Reagan's first month in office was a whirlwind of meetings with mayors, congressional caucuses, governors, and union leaders. In Sacramento, he had learned the importance of building bridges with legislators. Before taking office Reagan told his incoming congressional liaison Max Friedersdorf that "the first social event" he wanted to arrange was "a one-on-one sit-down dinner in the president's residence with Tip O'Neill and his wife, just as soon as he was sworn in."[3] Reagan visited Capitol Hill, offered to brief former presidents Carter, Ford, and Nixon, gave a televised speech to the nation on his economic program, and launched a public relations campaign to revitalize the economy. Federal Reserve chairman Paul Volcker announced tightening money supply would be a key element of the administration's economic plan. Goal one was to wring inflation from the bloodstream of the financial system.

In foreign affairs, a communist insurgency forming in Central America was the primary concern. Overseas, there were rumblings of democracy in communist Poland, where Lech Walesa was emerging as a leader of an anti-Soviet movement called Solidarity. On February 25, Reagan's key ally British prime minister Margaret Thatcher arrived for a three-day meeting on relations with the Soviet Union and economic challenges facing both countries. They had first met in London in 1975, shortly after Thatcher was elected leader of the Conservative Party. Thatcher's step-by-step effort to rein in Britain's government had met with defeat. She applauded and encouraged Reagan's approach—"all or nothing."[4] Reagan came away from the February meeting with a sense that a "real friendship exists between the PM, her family, and us."[5]

Americans responded to the administration's energy and clear message. They understood there was a plan in place and that it was being actively implemented. In March, a poll showed 66 percent of Americans were pleased with Reagan's economic programs. Then, on Monday, March 30, 1981, as he left the Washington Hilton after speaking to the Construction Trades Council, four shots rang out. Reagan and three others were hit by bullets fired by a deranged young man. It proved to be the Gipper's finest hour, as Americans watched their president respond with courage and grace to a gunshot wound that almost killed him.

At first, he didn't realize he had been hit. He blamed the piercing pain in his side on his Secret Service agent Jerry Parr. At the sound of gunfire, Parr had shoved Reagan into the limousine and jumped in behind him to shield the president with his body. Reagan's chest had slammed into the car's console. Reagan thought he'd broken a rib. The car sped away from the hotel, heading for the White House, but the bright red blood bubbling from Reagan's mouth indicated a serious internal injury. Parr directed the driver to George Washington University Hospital, three and a half minutes away, and saved the president's life. Pulling up at the emergency entrance, Reagan shook off his Secret Service agents and insisted on walking into the hospital unaided. Out of sight of onlookers and cameras, his knees buckled. Catching him, the agents helped him to a gurney. The bullet had torn through his lung and lodged an inch from his heart. His escape from death was much narrower than the public knew.

In the tumult of his arrival, it took a while for hospital staff to realize who their patient was. As Reagan's breathing was stabilized with oxygen, an intern approached Mike Deaver and asked if he knew the name of the patient. Deaver, with disbelief, said, "It's Reagan. R-E-A-G-A-N."

Despite massive internal bleeding—he lost almost half his blood—the president was soon joking with doctors, nurses, White House staffers, and Nancy Reagan. Opening his eyes to find Nancy gazing down at him, he reached back to his radio-listening youth and quoted boxer Jack Dempsey's quip to his wife after the 1926 championship fight with Gene Tunney: "Honey, I forgot to duck." Going into surgery, he joked with the doctors that he hoped they were Republicans. The surgeon replied, "Mr. President, today we're all Republicans."

As Reagan was recovering at the hospital, Tip O'Neill was one of the first people allowed in for a visit. He "got down on his knees next to the bed and said a prayer for the president and he held his hand and kissed him."[6] Together they recited Psalm 23, and O'Neill said, "God bless you, Mr. President, we're all praying for you."[7] Then O'Neill sat at the president's bedside for quite a while, holding his hand.

Reagan and O'Neill were close in age and had similar roots. They connected over their middle-class Irish backgrounds and upbringings. Both families had dealt with the scourge of alcoholism—the Irish curse. O'Neill marveled over how they had started out at the same point and come to such different conclusions. Over the next eight years, the two traded barbs, zingers, and insults back and forth through the media. Reagan once joked he had received a Valentine from the Speaker. He knew it was from Tip because "the heart was bleeding." When Reagan proposed a tax cut, O'Neill growled, "He has no concern, no regard, no care for the little man of America. And I understand that. Because of his lifestyle, he never meets those people."

Paler and thinner, Reagan left George Washington University Hospital on April 11 wearing a cheerful red sweater. Smiling and waving to hospital staff, he headed back to the White House to continue recovering. The next day he watched the *Columbia* take off on the maiden voyage of America's space shuttle program. The historic launch reignited his sense of the nation's remarkable accomplishments and reaffirmed his feelings about rekindling American patriotism.

Reagan came away from the assassination attempt more convinced than ever that his mother had been right. There was a plan for his life. He told a number of people, "I have decided that whatever time I may have left is left for Him."[8] In Mike Deaver's estimation, he "became less willing to be moved by arguments of others on issues that he felt very strongly about."[9] Senior advisor Ken Adelman summed up Reagan's thinking after the attempt on his life: "He felt he was on a mission. The first mission was the revitalization of the economy, then the mission was the Soviet Union and the attack on communism."[10] Deaver was convinced that "he got much more stubborn on issues after the shooting."[11]

Reagan's most urgent concern was to rid the world of nuclear weapons. Recovering in the White House solarium, he composed a letter to Soviet premier Leonid Brezhnev inviting him to engage in a dialogue. The essence of Reagan's letter was, "I want to sit down and explain why we're not a threat."[12] He circulated the letter to his top advisors, asking for their thoughts and feedback. They passed it along for review within their departments. Eventually a heavily revised version of his letter came back to him. It was unrecognizable. He read over the new letter, considered it, and told them to send the letter as he had originally written it.[13]

As president, Reagan remained the same person he had always been—friendly and gracious, treating everyone with dignity and respect. Still Nelle's son, he insisted on seeing the best in people. When people let him down, he didn't write them off. He believed everyone deserved a chance to overcome their mistakes. In the Oval Office, he'd ask rhetorically, "I wonder what Nelle would think of this?" He valued cooperation across political lines and firmly believed in a common purpose. He countered slights and insults with courtesy. Ted Kennedy railed against his policies and appointments; Reagan went to Boston to raise money for the Kennedy Library. Former president Carter kept up a steady stream of criticism; Reagan went to the opening of the Carter Library. House Speaker Tip O'Neill told the press, "The Reagan program is not working because it is not fair." Reagan shrugged. As Reagan saw it, with O'Neill it was "cocktails at dusk, pistols at dawn."[14] At George Washington University Hospital, waiting to go into surgery, he prayed for seriously injured press secretary Jim Brady and for Secret Service agent Tim McCarthy but he also prayed for "that boy who shot us, too."[15]

Less than a month after he was shot, on April 28, he gave a brief televised address before a joint session of Congress to reassure the nation about his recovery and to re-energize his economic plan. To thunderous applause from both sides of the aisle, he made it clear his priority was getting Americans back to work. The cure, he said, "begins with the federal budget. . . . Our government is too big, and it spends too much." A few weeks later, he made his first trip outside Washington since the assassination attempt, traveling to Notre Dame to give the commencement address. With Pat O'Brien seated on the platform behind him, he reminisced about Knute Rockne and football before turning his attention to the Founding Fathers. He talked about the contributions the graduates would make during their working lives and predicted a bright future, saying, "The years ahead are great ones for this country, for the cause of freedom and the spread of civilization. The West won't contain communism, it will transcend communism. It will dismiss it as some bizarre chapter in human history whose last pages are even now being written." The long standing ovation at the end was a heartwarming boost for the Gipper.

Leader of the Free World

A few weeks later, former White House speechwriter and *New York Times* editorial writer William Safire gave Reagan a new nickname, "the Great Communicator," in an article, ironically, criticizing his speeches.[16] In September, the *Times* economist Leonard Silk picked up Safire's term and gave it momentum. Silk warned Congress to "be wary of the public relations skills of the Great Communicator."[17] In 1983, Colorado congresswoman Patricia Schroeder added another nickname to the growing list when she dubbed Reagan "the Teflon president." Schroeder meant it to be unflattering but, as the term indicated, criticism rolled off Reagan. Political opponents and the press might nip at his heels, but America had seen how Reagan dealt with the attempt on his life and liked what it saw.

Just as an image was settling in of Reagan as a benign, kindly grandfather figure, the country suddenly saw another side of him—the fierce, determined fighter. On August 3, 1981, the Professional Air Traffic Controllers Organization (PATCO) declared an illegal strike and paralyzed air travel. As others had in the past, PATCO union officials underestimated Reagan. Lulled into thinking they were dealing with an amiable statesman always ready with a joke, they ran into a human buzz saw. With Secretary of Labor Drew Lewis acting as a go-between, Reagan informed the union in advance of the strike that he understood the pressures of their demanding jobs but he would not agree to a raise and corresponding tax increase of $700 million a year. Under no circumstances would he tolerate a strike. Reagan suggested Lewis remind the union executives that he had been the head of a union and a labor negotiator.

Ignoring the warning signals, the union's executive board flouted the law forbidding strikes by government employees and 70 percent of PATCO union members walked off their jobs. Visibly furious, Reagan marched out to a bank of microphones in the Rose Garden and delivered a strong message to union workers, "They are in violation of the law and if they do not report for work within forty-eight hours they have forfeited their jobs and will be terminated." Two days later, Reagan fired 11,345 striking workers. Supervisors, military, and a surplus force of six thousand controllers filled in. Over the next two years, a new crop of controllers was trained as replacements. Reagan's message went beyond the immediate audience and issue. Kremlin graybeards heard him loud and clear. He was no pushover.

That fall, Soviet leaders had their own union problems. Inspired in part by the 1979 elevation of Polish native Cardinal Karol Wojtyla to the papacy as Pope John Paul II, democracy was stirring in the shipyards of Gdansk, Poland. Lech Walesa emerged as the leader and ship-workers rose against Soviet-backed military forces. Thirty years later, Walesa said the Soviets "didn't stand a chance." He felt Solidarity prevailed because its "principles and values were stronger." This time Reagan came out strongly in favor of the labor union. On January 20, 1982, Reagan backed up the ship-workers with a strong proclamation. George Shultz, later secretary of state, described it as "an articulated view that we were in favor of freedom, that people living under the communist yoke we felt would want to get out from under it. To the extent that there were people willing to stand up and fight, we were ready to help them."[18]

In speeches and proclamations, State of the Union addresses and press conferences, Reagan "spoke incessantly of America's grand potential, that government needs to be tolerated and managed by the people, not the other way around, and that freedom superseded almost anything."[19] His message was consistent, and it resonated around the world. By this point in his career, Reagan had a tremendous amount of experience speaking to audiences. He might have been jaded, but according to Deaver, "Every speech was a new adventure. . . . He would be the first to admit it."[20] Before every event, he rehearsed. For speechwriters it was like "watching Babe Ruth take batting practice."[21]

Though his audience was now global, Reagan continued to speak with directness and intimacy. Any changes he made to the speechwriters' drafts were "intelligent changes" that smoothed out the cadence and flow "or added an element of feeling." Sometimes Reagan rewrote whole paragraphs, other times he just changed a word, but whatever the scope of his revisions, he made the words more accessible to the listener and gave the speeches a more conversational tone. He preferred simpler words that sounded natural to the ear. For speechwriters the goal was to "keep it very compact, concise, clear, snappy."[22]

Major policy addresses would be passed around the various cabinet departments for review and approval and inevitably translated into "bureaucratese." Reagan's speechwriters fought them "back into good spoken English."[23] Speechwriter Aram Bakshian said Reagan's talent for speaking was "like a singing voice with a wide range and also a set of several styles." For

Bakshian, writing for Reagan was like playing on a "perfectly tuned Steinway." Speaking to a camera, Reagan focused on a few people he knew would be listening. Just as in his early days as a sportscaster, he had pictured a group of guys listening in a barber shop. Bakshian says, "He had an incredible memory and he always knew how to relate to his audiences. It goes back to his sportscasting days."[24] It was helpful that as a broadcaster and actor he had learned how to use a script, but there was more to it than that. A lifetime of experience—living through war and peace and the Great Depression—gave Reagan an ability to connect with people. A warm heart gave him genuine emotion and empathy.

Bakshian, who had also served in the Nixon and Ford administrations as a speechwriter, noted another difference in working with Reagan: he kept the lines of communication open. Reagan was unusual in that he made it clear from the beginning that he didn't want Bakshian to be a "yes man." In fact, he wanted the opposite. If Bakshian had something to add, contribute, or correct, he should by all means do so.

Peace through Strength

In 1982, at the suggestion of Margaret Thatcher, Reagan was invited to London for a rarely offered full state visit—including an overnight stay at Windsor Castle with Queen Elizabeth II—and to address the British Parliament. Chief speechwriter Anthony R. Dolan was assigned to write a draft. As with the proclamation in support of Solidarity, Reagan used the occasion to take aim at tyranny. Formally known as "Westminster," the speech to the British Parliament is often referred to as the "ash heap of history" speech.

Framed as a bookend to Leon Trotsky's 1917 rebuke to opponents at the Second Congress of Soviets, "Go out where you belong—into the ash heap of history,"[25] the address for Parliament laid the groundwork for future speeches and was designed to be a blueprint on how the West should deal with totalitarian regimes. Speaking to a packed audience in the Royal Gallery of Parliament on June 8, 1982, Reagan said, "What I am describing now is a plan and a hope for the long term—the march of freedom and democracy which will leave Marxism-Leninism on the ash heap of history as it has left other tyrannies which stifle the freedom and muzzle the self-expression of the people." The speech provoked a strong reaction. The British Labour Party "completely rejected it." Thatcher lauded it as a "triumph." The *London Times* reported, "President Ronald Reagan launched a crusade for freedom and democracy."[26] Speechwriter Tony Dolan called it a "forward strategy for freedom," representing a sea change in the approach to negotiating with the Soviet Union. As Dolan said, "For a decade there had been nothing but pessimism. And here suddenly was Reagan saying the Soviets were doomed, freedom was on the march—a Western leader was offering hope."[27]

Later that year, the U.S. economy finally showed signs of a recovery as Reagan's much-derided economic policies unleashed an economic expansion that lasted for ninety-three consecutive months—setting a record for economic growth in peacetime. Less welcome news for the administration was that the concept of a "nuclear freeze" was gaining ground. Peace-loving clergy members proved to be particularly fertile territory. The fear at the White House was that, as Reagan put it, "A freeze would reward the Soviet Union for its enormous and unparalleled military buildup. It would prevent the essential and long-overdue modernization of United States and allied defenses and would leave our aging forces increasingly vulnerable."

Searching for an opportunity to tackle the nuclear-freeze issue head-on, Reagan found it in a B-list speech for a B-list audience in a B-list location. The audience was the National Association of Evangelicals in Orlando, Florida, on March 8, 1983. The text hammered away at the evil of an authoritarian regime—using the word "evil" eight times—and came to be known as the "Evil Empire" speech. Picking up the themes of the 1982 "Westminster" speech, it was the defining speech of the administration. The simple, straightforward words of the "Evil Empire" speech set the tone for an address at the Berlin Wall in 1987. The stand-out line urged the ministers "to beware the temptation of pride—the temptation of blithely declaring yourselves above it all and label both sides equally at fault, to ignore the facts of history and the aggressive impulses of an evil empire, to simply call the arms race a giant misunderstanding and thereby remove yourself from the struggle between right and wrong and good and evil." Echoing the commencement speech at Notre Dame, Reagan concluded, "I believe that communism is another sad, bizarre chapter in human history whose last pages even now are being written."

At first glance, the speech to a gathering of ministers looked like a snoozer. Dolan submitted it for review on Thursday, March 5, as the president was on *Air Force One* returning to

Washington from California. Reagan got to it first. By the time staffers at the State Department and NSA reviewed the speech, it was too late. The president had approved the wording. Given the opportunity, administration moderates would have gutted the speech of its take-no-prisoners language, as the "Westminster" speech had been toned down a year earlier. "Evil Empire" echoed and reverberated and seeped into the bloodstream of America. Suddenly a vague, looming threat had an identity.

Once again, the intended, more important audience was thousands of miles away in the Kremlin. It was a shot over the bow, as Reagan put it, "With malice aforethought." The goal was "to let Andropov know we recognized the Soviets for what they were. Frankly, I think it worked, even though some people—including Nancy—tried persuading me to lower the temperature of my rhetoric."[28]

"Evil Empire" burrowed into the network of the Russian gulags where it met an enthusiastic audience. Natan Sharansky, human rights champion and founder of Moscow's Jewish and "refusenik" movements, was serving thirteen years of hard labor for spying. In a Siberian prison, he and a Christian were reading the Bible together. In his 1988 memoir, *Fear No Evil,* he wrote: "We called our sessions Reaganite readings . . . we realized that even the slightest improvement in our situation could be related only to a firm position on human rights by the West, especially by America, and we mentally urged Reagan to demonstrate such resolve."

Two weeks later, on March 23, 1983, Reagan gave dissidents in the Eastern Bloc countries another reason to cheer with a televised address on the Strategic Defense Initiative—a missile shield designed to protect against nuclear attacks. SDI was the brainchild of theoretical physicist Edward Teller, whose work had impressed Reagan on a 1979 visit to the Lawrence Livermore National Laboratory. Teller sat in the Oval Office as Reagan gave what became known as the "Star Wars" speech. Reagan called upon "the scientific community who gave us nuclear weapons to turn their great talents to the cause of mankind and world peace: to give us the means of rendering these nuclear weapons impotent and obsolete." Reagan's critics saw it as provocation, escalating the rhetoric of the Cold War. Strobe Talbot wrote in *Time* magazine: "To many experts, however, Reagan's dream of a 'truly lasting stability' is a nightmare of a new, and highly destabilizing, arms race."[29] Reagan viewed the speech as a key tool in his strategy of pursuing peace through strength and saw it as a way to protect the world from nuclear weapons. He offered to share the missile shield technology with the rest of the world.

As always, Reagan reviewed the speech line by line, deleting paragraphs and writing new ones. He inserted "We can't afford to believe we will never be threatened. There have been two world wars in my lifetime. We didn't start them and indeed did everything we could to avoid being drawn into them. We were ill-prepared for both." He emphasized that the Russians were continuing to acquire weapons. He changed a reference to the Soviets' "new Blackjack bomber" to the Soviets' "brand new Blackjack bomber," a seemingly minor change, but one that stressed the Soviets' unrelenting action. He drilled home the point by replacing "in March 1982" with "a year ago this month" in a sentence that continued "Mr. Brezhnev pledged a moratorium or freeze on SS-20 deployment." He completely rewrote the next two sentences, which became, "but by last August their 800 warheads had become more than 1,200." The original draft's "we still had none" became "we have none."

Americans got the point. A Wirthlin poll found 63 percent of respondents agreed with the statement, "The best way to guarantee peace is for the U.S. to be so strong that no one will dare attack us."[30] Reagan had successfully "communicated a 'can-do' message rooted in hope."[31] Phone calls, telegrams, and letters of congratulation and support poured into the White House. The American Legion telegraphed, "Your television speech last night was the greatest ever delivered by an American president for peace." A television station in Texas wired the results of their computerized poll, which had asked viewers if the president convinced them the "USA should spend more for defense." Of the more than nine hundred responses, 88 percent voted yes. Reagan wrote a note of thanks to the station's president, saying, "I'm especially gratified since some of the Eastern press insist the result was contrary to what your poll shows."

Two days after the speech, Wayne Gilley, a mayor and minister from Lawton, Oklahoma, who had been in the audience at the "Evil Empire" speech in Orlando, wrote to say, "On that occasion, you had the most applause I have ever heard. I heard a spiritual Gettysburg Address from your lips that day." Reagan wrote back and, responding to another part of Gilley's letter about the state of the economy and the Depression, said, "I too recall those days in '32 & '33. I entered the work force in 1932—not exactly the happiest time for job hunting. We survived that as a nation & and as a people and we are surviving this time of trouble. I know you must be encouraged as I am by the evident signs of [economic] recovery." Throughout his years in politics, Reagan remained committed to connecting with his constituents and was always interested in hearing from them. He insisted on seeing a sampling of the mail sent to the White House and often responded personally.

Keeping Information Flowing

As governor and president, Reagan believed in connecting with people in one-on-one conversations. Just as with his Sacramento speechwriter Jerry Martin, in his first meeting with pollster Dick Wirthlin he spent fifteen minutes getting to know him. Wirthlin wrote many years later: "To him, getting to know someone was his business. He asked questions and listened."[32] With staff at the White House, he started meetings with a few jokes to loosen up the atmosphere and encourage everyone to relax.

Samora Machel, president of Mozambique, came to visit Reagan at the White House. Machel's flirtations with communism had conservatives in a flurry, but he and Reagan hit it off when Machel launched into telling anti-Soviet jokes and funny stories about things he had seen in Moscow. In informal meetings, Reagan relied as much on his own intuition as on background information supplied by his staff. His perspective was that "this meeting is about me getting to know that person and figuring out what kind of a person this is. Is this a person who will stand up to his word if the going gets tough or will he run for cover? What am I dealing with?"[33]

Another leader of an impoverished African nation came by for a visit. Reagan asked his awed visitor, "What kind of business are you doing over there?"[34] The country's main business was selling camel meat to Saudi Arabia. Cautioning his visitor against taxing ranchers too much, Reagan asked how they got the camels to the ports. The two happily compared notes on the fine points of camel and cattle driving. The African president left delighted with his meeting. Reagan had engaged him by talking about his interests and what he knew about. Informal meetings kept Reagan limber for more substantive talks with Soviet general secretary Mikhail Gorbachev and Prime Minister Yasuhiro Nakasone of Japan.

Reagan reached out to ordinary Americans. On one occasion he called a little boy who had been badly burned in a fire while saving his brother. After talking for a while, the boy said he wished he had thought to turn his tape recorder on. The president asked if he had it handy—he did—and the leader of the free world said, "Let's chat some more."[35] In personal conversations or in dealing with a crisis or catastrophe, Reagan had an instinct for the right thing to do.

On September 1, 1983, he was on vacation at his ranch near Santa Barbara when the Soviet Union shot down a Korean Air Lines jetliner, filled with 269 passengers and crew, that had inadvertently strayed into Soviet airspace. He headed back to the White House and listened as aides debated a response. He finally said, "Fellas, I don't think we need to do a damn thing. . . . The entire world will rightly and vigorously condemn the Soviets for this barbarism. We need to remember our long-term objectives." He issued a formal statement denouncing the tragedy as a "crime against humanity." Secretary of State George Shultz remembered Reagan's attitude was, "What do you expect of an evil empire. Nevertheless, we should continue our arms negotiations."[36] In Shultz's opinion, "From the standpoint of the European perception of the genuineness of the U.S. desire to negotiate, that made a big impact."

On October 23, 214 U.S. Marines were murdered by a suicide bomber as they slept in their quarters in Beirut, Lebanon. At the same time, the United States was in the advance stages of planning an invasion of Grenada at the request of the Organization of Eastern Caribbean States. On October 27, the president delivered a prime-time television address to discuss the KAL disaster and the events of the previous week in Lebanon and Grenada.

He started by explaining the marines were in Lebanon as part of a multinational force trying to "restore order and stability to that troubled land." He outlined the strategic importance of the Middle East and added that the United States has "a moral obligation to assure the continued existence of Israel as a nation." He reminded America that "our main goal and purpose is to achieve a broader peace in all of the Middle East."

Turning to Grenada, Reagan started with background information. "In 1979, trouble came to Grenada. Maurice Bishop, a protégé of Fidel Castro, staged a military coup and overthrew the government which had been elected under the constitution left to the people by the British." Bishop had recently indicated an interest in improving relations with the United States. Bishop's overture was thwarted when he and members of his cabinet were executed on October 19, 1983. But the most pressing concern was the safety of one thousand U.S. citizens living in

Grenada, among them eight hundred medical students. Reagan concluded by bringing the focus back to his long-term objectives: "Not only has Moscow assisted and encouraged the violence in both countries, but it provides direct support through a network of surrogates and terrorists." Wirthlin reported a "dramatic" shift in public opinion following the speech—71 percent had a favorable reaction.[37]

In late November 1983, Pershing II missiles were deployed in West Germany and at other sites in Europe as the result of an agreement reached earlier in the year at a summit conference Reagan hosted in Williamsburg. The missile deployment brought the United States and Western Europe to parity with the Soviet Union. The Reagan team saw the moment as a turning point in the Cold War, as the shaky NATO alliance stood together. Reagan particularly appreciated the efforts of Helmut Kohl, the newly elected leader of West Germany. He understood it hadn't been a popular or easy decision. In response to the missile deployment, the Soviet Union walked out of the International Nuclear Forces (INF) talks in Geneva.

Author and Russian expert Suzanne Massie asked to meet Reagan in January 1984. She networked her way into the Oval Office via an old friend, Senator William Cohen of Maine, who introduced her to national security advisor Robert C. McFarlane. A five-minute appointment stretched to forty-five minutes. Reagan asked, "How much do they believe in communism over there?"[38] Her welcome reply was, not much. Like many, she underestimated Reagan and thought she "helped persuade the president to peer beyond his 'evil empire' cue cards and get a more balanced handle on Mikhail Gorbachev and the Soviet people." Intrigued by her personal connections with the Russian people, Reagan sent her to Moscow on a "back channel mission" and found her a valuable source of information. Over the next four years, Massie had eighteen more meetings at the White House. According to Mike Deaver, "She was the one who was responsible for getting Reagan ready for the summits, not the experts over in the State Department or the CIA."[39]

Years later George Shultz admitted he, too, underestimated Reagan. After reading excerpts from the diaries Reagan kept during his White House years, Shultz said, "I had no idea how much he wrote . . . that he liked to think things through, work them through his mind, and write them down. . . . The whole kind of conceptual understructure of the Reagan administration right there. It wasn't something that somebody had to tell him about, he had thought it through for himself."[40] Shultz, though, had noted that in preparing for a September 1984 meeting with Soviet foreign secretary Andrei Gromyko, Reagan set aside time during a busy re-election campaign to study the briefing books. He took the material with him to Camp David, read it over, internalized it, came up with his own talking points for the discussion with Gromyko, and asked for feedback.[41] Shultz said, "He knew what he thought and he knew why he thought what he thought."[42]

The year 1984 was a whirlwind of traveling and campaigning, but the Great Communicator was brought up short on October 7 in Louisville, Kentucky, at his first debate with his Democratic challenger, former vice president Walter Mondale. The Gipper had a bad night. Nancy Reagan called it "the worst night of Ronnie's political career."[43] America shrugged it off. He was too well known, too well established to let one bad performance make a difference. Two weeks later in Kansas City he spectacularly redeemed himself when Henry Trewhitt of the *Baltimore Sun* asked, "Mr. President, I want to raise an issue that I think has been lurking out there for two or three weeks and cast it specifically in national security terms. You already are the oldest president in history. And some of your staff say you were tired after your most recent encounter with Mr. Mondale. I recall yet that President Kennedy had to go for days on end with very little sleep during the Cuban missile crisis. Is there any doubt in your mind that you would be able to function in such circumstances?" Reagan stepped up to the plate and blasted the hardball out of the park, "Not at all, Mr. Trewhitt, and I want you to know that also I will not make age an issue of this campaign. I am not going to exploit, for political purposes, my opponent's youth and inexperience." Even Mondale laughed.

On his last run, the seventy-three-year-old campaigner would blow into an event, glance briefly at the notes handed to him by an organizer, step up to the podium, shake his head to loosen up, grin, and give his stump speech. Some candidates need to protect their home turf; Reagan had room to spare. He rolled into Boston's City Hall Plaza—right under the noses of his staunchest adversaries, Ted Kennedy and Tip O'Neill. He wrapped up his speech with, "You ain't seen nothing yet." The crowd roared "FOUR MORE YEARS, FOUR MORE YEARS!" "You talked me into it!"

Wirthlin's polls indicated a major win in the offing. The campaign had the option of spending the final weekend before the election in Minnesota, Mondale's home state, and sweeping every state in the country. The Gipper generously decided against it.[44] He settled for winning forty-nine states, 525 electoral votes, and a decisive 58.8 percent of the vote. He lost Minnesota by less than four thousand votes.

A few weeks after the election German chancellor Helmut Kohl arrived in Washington for a two-day visit. He and Reagan had met a few times before—notably at the Williamsburg summit—and they liked each other. Since taking office, Kohl had been attempting to heal old wounds. In January, he had addressed the Israeli Knesset. In September, he'd met François Mitterrand at Verdun, a World War I battlefield. In a lengthy handshake, they commemorated the war dead and symbolized reconciliation between old enemies. Kohl's goal was to "project a forward-looking image of hope and reconciliation."[45] With no sense of trouble ahead, Kohl invited Reagan to Germany in observance of the fortieth anniversary of the end of World War II in Europe on May 8, 1985. He suggested they visit a cemetery. It was the beginning of the first major public relations crisis of the Reagan administration.

THE GREAT COMMUNICATOR: EXCERPTS FROM REAGAN SPEECHES

I, in my own mind, have thought [of] America as a place in the divine scheme of things that was set aside as a promised land.

—Ronald Reagan, "America the Beautiful," commencement address, William Woods College, June 2, 1952

Looming large in your inheritance is this country, this land America, placed as it is between two great oceans. Those who discovered and pioneered it had to have rare qualities of courage and imagination, nor did these qualities stop there. Even the modern-day immigrants have been possessed of courage beyond that of their neighbors. The courage to tear up centuries-old roots and leave their homelands, to come to this land where even the language was strange. Such courage is part of our inheritance, all of us spring from these special people and these qualities have contributed to the make-up of the American personality.

—Ronald Reagan, "Your America to Be Free," commencement address at Eureka College, 1957, delivered on the occasion of his twenty-fifth reunion

The path we will chart is not an easy one. It demands much of those chosen to govern, but also from those who did the choosing. And let there be no mistake about this: We have come to a crossroad—a time of decision—and the path we follow turns away from any idea that government and those who serve it are omnipotent. It is a path impossible to follow unless we have faith in the collective wisdom and genius of the people. Along this path government will lead but not rule, listen but not lecture.

—Ronald Reagan, Inaugural Address,
Sacramento, California, 1967

When we first set foot on that path I expressed a belief that the most meaningful words in our Constitution are three in number, contained in the phrase, "We the people." Those of us who faced you from these historic steps then, and we today who have been elected to constitutional office or legislative position, are in that three-word phrase. We are of the people, chosen by them to see that no permanent structure of state government ever encroaches upon freedom or assumes a power beyond that freely granted by the people.

—Ronald Reagan, Inaugural Address,
Sacramento, California, 1971

In this election season the White House is telling us a solid economic recovery is taking place. It claims a slight drop in unemployment. It says that prices aren't going up as fast, but they are still going up, and that the stock market has shown some gains. But, in fact, things seem just about as they were back in the 1972 election year. Remember, we were also coming out of a recession then. Inflation had been running at round 6 percent. Unemployment about 7 [percent]. Remember, too, the upsurge and the optimism lasted through the election year and into 1973. And then the roof fell in. Once again we had unemployment. Only this time not 7 percent, more than 10 [percent]. And inflation wasn't 6 percent, it was 12 percent. Now, in this election year 1976, we're told we're coming out of this recession just because inflation and unemployment rates have fallen, to what they were at the worst of the previous recession. If history repeats itself, will we be talking recovery four years from now merely because we've reduced inflation from 25 percent to 12 percent?

—Ronald Reagan, "To Restore America," March 31, 1976

If I could just take a moment; I had an assignment the other day. Someone asked me to write a letter for a time capsule that is going to be opened in Los Angeles a hundred years from now, on our Tricentennial.

It sounded like an easy assignment. They suggested I write something about the problems and the issues today. I set out to do so, riding down the coast in an automobile, looking at the blue Pacific out on one side and the Santa Ynez Mountains on the other, and I couldn't help but wonder if it was going to be that beautiful a hundred years from now as it was on that summer day.

Then, as I tried to write—let your own minds turn to that task. You are going to write for people a hundred years from now, who know all about us. We know nothing about them. We don't know what kind of a world they will be living in.

And suddenly I thought to myself, if I write of the problems, they will be the domestic problems the president spoke of here tonight; the challenges confronting us, the erosion of freedom that has taken place under Democratic rule in this country, the invasion of private rights, the controls and restrictions on the vitality of the great free economy that we enjoy. These are our challenges that we must meet.

And then again, there is that challenge of which he spoke, that we live in a world in which the great powers have poised and aimed at each other horrible missiles of destruction, nuclear weapons that can in a matter of minutes arrive at each other's country and destroy, virtually, the civilized world we live in.

And suddenly it dawned on me, those who would read this letter a hundred years from now will know whether those missiles were fired. They will know whether we met our challenge. Whether they have the freedoms that we have known up until now will depend on what we do here.

Will they look back with appreciation and say, "Thank God for those people in 1976 who headed off that loss of freedom, who kept us now 100 years later free, who kept our world from nuclear destruction"?

—Ronald Reagan, impromptu address
at the GOP Convention, 1976

FINE-TUNING YOUR COMMUNICATION SKILLS

Brave men who work while others sleep,
Who dare while others fly . . .
They build a nation's pillars deep
And lift them to the sky.

—Ralph Waldo Emerson, "A Nation's Strength"

- Have a clearly defined goal.
- Gain the cooperation of others by reaching out and asking for support.
- Work at articulating your thinking. Speak in clear, lucid, simple-to-understand words. To connect with your audience, be sure you are close enough and that the lighting is arranged so you can see your audience clearly.
- Success comes from focusing on your most important goals.
- Working out your beliefs, values, and core principles will give consistency and harmony to your positions and speeches.
- Your message goes beyond the immediate audience.
- Work at developing good relations with the press and with audiences. Learn as much as possible about your audience in advance of a speech.
- Fine-tune your message for each audience.

Working It In

Identify an individual or group you want to communicate with. What's the current status of your interaction? How can you improve your communication strategies?

What is it you want to communicate? The U.S. Marines have a short-cut method for successful communication. Simply ask yourself, "What do I know? Who needs to know it? Have I told them?"

What is the overarching message you are most interested in communicating?

Chapter 9

Challenges

The White House Years, the Second Administration, 1985–89

> Over a lifetime spent communicating to the public, he had developed a rhetorical method best summed up in six simple words: *Persuade through reason. Motivate through emotion.*
>
> —Richard Wirthlin, Reagan pollster, *The Greatest Communicator*

The Second Administration

Reagan's second term began with a round of musical chairs. By May 1985, all three members of the first administration's troika had left the White House. Chief of staff Jim Baker was anxious to move on and swapped jobs with Treasury secretary Donald Regan. Ed Meese headed over to the Justice Department as attorney general. After twenty years with Reagan, Mike Deaver left the administration to set up his own public relations firm.

By the end of 1985, the once smoothly running administration was staffed by "strangers, newcomers who brought it to a standstill through bad staffing decisions."[1] Reagan's weaknesses had intersected. He always recoiled from dealing with personnel problems. He was loath to fire anyone. His attitude was that people should figure out for themselves how to get along. He was long used to being surrounded by a seasoned, top-notch staff. He took that for granted. But at some point in his second term, he must have looked around and wondered where all his longtime staffers had gone. If they hadn't left on their own, they had been pushed out by Don Regan and his handpicked team of cutthroat flunkeys who had unleashed a reign of terror throughout the West Wing from the vice president on down. To his detriment, Reagan's attention was focused far beyond his immediate surroundings.

That March, the leadership of the Soviet Union changed hands for the fourth time in two and a half years when fifty-four-year-old Mikhail Gorbachev became leader of the Soviet Union after Konstantin Chernenko died. Leonid Brezhnev's eighteen-year reign as general secretary of the Communist Party ended with his death in November 1982. He was replaced by Yuri Andropov, who succumbed to kidney failure in February 1984. In Gorbachev's first public speech, on March 11, 1985, he talked of "glasnost." A new day was dawning in the Soviet Union. Gorbachev was instituting a policy of candor and openness in dealing with Russia's internal challenges. For the fourth time, Reagan sent a letter via the State Department suggesting the two leaders meet.

In an astute move a year earlier, Margaret Thatcher had flown to Russia for Andropov's funeral. Her goal was to get a firsthand look at Russia's leadership. Looking past the visibly ailing Chernenko to the next generation of leaders, she focused on the party's rising star, Andropov's protégé, Mikhail Gorbachev. In December 1984, a few days before she was due at a scheduled meeting with Reagan at Camp David, Thatcher met with Gorbachev and his wife at Chequers, the British equivalent of Camp David. She noted Gorbachev's "personality could not have been more different from the wooden ventriloquism of the average Soviet *apparatchik*."[2] Following their meeting, Thatcher told the press, "I like Mr. Gorbachev. We can do business together." In conversation, though, she picked up on Gorbachev's poorly disguised anxiety about Reagan's pet project, the Strategic Defense Initiative.

Early in 1985, following up on Helmut Kohl's invitation, Deaver and an experienced advance team flew to Germany to scout potential venues for Reagan's upcoming visit. At Kohl's suggestion, they visited Bitburg, where eleven thousand Americans were stationed at an airbase. Nearby was a snow-dusted cemetery called Kolmeshohe. It appeared to be a good choice. Deaver and his team weren't aware that forty-nine Nazi SS officers were buried there. At a press conference in early April, press secretary Larry Speakes was asked who was buried at Kolmeshohe—the first indication of an impending problem. On April 19, Holocaust survivor Elie Wiesel, at the White House to receive a Congressional Gold Medal from Reagan, was asked about the upcoming visit. Standing beside Reagan on the podium, Wiesel said, "Mr. President, if it's possible at all, I implore you to do something else, to find a way, to find another way, another site? That place, Mr. President, is not your place. Your place is with the victims of the SS." With that, the seemingly harmless trip to Bitburg exploded into a full-fledged controversy.

The well-connected Jim Baker could have made a few well-placed calls to damp down the media furor. Don Regan could not. He didn't have the connections and he had drawn a clear line from the start. He would not have any back-corridor dealings with the press. By the end of May, an unnamed former White House official was quoted in the *Los Angeles Times* as saying, "He's the wrong guy for the job. He's got a short fuse and a big ego and no political instincts."[3] The criticism seemed like the usual sniping; it was in fact prescient. At the time of Reagan's second inauguration, his approval rating was close to 70 percent, and the successes of his first term were widely lauded. Suddenly, he was swamped by controversies on the Bitburg visit, defense spending, the budget, and aid to the Nicaraguan Contras.

Taking On Challenges

Resisting enormous pressure from Congress, Jewish groups, and veterans to cancel the visit to Bitburg, Reagan stood fast, saying it was "morally right" to visit the cemetery and that it symbolized "the great reconciliation that has taken place" between the two nations. Kohl told the *New York Times,* "I will not give up the idea. If we don't go to Bitburg, if we don't do what we jointly planned, we will deeply offend the feelings of [my] people." A poll of West Germans confirmed that 72 percent thought Reagan should go ahead with the visit. Americans saw it differently, starting with Nancy Reagan, who "was furious at Helmut Kohl" and "urged Ronnie to cancel the visit. I wasn't alone: Fifty-three senators and almost four hundred members of the House asked Ronnie not to go. But the previous November, in the Oval Office, Ronnie had given his word to Kohl, and he felt duty-bound to honor his commitment."[4]

Opposition energized Reagan. It was an unlikely twist to Reagan's character. His pollster Richard Wirthlin observed, "Reagan was never more energized than when confronting opposition. His enthusiasm would soar, his sights would focus, and his passion would stir. He was one of the few leaders I've ever known who actually derived pleasure from confrontation."[5] As with other controversial decisions, the audience and issues went far beyond the immediate problem. George Shultz said, "So he was doing something that he knew, and everybody knew, was tough politics. But he was doing it because he had made a commitment and he was carrying out the commitment. . . . That's a big point."[6] His resolve proved farsighted. Reagan's strategic alliance with Kohl and rapprochement with Germany led to his greatest triumph.

Deaver was heartsick that as head of the advance team, he had let his boss down. Reagan, as always, was phlegmatic, saying to Deaver, "What happened in Europe forty years ago was horrible, but it was forty years ago. If we can't put that war behind us now, if we can't reconcile and look forward, then we'll always think about the war, never the peace."[7] Arriving at the Bitburg airbase, Reagan acknowledged the passions that had been inflamed, saying, "This visit has stirred many emotions in the American and German people, too. I've received many letters since first deciding to come to Bitburg cemetery; some supportive, others deeply concerned and questioning, and others opposed. Some old wounds have been reopened, and this I regret very much because this should be a time of healing." He concluded, "There's much to make us hopeful on this historic anniversary. One of the symbols of that hate—that could have been that hope, a little while ago, when we heard a German band playing the American National Anthem and an American band playing the German National Anthem. While much of the world still huddles in the darkness of oppression, we can see a new dawn of freedom sweeping the globe. And we can see in the new democracies of Latin America, in the new economic freedoms and prosperity in Asia, in the slow movement toward peace in the Middle East, and in the strengthening alliance of democratic nations in Europe and America that the light from that dawn is growing stronger. Together, let us gather in that light and walk out of the shadow. Let us live in peace."[8]

Bitburg was a summer squall compared to the hurricane that lay ahead.

On June 14, 1985, a young navy diver boarded a flight in Athens, Greece, bound for Rome. Shortly after takeoff, Muslim terrorists hijacked the plane and forced the pilot to fly to Beirut, Lebanon. Singling out twenty-three-year-old Robert Stethem, the terrorists savagely beat him, shot him between his eyes, and dumped his body on the tarmac. The hostage crisis lasted for seventeen days as the plane shuttled back and forth from Beirut to Algiers. Israel was at the center of the furor. The terrorists were demanding the release of more than seven hundred Palestinians and Lebanese held in Israeli prisons. Negotiating with terrorists was out of the question; that would reward terrorism and encourage future hostage-takings and hijackings. In an account of the incident in its July 1, 1985, issue, *Time* framed the problem: "For Ronald Reagan, the hard question is whether retaliating against terrorists will deter terrorism—or only provoke more of it."[9] Stethem's brutal death set the stage for the major crisis of the Reagan administration, Iran-Contra.

A few weeks later, on July 13, Reagan was operated on for colon cancer. As he was recovering from surgery at Bethesda Navy Medical Center, National Security Advisor Robert McFarlane asked him to okay a plan suggested by the Israelis, whereby Israel would ship weapons through an intermediary, Menucher Ghorbanifar, to a moderate Iranian group opposed to Ayatollah Khomeini. Secretary of Defense Caspar Weinberger and Secretary of State George Shultz were strongly against any suggestion of supplying weapons to Iran—they had worked hard to prevent other countries from selling arms to Iran. But McFarlane and like-minded officials hoped to generate goodwill in the troubled region and lure Iran away from the influence of the Soviets into better relations with the West. At the time, Iran was at war with Iraq and anxious to receive the weapons. The idea had been proposed to McFarlane by the Israelis, who offered to act as intermediaries on an initial shipment of ninety-six antitank missiles. In August, 508 more antitank missiles were delivered to Iran.

Negotiator in Chief

In mid-November 1985, Reagan finally had the meeting he had long dreamed of—a summit with Russian counterpart Mikhail Gorbachev. At Reagan's insistence, they started with a one-on-one session scheduled to last fifteen minutes—their conversation lasted for an hour. Reagan used the time to confront Gorbachev on "freedom of religion"—a shorthand way of dealing with human rights abuses in the Soviet Union. They spent the afternoon arguing about SDI. Gorbachev took the position, "It opens up an arms race in space." Like many before him, Gorbachev may have expected to meet a jovial, kindly old man. Instead he ran into a bruising negotiator. Each time they met, "Reagan took him to the cleaners."[10] They agreed to disagree for the time being on SDI. Each issued an invitation to the other for further meetings. They pledged to seek a 50 percent reduction in nuclear arms and issued a joint statement that "a nuclear war cannot be won and must not be fought."

Reporting on the meeting at a Joint Session of Congress on November 21, Reagan was roundly applauded. He said there had been more than "three thousand reporters in Geneva, so it's possible there will be three thousand opinions on what happened. So, maybe it's the old broadcaster in me, but I decided to file my own report directly to you." He continued, "I welcomed the chance to tell Mr. Gorbachev that we are a nation that defends, rather than attacks; that our alliances are defensive, not offensive." He cautioned patience with a trademark Reaganism, "Quick fixes don't fix big problems," and ended, "We traveled to Geneva with peace as our goal and freedom as our guide. For there can be no greater good than the quest for peace and no finer purpose than the preservation of freedom." Aides negotiated a follow-up summit eleven months later in Reykjavik.

In December 1985, Bud McFarlane suddenly resigned as national security advisor. The press reported he was a victim of burnout, like others who had left the administration. Admiral John Poindexter, McFarlane's former deputy, stepped up to take his place. It was the first sign of problems to come.

For the Reagan administration, 1986 seemed to consist of one crisis after another. In January, as the nation's schoolchildren watched attentively, the space shuttle *Challenger* exploded seventy-three seconds after takeoff. Reagan postponed his State of the Union speech scheduled for that night and replaced it with a televised address focused on the concerns of the children. In April, a poorly tended nuclear power plant exploded at Chernobyl in the Soviet Union. Despite the overtures to Iran, throughout the year, Americans continued to be kidnapped in the Middle East.

Still the weapon shipments went on—in February 1986, the United States shipped one thousand antitank missiles to Iran, in October, another five hundred. On June 25, 1986, the House of Representatives reversed its long-standing opposition to funding the Nicaraguan Contras and passed a $100 million bill approving aid for the Contras by twelve votes. Reagan saw it as a "a step forward in bipartisan consensus in American foreign policy." In September, McFarlane, now outside the administration, delivered twenty-three tons of weapons to Iran.

On October 11, Reagan and Gorbachev met in Reykjavik for follow-up discussions on arms control. Gorbachev proposed deep cuts in stockpiles of nuclear weapons. Reagan agreed. They appeared to be moving toward an agreement that would create a more peaceful and stable world. Then Gorbachev blindsided Reagan. His proposal was only good if the United States limited work on the Strategic Defense Initiative to laboratory testing. Thousands of journalists hovered around the building waiting for news of a historic agreement, but in "a moment of great courage"[11] Reagan walked away. "If he wanted it that much then we weren't giving it away."[12] The summit was widely viewed as a failure and the blame was put squarely on Reagan.

On November 3, three days before the 1986 midterm elections, a pro-Syrian Lebanese magazine broke the story that the Reagan administration had been selling arms to Iran. The Iranian government confirmed the story, and the Iran-Contra controversy burst into headlines around the world. The Democrats picked up five seats in the House and won back the Senate.

Funding the Contras was in line with Reagan's thinking and everyone knew it. A January 10, 1980, *Los Angeles Times* article was headlined, "Reagan Would Supply Arms to Rebels in Afghanistan," and quoted him as saying, "I think that there's nothing wrong with giving free people weapons to defend their freedom."

Reagan never was good at defending himself, even when the facts were on his side, as in the 1966 flare-up with primary opponents George Christopher and William Patrick in Santa Monica and the long-simmering debate over the 1952 waiver for MCA. He may not have known all the details of the sales of arms to Iran or the funding of the Contras but he, or his chief of staff, should have. Thrown on the defensive on Iran-Contra, he could not seem to get traction in explaining his perspective on the issue. The Great Communicator struggled with how to explain Iran-Contra to the American people. For once the right words eluded him. His popularity suffered badly. On December 1, 1986, a *New York Times* poll showed a drop in Reagan's approval rating from 67 percent to 46 percent in the space of a month.

In truth the situation was incredibly complicated. Attorney General Ed Meese, put in charge of investigating the matter, characterized it as fraught with "legal complexities and policy ambiguities." And that was just on the Iranian side of the transaction. Coming into office, a top Reagan goal was to push back the communist insurgency forming in Central America. Nicaragua was the frontline in the battle. There, communist-backed Sandinistas were fighting a loosely coordinated resistance movement known as the Contras. Neither side was composed of angels. The Boland Amendment, sponsored by Tip O'Neill's lifelong associate Congressman Edward P. Boland, consisted of three separate pieces of legislation enacted between 1983 and 1985. Designed to prohibit the CIA and Department of Defense from funding the Contras, the amendment was inspired by O'Neill's connection to Maryknoll nuns who had worked in Nicaragua under the heavy-handed rule of the Samoza regime. As the administration saw it, the legislation would allow the Sandinistas, who were heavily funded by the Soviet Union, Cuba, and other communist countries, to take over Nicaragua and, from there, the rest of Central America. But there was a loophole. The amendment could be, and was, circumvented by operating through the National Security Council.

On November 13, 1986, Reagan again addressed the nation on Iran-Contra. "Our government has a firm policy not to capitulate to terrorist demands. . . . We did not—repeat, did not—trade weapons or anything else for hostages, nor will we." Polls showed Americans weren't convinced. Attorney General Meese established within twenty-four hours that McFarlane, Poindexter, and Marine colonel Oliver North were the links between weapon sales to Iran and supplying funds to the Nicaraguan Contras. They had been working under the National Security

Council, which was outside the parameters of the legislation. In rapid succession, Poindexter resigned, North was fired, and Reagan appointed Senator John Tower of Texas to review how weapons sales to Iran were used to support freedom fighters in Nicaragua. Shultz summed it up: "The Iran-Contra business was worked by the NSC staff with the CIA . . . in a sense it was a major activity carried on off-line."[13]

With the West Wing under siege, Don Regan was soon under the intense glare of the spotlight. The White House chief of staff's job was to know what was going on within the administration, massage press contacts, and shelter the president from criticism. With the high-handed Regan in place, the once Teflon-coated president suddenly could do nothing right. Testifying before the Tower Board for a second time on February 2, 1987, the president appeared confused. When asked to explain inconsistencies in his statements, Reagan picked up a memo and read aloud, "If the question comes up at the Tower Board meeting, you might want to say that you were surprised." It was a disastrous repetition of the first debate with Mondale.

Former budget director David A. Stockman colorfully described Regan as "an ideological neuter" with an "insatiable ego." On November 29, 1986, the *Los Angeles Times* reported: "Only the president or his chief of staff, Donald Regan, was in a position to oversee such programs. One of the great unanswered questions about the Iranian arms scandal is whether such oversight actually occurred or whether White House superiors of the council were ignorant of what their subordinates were doing." A savvier manager would have had listening posts strategically set up throughout the ranks of the administration. That was a moot point. Regan had been at most of the NSC meetings where Iran-Contra was discussed.

Despite a torrent of criticism, Don Regan refused to step down. Hoping the storm would blow over, he hunkered down in his office and repeatedly postponed his departure date. The crisis hit right at Reagan's weak spot. He couldn't bring himself to deal with the problem head-on. He only saw the jovial side of his chief of staff and former secretary of treasury. Reagan thought he knew Regan well. He was unaware, for example, that Regan had assigned a staffer to come up with a new joke every morning to greet the president with. Reagan, who only saw the good in people, couldn't bring himself to believe there was another side of Regan that was invisible to him.

Plenty of people, though, were well aware of Regan's dark side. Reportedly the cabinet, in unison, asked Regan to step down. He didn't. Washington operative Bob Strauss was brought in to talk to Reagan about firing Regan. Strauss took to the task with unusual bluntness. Even longtime White House staffer Rex Scouten, in a highly unusual move, approached the First Lady about problems with Regan. Maureen Reagan had squabbled with the volatile chief of staff. She recounted the particulars to her father. It finally began to sink in that there was a real problem. Yet Reagan still remained reluctant to fire Regan. The only person left to deal with the problem was Nancy Reagan. Then, in a heated phone conversation with the First Lady, Regan hung up on her. That was it.

On February 26, the Tower Commission Report was delivered to Reagan and charged that as president he had failed to "insist upon accountability and performance review." The commission found that "the arms transfers to Iran and the activities of the N.S.C. staff in support of the contras are case studies in the perils of policy pursued outside the constraints of orderly process." The report said, "Mr. Regan also shares in this responsibility. More than almost any chief of staff of recent memory, he asserted personal control over the White House staff and sought to extend this control to the national security adviser. He was personally active in national security affairs and attended almost all the relevant meetings regarding the Iran initiative. He, as much as anyone, should have insisted that an orderly process be observed. In addition, he especially should have ensured that plans were made for handling any public disclosure of the initiative. He must bear primary responsibility for the chaos that descended upon the White House when such disclosure did occur."

The next day, word that Regan was being replaced by Senator Howard Baker was strategically leaked to CNN. In a fury, Regan whipped off a one-sentence letter of resignation. From the West Wing to Capitol Hill, there was a huge sigh of relief. Nancy Reagan described Baker as "calm, easygoing, congenial, and self-effacing"[14]—in short, everything that Don Regan was not. Baker was adept at smoothing over differences and had a rapport with the press. It helped that, as a three-time senator, he had friends on Capitol Hill. Baker got right down to work restoring morale in the West Wing.

In a televised address on March 4, Reagan resolutely put the affair behind him by acknowledging mistakes on Iran-Contra. He told the nation, "You know, by the time you reach my age, you've made plenty of mistakes. And if you've lived your life properly—so, you learn. You put things in perspective. You pull your energies together. You change. You go forward."

And that's what he set about doing. Though his once spectacularly successful presidency seemed mired in difficulties and doomed to be defined by controversies, he looked ahead. In January, the White House press office had announced the president would be giving a speech in Berlin to mark the city's 750th anniversary on June 12, 1987.

In early June, the Reagans flew to Italy for a G7 summit in Venice. Stopping in Rome for a meeting with John Paul II, the president briefly nodded off. The London *Guardian* sniped: "A shadow of his former self. . . . His leadership is compared unfavorably with that of Mr. Gorbachev." Longtime observer Lou Cannon headlined an article on the summit, "Much Ado About Nothing." The old warrior was weary but he could still pull it together for the issues he cared about, revitalizing the economy, matters of faith, and for his trademark punch lines. There was one last great speech left in him. Reagan went to Berlin armed with it. Nine years earlier Reagan had visited Berlin shortly after a young East Berliner was shot attempting to escape and left to die entangled in the wall's barbed wire. Looking out over the wall that held its citizens hostage, Reagan had silently listened as West German guards recounted the young man's ordeal and the horror of East Germans who could only watch as he suffered and died. The incident, which succinctly captured the battle between freedom and the brutal oppression of totalitarian regimes, had made an enduring impression on Reagan. Now he thundered, "Mr. Gorbachev, tear down this wall!" The press, for the most part, dismissed the speech as a meaningless gesture.

Reagan's staunchest ally, Prime Minister Thatcher, thought he had gone too far.

Approaching the end of a storied career, it should have been the best of times. Instead it seemed like the worst. Personal problems piled on matters of state. Iran-Contra was still in the headlines and poised to leave an indelible stain on his presidency. That fall he was devastated when Nancy Reagan was diagnosed with breast cancer. Ten days later, he had to tell Nancy her mother had passed away. In between the two events, the stock market had plummeted five hundred points. He casually dismissed it as "a buying opportunity." In January 1988, the bad news continued with the sudden death from a heart attack of close friend Ed Hickey. Oliver North and Admiral Poindexter were indicted for crimes relating to the Iran-Contra affair. In May, Don Regan's score-settling memoir was published.

Still, there were successes. In December 1987, Premier Gorbachev arrived in Washington for another summit. They signed the INF treaty, eliminating an entire class of weapons. It was the first arms-control agreement to be signed and ratified by the Senate since 1972. In May 1988, Reagan flew to Moscow for a fourth summit with Gorbachev and was gratified that Russians lined the route of his motorcade and cheered as he passed by. Speaking to students at Moscow State University, he said, "We do not know what the conclusion will be of this journey, but we're hopeful that the promise of reform will be fulfilled. In this Moscow spring, this May 1988, we may be allowed that hope: that freedom, like the fresh green sapling planted over Tolstoy's grave, will blossom forth at last in the rich fertile soil of your people and culture." That fall he was pleased when his vice president,

George H. W. Bush, was elected to succeed him. The election was widely seen as an endorsement of Reagan's policies.

On January 11, 1989, forty years after he'd been galvanized into action by a vicious union strike and twenty-five years after The Speech, Reagan gave a final address from the Oval Office. Like a magnet drawn to true north, he returned to his most cherished themes. He summed up his eight years in office with "a small story about a big ship, and a refugee, and a sailor." It was a story from the early 1980s, "at the height of the boat people" fleeing oppression in Indochina. A sailor scanning the horizon from the deck of the aircraft carrier *Midway* spotted a "leaky little boat" overloaded with refugees "hoping to get to America." A motor launch was dispatched to bring the strugglers to the ship and safety. "As the refugees made their way through the choppy seas, one spied the sailor on deck, and stood up, and called out to him. He yelled, 'Hello, American sailor. Hello, freedom man.'" America in the 1980s, Reagan said, "stood, again, for freedom."

For him the "Reagan revolution" was simply "a rediscovery of our values" and return to "common sense." He said, "Common sense told us that when you put a big tax on something, the people will produce less of it. So we cut the people's tax rates, and the people produced more than ever before. The economy bloomed like a plant that had been cut back and could now grow quicker and stronger." He continued, "Common sense also told us that to preserve the peace, we'd have to become strong again after years of weakness and confusion."

He concluded his review of his presidency with his favorite metaphor for America, "the shining city upon a hill."

Describing the country he knew so well as "a tall, proud city built on rocks stronger than oceans, windswept, God-blessed, and teeming with people of all kinds living in harmony and peace; a city with free ports that hummed with commerce and creativity. And if there had to be city walls, the walls had doors and the doors were open to anyone with the will and the heart to get here. That's how I saw it, and see it still."

Ten days later, he watched George H. W. Bush's inauguration. As he boarded a helicopter to begin the journey back to California, he turned and snapped off a salute. His job was done. He had put America back to work, rekindled American patriotism, and using only words had cracked the wall that divided Europe like a scar, separating free people of the West from those living under the tyranny of brutal regimes.

FAREWELL SPEECH FROM THE OVAL OFFICE, JANUARY 11, 1989

This is the thirty-fourth time I'll speak to you from the Oval Office and the last. We've been together eight years now, and soon it'll be time for me to go. But before I do, I wanted to share some thoughts, some of which I've been saving for a long time.

It's been the honor of my life to be your President. So many of you have written the past few weeks to say thanks, but I could say as much to you. Nancy and I are grateful for the opportunity you gave us to serve.

One of the things about the Presidency is that you're always somewhat apart. You spent a lot of time going by too fast in a car someone else is driving, and seeing the people through tinted glass—the parents holding up a child, and the wave you saw too late and couldn't return. And so many times I wanted to stop and reach out from behind the glass, and connect. Well, maybe I can do a little of that tonight.

People ask how I feel about leaving. And the fact is, "parting is such sweet sorrow." The sweet part is California and the ranch and freedom. The sorrow—the goodbyes, of course, and leaving this beautiful place.

You know, down the hall and up the stairs from this office is the part of the White House where the President and his family live. There are a few favorite windows I have up there that I like to stand and look out of early in the morning. The view is over the grounds here to the Washington

Monument, and then the Mall and the Jefferson Memorial. But on mornings when the humidity is low, you can see past the Jefferson to the river, the Potomac, and the Virginia shore. Someone said that's the view Lincoln had when he saw the smoke rising from the Battle of Bull Run. I see more prosaic things: the grass on the banks, the morning traffic as people make their way to work, now and then a sailboat on the river.

I've been thinking a bit at that window. I've been reflecting on what the past eight years have meant and mean. And the image that comes to mind like a refrain is a nautical one—a small story about a big ship, and a refugee, and a sailor. It was back in the early eighties, at the height of the boat people. And the sailor was hard at work on the carrier *Midway,* which was patrolling the South China Sea. The sailor, like most American servicemen, was young, smart, and fiercely observant. The crew spied on the horizon a leaky little boat. And crammed inside were refugees from Indochina hoping to get to America. The *Midway* sent a small launch to bring them to the ship and safety. As the refugees made their way through the choppy seas, one spied the sailor on deck, and stood up, and called out to him. He yelled, "Hello, American sailor. Hello, freedom man."

A small moment with a big meaning, a moment the sailor, who wrote it in a letter, couldn't get out of his mind. And, when I saw it, neither could I. Because that's what it was to be an American in the 1980s. We stood, again, for freedom. I know we always have, but in the past few years the world again—and in a way, we ourselves—rediscovered it.

It's been quite a journey this decade, and we held together through some stormy seas. And at the end, together, we are reaching our destination.

The fact is, from Grenada to the Washington and Moscow summits, from the recession of '81 to '82, to the expansion that began in late '82 and continues to this day, we've made a difference. The way I see it, there were two great triumphs, two things that I'm proudest of. One is the economic recovery, in which the people of America created—and filled—19 million new jobs. The other is the recovery of our morale. America is respected again in the world and looked to for leadership.

Something that happened to me a few years ago reflects some of this. It was back in 1981, and I was attending my first big economic summit, which was held that year in Canada. The meeting place rotates among the member countries. The opening meeting was a formal dinner of the heads of government of the seven industrialized nations. Now, I sat there like the new kid in school and listened, and it was all François this and Helmut that. They dropped titles and spoke to one another on a first-name basis. Well, at one point I sort of leaned in and said, "My name's Ron." Well, in that same year, we began the actions we felt would ignite an economic comeback—cut taxes and regulation, started to cut spending. And soon the recovery began.

Two years later, another economic summit with pretty much the same cast. At the big opening meeting we all got together, and all of a sudden, just for a moment, I saw that everyone was just sitting there looking at me. And then one of them broke the silence. "Tell us about the American miracle," he said.

Well, back in 1980, when I was running for President, it was all so different. Some pundits said our programs would result in catastrophe. Our views on foreign affairs would cause war. Our plans for the economy would cause inflation to soar and bring about economic collapse. I even remember one highly respected economist saying, back in 1982, that "The engines of economic growth have shut down here, and they're likely to stay that way for years to come." Well, he and the other opinion leaders were wrong. The fact is what they call "radical" was really "right." What they called "dangerous" was just "desperately needed."

And in all of that time I won a nickname, "the Great Communicator." But I never thought it was my style or the words I used that made a difference: it was the content. I wasn't a great communicator, but I communicated great things, and they didn't spring full bloom from my brow, they came from the heart of a great nation—from our experience, our wisdom, and our belief in the principles that have guided us for two centuries. They called it the Reagan revolution. Well, I'll accept that, but for me it always seemed more like the great rediscovery, a rediscovery of our values and our common sense.

Common sense told us that when you put a big tax on something, the people will produce less of it. So, we cut the people's tax rates, and the people produced more than ever before. The economy bloomed like a plant that had been cut back and could now grow quicker and stronger. Our economic program brought about the longest peacetime expansion in our history: real family income up, the poverty rate down, entrepreneurship booming, and an explosion in research and new technology. We're exporting more than ever because American industry became more competitive, and at the same time, we summoned the national will to knock down protectionist walls abroad instead of erecting them at home.

Common sense also told us that to preserve the peace, we'd have to become strong again after years of weakness and confusion. So, we rebuilt our defenses, and this New Year we toasted the new peacefulness around the globe. Not only have the superpowers actually begun to reduce their stockpiles of nuclear weapons—and hope for even more progress is bright—but the regional conflicts that rack the globe are also beginning to cease. The Persian Gulf is no longer a war zone. The Soviets are leaving Afghanistan. The Vietnamese are preparing to pull out of Cambodia, and an American-mediated accord will soon send 50,000 Cuban troops home from Angola.

The lesson of all this was, of course, that because we're a great nation, our challenges seem complex. It will always be this way. But as long as we remember our first principles and believe in ourselves, the future will always be ours. And something else we learned: Once you begin a great movement, there's no telling where it will end. We meant to change a nation, and instead, we changed a world.

Countries across the globe are turning to free markets and free speech and turning away from the ideologies of the past. For them, the great rediscovery of the 1980s has been that, lo and behold, the moral way of government is the practical way of government: Democracy, the profoundly good, is also the profoundly productive.

When you've got to the point when you can celebrate the anniversaries of your thirty-ninth birthday, you can sit back sometimes, review your life, and see it flowing before you. For me there was a fork in the river, and it was right in the middle of my life. I never meant to go into politics. It wasn't my intention when I was young. But I was raised to believe you had to pay your way for the blessings bestowed on you. I was happy with my career in the entertainment world, but I ultimately went into politics because I wanted to protect something precious.

Ours was the first revolution in the history of mankind that truly reversed the course of government, and with three little words: "We the People." "We the People" tell the government what to do; it doesn't tell us. "We the People" are the driver; the government is the car. And we decide where it should go, and by what route, and how fast. Almost all the world's constitutions are documents in which governments tell the people what their privileges are. Our Constitution is a document in which "We the People" tell the government what it is allowed to do. "We the People" are free. This belief has been the underlying basis for everything I've tried to do these past eight years.

But back in the 1960s, when I began, it seemed to me that we'd begun reversing the order of things—that through more and more rules and regulations and confiscatory taxes, the government was taking more of our money, more of our options, and more of our freedom. I went into politics in part to put up my hand and say, "Stop." I was a citizen politician, and it seemed the right thing for a citizen to do.

I think we have stopped a lot of what needed stopping. And I hope we have once again reminded people that man is not free unless government is limited. There's a clear cause and effect here that is as neat and predictable as a law of physics: As government expands, liberty contracts.

Nothing is less free than pure communism—and yet we have, the past few years, forged a satisfying new closeness with the Soviet Union. I've been asked if this isn't a gamble, and my answer is no, because we're basing our actions not on words but deeds. The detente of the 1970s was based not on actions but promises. They'd promise to treat their own people and the people of the world better. But the gulag was still the gulag, and the state was still expansionist, and they still waged proxy wars in Africa, Asia, and Latin America.

Well, this time, so far, it's different. President Gorbachev has brought about some internal democratic reforms and begun the withdrawal from Afghanistan. He has also freed prisoners whose names I've given him every time we've met.

But life has a way of reminding you of big things through small incidents. Once, during the heady days of the Moscow summit, Nancy and I decided to break off from the entourage one afternoon to visit the shops on Arbat Street—that's a little street just off Moscow's main shopping area. Even though our visit was a surprise, every Russian there immediately recognized us and called out our names and reached for our hands. We were just about swept away by the warmth. You could almost feel the possibilities in all that joy. But within seconds, a KGB detail pushed their way toward us and began pushing and shoving the people in the crowd. It was an interesting moment. It reminded me that while the man on the street in the Soviet Union yearns for peace, the government is Communist. And those who run it are Communists, and that means we and they view such issues as freedom and human rights very differently.

We must keep up our guard, but we must also continue to work together to lessen and eliminate tension and mistrust. My view is that President Gorbachev is different from previous Soviet leaders. I think he knows some of the things wrong with his society and is trying to fix them. We wish him well. And we'll continue to work to make sure that the Soviet Union that eventually emerges from this process is a less threatening one. What it all boils down to is this: I want the new closeness to continue. And it will, as long as we make it clear that we will continue to act in a certain way as long as they continue to act in a helpful manner. If and when they don't, at first pull your punches. If they persist, pull the plug. It's still trust but verify. It's still play, but cut the cards. It's still watch closely. And don't be afraid to see what you see.

I've been asked if I have any regrets. Well, I do. The deficit is one. I've been talking a great deal about that lately, but tonight isn't for arguments, and I'm going to hold my tongue. But an observation: I've had my share of victories in the Congress, but what few people noticed is that I never won anything you didn't win for me. They never saw my troops, they never saw Reagan's regiments, the American people. You won every battle with every call you made and letter you wrote demanding action. Well, action is still needed. If we're to finish the job. Reagan's regiments will have to become the Bush brigades. Soon he'll be the chief, and he'll need you every bit as much as I did.

Finally, there is a great tradition of warnings in Presidential farewells, and I've got one that's been on my mind for some time. But oddly enough, it starts with one of the things I'm proudest of in the past eight years: the resurgence of national pride that I called the new patriotism. This national feeling is good, but it won't count for much, and it won't last unless it's grounded in thoughtfulness and knowledge.

An informed patriotism is what we want. And are we doing a good enough job teaching our children what America is and what she represents in the long history of the world? Those of us who are over thirty-five or so years of age grew up in a different America. We were taught, very directly, what it means to be an American. And we absorbed, almost in the air, a love of country and an appreciation of its institutions. If you didn't get these things from your family, you got them from the neighborhood, from the father down the street who fought in Korea or the family who lost someone at Anzio. Or you could get a sense of patriotism from school. And if all else failed, you could get a sense of patriotism from the popular culture. The movies celebrated democratic values and implicitly reinforced the idea that America was special. TV was like that, too, through the mid-sixties.

But now, we're about to enter the nineties, and some things have changed. Younger parents aren't sure that an unambivalent appreciation of America is the right thing to teach modern children. And as for those who create the popular culture, well-grounded patriotism is no longer the style. Our spirit is back, but we haven't reinstitutionalized it. We've got to do a better job of getting across that America is freedom—freedom of speech, freedom of religion, freedom of enterprise. And freedom is special and rare. It's fragile; it needs [protection].

So, we've got to teach history based not on what's in fashion but what's important—why the Pilgrims came here, who Jimmy Doolittle was, and what those thirty seconds over Tokyo meant. You know, four years ago on the fortieth anniversary of D-Day, I read a letter from a young woman writing to her late father, who'd fought on Omaha Beach. Her name was Lisa Zanatta Henn, and she said, "We will always remember, we will never forget what the boys of Normandy did." Well, let's help her keep her word. If we forget what we did, we won't know who we are. I'm warning of an eradication of the American memory that could result, ultimately, in an erosion of the American spirit. Let's start with some basics: more attention to American history and a greater emphasis on civic ritual.

And let me offer lesson number one about America: All great change in America begins at the dinner table. So, tomorrow night in the kitchen, I hope the talking begins. And children, if your parents haven't been teaching you what it means to be an American, let 'em know and nail 'em on it. That would be a very American thing to do.

And that's about all I have to say tonight, except for one thing. The past few days when I've been at that window upstairs, I've thought a bit of the "shining city upon a hill." The phrase comes from John Winthrop, who wrote it to describe the America he imagined. What he imagined was important because he was an early Pilgrim, an early freedom man. He journeyed here on what today we'd call a little wooden boat; and like the other Pilgrims, he was looking for a home that would be free. I've spoken of the shining city all my political life, but I don't know if I ever quite communicated what I saw when I said it. But in my mind it was a tall, proud city built on rocks stronger than oceans, windswept, God-blessed, and teeming with people of all kinds living in harmony and peace; a city with free ports that hummed with commerce and creativity. And if there had to be city walls, the walls had doors and the doors were open to anyone with the will and the heart to get here. That's how I saw it, and see it still.

And how stands the city on this winter night? More prosperous, more secure, and happier than it was eight years ago. But more than that: After 200 years, two centuries, she still stands strong and true on the granite ridge, and her glow has held steady no matter what storm. And she's still a beacon, still a magnet for all who must have freedom, for all the pilgrims from all the lost places who are hurtling through the darkness, toward home.

We've done our part. And as I walk off into the city streets, a final word to the men and women of the Reagan revolution, the men and women across America who for eight years did the work that brought America back. My friends: We did it. We weren't just marking time. We made a difference. We made the city stronger, we made the city freer, and we left her in good hands. All in all, not bad, not bad at all.

And so, goodbye, God bless you, and God bless the United States of America.

OVERCOMING YOUR CHALLENGES

> Develop success from failures. Discouragement and failure are two of the surest stepping stones to success.
>
> —Dale Carnegie

- Resolve to continue learning throughout your career. Be strategic in choosing courses and programs that will enhance your natural talents.
- Continue to develop new skills as you progress in your career. An apprenticeship provides a path to learning new skills and gives you the opportunity to learn firsthand about a business and to develop contacts.
- Use down time to polish your image and stay on top of your game. Develop strategies, habits, and hobbies conducive to maintaining your health.
- To get through tough times and life's inevitable challenges, resolve to put one foot in front of the other and take the next step. Find an exercise program you enjoy and that fits into your schedule so you can stick with it.
- Be open to trying new approaches and exploring new ideas but wait for the right opportunity that is in harmony with your values to come along.
- Never flinch from a challenge. You may find that rising to meet a challenge unleashes your greatest strengths.

Working It In

Identify someone you can confide in, who will listen supportively and provide you with helpful feedback and practical advice.

List three networks that you are connected with that you can tap for support.

Think of an example of a time you successfully dealt with a challenge. What skills did you use? What lessons did you learn that you can use again in the future?

Chapter 10

Legacy

> Whatever else history may say about me when I'm gone, I hope it will record that I appealed to your best hopes, not your worst fears; to your confidence rather than your doubts. My dream is that you will travel the road ahead with liberty's lamp guiding your steps and opportunity's arm steadying your way.
>
> —Ronald Reagan, Republican National Convention, August 17, 1992

His image lingers. Striding through halls of power, mingling with heads of state, standing against a backdrop of American flags. Easily forgotten are the long train rides, nerve-racking flights, and lonely nights far from home. Though he rose to the pinnacle of power, celebrated and honored around the world, he never changed. The gloss of Hollywood and polished veneer of a successful executive concealed the inner Reagan—the man from Dixon "shaped by a river and a church."[1]

In Dixon he developed the values that stayed with him for a lifetime and "a profound spiritual faith that grounded him and left him with a nearly perpetual peace of mind."[2] There was nothing easy or straightforward about Ronald Reagan's life journey. Like everyone, he suffered setbacks, controversies, and a full share of heartache. The son of a troubled alcoholic, he spent the summers of his youth working long hours, seven days a week, to help support his family and put himself through college. Battling the Rock River and saving lives instilled in him an enduring self-confidence that never teetered into arrogance.

Early on, his strengths were evident to others. Watching him fight his way through the tough primaries of 1976, his old mentor, Bernard Fraser, told a reporter, "He hasn't changed. He's essentially interested in people and wants them to have their destiny in their own hands, which is what he wants in government."[3] At Eureka, Moon Reagan noted his brother's "swashbuckling self-confidence," and "ability to lead" and "inspire."[4] He had come through childhood challenges strong but not hard. By the time he graduated from Eureka at the bottom of the Depression, he had an internal toughness that gave him the strength to resist the siren song of an easier path and set his sights on finding his dream job.

His distinguishing qualities had already emerged—perseverance and optimism. When times were tough, when his career hit a snag, instead of changing course or giving up, he dug in, muscled on, and figured out how to get ahead. As an actor faced with a crumbling career, he adjusted his focus, tapped his strengths and interests, reached out to others, got involved with industry associations and began speaking out. Step by step, speech by speech, he polished his abilities and fine-tuned his skills. Confronted by challenges, he refused to give up. Putting one foot in front of the other, he drove toward a positive outcome. Nothing just happened for him. His success came from blending strategic thinking with a matter-of-fact, businesslike attitude. He backed those traits with "sheer force of will."[5] His overarching goal was a world where everyone could flourish by using his or her gifts.

In choosing his first postcollege job, he displayed a knack for identifying growing industries and spotting opportunities in a confusing and changing world. As an early sportscaster, star in the dawn of television, and politician in a new world of mass media, he was at the forefront of trends and a master of emerging technology. By identifying his inherent talents, he could see how those strengths could best be used in service to others. With unusual clarity he kept his eye on his long-range goals. If a career as a movie star seemed like a pipe dream, he figured out the interim steps he needed to take to reach his goal, put his plan into action, and stayed focused. Throughout his life, he refused to be daunted by challenges. In 1978, when he told Nancy Clark Reynolds he would be running again for president in 1980, she gasped, "But, Governor, you're sixty-seven years old!" he patiently responded, "I know how old I am, Nancy."

Dragged into politics in his midfifties, he unexpectedly found it "the most fulfilling thing I've done in life." After eight years in Sacramento, he said, "It's been the greatest experience of my life and the most challenging."[6] Yet, throughout his career in politics, easterners and the media elite sneered at the B-list actor. In a 1967 profile of California's newly elected governor, CBS newscaster Harry Reasoner said, "American sophisticates couldn't take Ronald Reagan seriously. As an actor, he had seemed corny to them. As a politician, he had seemed improbable." During the 1980 primary campaign, *Time* described Reagan as "that crinkly and blandly familiar face from scores of old movies on afternoon TV, that two-time loser for the Republican presidential nomination who has not been elected to any public office for a decade." But a group of savvy businessmen saw him differently. Kitchen cabinet member William French Smith spoke for those who had taken his measure and were impressed. Those early supporters admired "his basic philosophy that everybody agreed with, which he articulated so well. . . . You don't sit down and hatch it up. It just develops."[7]

Reagan came to understand the challenges involved in running a business in the course of countless breakfast meetings with corporate executives and luncheons and dinners with business groups. His philosophy had evolved over years of talking to assembly-line workers at factories. He understood and respected their concerns and their thinking. As his supporters, these blue-collar workers came to be known as "Reagan Democrats." And he found ways to communicate with the wide range of people he met. On the road with General Electric, it didn't take long for him to notice that everyone wanted to meet the celebrity; nobody wanted to listen to a speech. Weary workers coming off the night shift just wanted to shake his hand and head for home. He made adjustments and adopted a more conversational, engaging tone in his remarks. Through these many conversations, he developed "an enormous ability to articulate what a very large number of men and women felt and thought and didn't articulate very well for themselves. He always spoke for them."[8]

He worked at honing his message. While speaking to an audience, he noted which parts of his speech provoked a reaction. On a speeding train or in a car, rushing from event to event, rather than rewrite the entire speech, he swapped out one file card for another. He perfected a system of shorthand, writing his speeches on four-by-six file cards, making it easy to fine-tune, change, and modify his comments for the next audience. Listening, thinking, adapting, responding. Along the way he became the Great Communicator.

He took office as president in 1981 with three big priorities: to unleash the economy, limit intrusion of government into people's lives, and defeat communism. He once told Mike Deaver he would heave the first two overboard to achieve the third. Thanks to his finely polished negotiating skills and extensive knowledge of economics, he left the world a more prosperous and peaceful place than he had found it.

It wasn't easy. To rescue the U.S. economy from the stranglehold of inflation, he made tough, and for a while, unpopular decisions, but his economic policies—once widely derided in the press and by opponents as "Reaganomics"—led the country out of a recession and produced a thriving economy. He joked, "You can tell our program is working, because they don't call it 'Reaganomics' anymore!" In a 1979 interview, he summed up his thinking on the American Revolution and the free enterprise system: "Our revolution was the philosophical revolution. For the first time in man's history, we unleashed the individual genius of every man to climb as high and as far as his own strength and ability will take him. This is the secret of our success. . . . When we were less than seventy years old scholars from Europe were coming to this country to find out what had created this great miracle."[9] During his years in office, inflation fell 70 percent and interest rates were cut in half. In June 1988, unemployment hit a fourteen-year low.

In January 1989, shortly after Reagan left office, the Soviet Union quietly packed up and left Afghanistan, as had been agreed in the Geneva Accords a year earlier. That June, Chinese students demonstrated for democracy in Tiananmen Square. Their protest was beaten back, but suddenly democracy was on the march around the world. Starting as a trickle with a handful of students, the movement gathered momentum. That August, it burst into a flood when Hungary lifted its border defenses and thirteen thousand East Germans escaped to the West. An attempt to clamp down on the refugees failed when East Germans swarmed the West German embassy in Budapest and refused to leave. The fever for freedom spread to Czechoslovakia and from there to East Germany. In November 1989, the Berlin Wall fell. In early 1990, the Marxist/Sandinista government was voted out of office in Nicaragua. Gorbachev was greeted by two hundred fifty thousand protesters on a visit to Lithuania. Suddenly the Evil Empire was in its death throes. That spring, Lithuania, Estonia, and Latvia, in rapid succession, declared their independence from the USSR. On December 25, 1991, the Soviet flag flew over the Kremlin for the last time.

Looking back on the hard-fought battles of the 1980s, Reagan's national security advisor and secretary of defense Frank Carlucci said, "Ronald Reagan was more right than I was in wanting to be forward leaning with Gorbachev."[10] The old warhorse's instincts had proven correct. Twenty years later, on November 9, 2009, German chancellor Angela Merkel celebrated the anniversary of the fall of the Berlin Wall and reunification of Germany by walking through the Brandenburg Gate with Russia's Mikhail Gorbachev and Poland's Lech Walesa.

Leaving the White House, Reagan looked forward to spending time at his ranch, giving speeches, and writing his memoirs. His old friend from Hollywood, Lew Wasserman, was again acting as his agent. In 1990, Reagan returned to Dixon and Tampico, this time to launch his book. On Mother's Day, 1992, he made a last, unannounced, trip to Tampico. The tiny community was astonished when former president and Mrs. Reagan arrived to attend a service at his mother's old church. Visiting the small museum below the second-floor apartment where he was born, the president noticed posters of his old movies on the walls. Pointing to each poster in turn, he regaled the museum's staff with stories from each of the film sets.[11]

Two years later, he was confronted with the devastating diagnosis of Alzheimer's Disease. He had seen the disease ravage the minds of his mother and brother. He was well aware of what lay ahead. Now a private citizen, he might have chosen to keep the news a personal matter. Instead, after absorbing the blow, he sat down and wrote a letter.

He said he had "recently been told that I am one of the Americans who will be afflicted with Alzheimer's Disease." He ended, "When the Lord calls me home, whenever that may be I will face it with the greatest love for this country of ours and eternal optimism for its future. I now begin the journey that will lead me into the sunset of my life. I know that for America there will always be a bright dawn ahead." Nancy Clark Reynolds, who knew him so well, says the Alzheimer's letter "shows the true measure of the man."[12] Anyone who wrote to President Reagan after the announcement received a note back from him in appreciation of the support.

Reagan's stunning letter was published in newspapers on November 5, 1994. Two days later, in the midterm elections, Democrats lost their majorities in both houses of Congress. Republicans picked up fifty-three seats in the House of Representatives and seven seats in the Senate. The vote was seen as a repudiation of the policies of the administration in office. But perhaps voters were also registering some nostalgia for the days of the Gipper.

For the next four years, President Reagan continued to go to his office and meet with supporters who wrote and asked for an appointment. A young intern in the president's Century City office noticed the increasingly frail former president might stumble on a name or title but he was happy to accommodate visitors by answering questions about his meetings with Prime Minister Thatcher and negotiating sessions with General Secretary Gorbachev. His eyes sparkled, though, when he was asked about his years in Hollywood.[13]

In the fall of 1998, two young pastors, Scott Porter, from Dixon, Illinois, and his friend Todd Bailey, were among the last outsiders to have an appointment with the president. The president lit up when Scott mentioned he had been to Dixon's Lowell Park recently for a picnic with his wife and daughters. A Reagan staffer commented that the president had saved seventy-seven lives in his days as a lifeguard at the park. Ronald Reagan, now eighty-seven, puffed up his chest and said, "Yes, I did!" Everyone laughed and everyone teared up.[14]

The former president said good-bye to Porter and Bailey with a wink and a wave. Still the Great Communicator, he sent an unspoken message that came through loud and clear: They shouldn't worry about him. A few months later, his office announced the president would no longer be receiving visitors. His Century City office was closed up and moved to the recently completed Reagan Library, set among the rolling hills he loved north of Los Angeles.

Over the next few years the elderly president faded from public view. On June 5, 2004, Nancy Reagan, in a brief statement, announced the president's death and added, "We appreciated everyone's prayers over the years." A few days later Jane Wyman broke her long-standing silence on her former husband, saying, "America has lost a great president and a great, kind, and gentle man."

Tributes poured in from around the world. Florida aeronautics executive David Thompson was in Los Angeles on business and joined the throng heading to the Reagan Library to pay their respects. The library had arranged for parking at a nearby college and buses to bring well-wishers to the library but had greatly underestimated the turnout. A cross-section of Americans—"all ages, all races, all social classes"[15]—waited patiently for hours to board a bus to the library. Halfway up the winding road that leads to the library, an impromptu shrine sprang up—a wreath from the Screen Actors Guild was next to one from the National Rifle Association—reminding visitors of the extraordinary breadth of Reagan's life and how many lives he had touched over the years. Personal mementos flanked the flowers—a remarkable collection of fading photographs, weather-worn campaign placards, and yard signs that had been stored in basements, attics, and garages for years.

His life was celebrated at a service at Washington's National Cathedral on June 11, 2004. As the great and mighty filed through the doors, the recessional hymn, "Jerusalem," soared through the cathedral and the choir sang—"bring me my bow of burning gold, bring me my arrows of desire." Church bells rang out across America—a tribute loosely coordinated through an informal network of churches. The New York Stock Exchange and the nation's financial markets closed in observance of Ronald Reagan's funeral. The president's body was flown back to the library in Simi Valley for burial. With fifteen minutes' notice, residents of Tampico were alerted the plane would be flying over his birthplace. Old friends and neighbors poured into the streets for a final wave and salute to Tampico's most famous son. The plane flew low overhead and dipped its wings.[16]

Reagan insiders were caught off-guard by the tremendous outpouring of affection and admiration for the former president. He had been off the public stage for ten years and some thought he might have been forgotten. But since he had left office, "So many of the things we had talked about and fought for had come to pass"[17]—the expansion of the economy, the fall of the Berlin Wall, freedom and democracy sprouting up all over the world. The goal that proved most elusive was containing the spread of the federal government.

Reagan saw America as a land where people help one another; where in times of crisis or tragedy, neighbors turn out to pitch in and do whatever they can. From his days as an economics major in college, wrestling with welfare reform as governor of California, and firsthand observation, he believed privately funded charities were the most effective and cost-efficient way to help the destitute. As governor, his signature reform was revising the state's welfare program. His administration gave the truly needy the first increase they had seen since 1958 and transferred the distribution of aid back to local governments where it could be done more efficiently—"eliminating the middlemen."

In a 1979 PBS interview, he cited a group of Mormons who owned farms near Sacramento as an example of how he thought charity should work. Church members down on their luck were given jobs on the farm or in a church-owned factory canning the harvest and distributing the food to the rest of the country. The soon-to-be candidate for president talked of how it was more economically efficient for the church or local governments to provide aid to the needy rather than rely on the federal government. Bill Moyers pressed him: "You're not suggesting we turn HEW[18] over to the Mormon Church?" Reagan responded with a question of his own: "What if every organized religion in America had done the same thing?" In an era when citizens rely increasingly on government intervention and mandates to solve problems, Reagan's worldview seems hopelessly outdated and naive, but that was the America he had grown up in and had seen close up in his travels around the country.

As a young boy he immersed himself in books and dreamed of becoming a hero. Longtime press aide Lyn Nofziger said Reagan often talked about his childhood during their travels. Nofziger thought Reagan would have made "a superb hermit."[19] Instead, inspired by heroes and mentors, from childhood on, he pushed himself out into the world, set high goals, and pursued his dreams. As a child, he refused to be held back by poor eyesight and drove himself in athletics, setting a swimming record that stood for years. In college he won three varsity letters and an "Oscar." In the depths of the Depression, he found his dream job. When necessary, he asked for guidance, listened carefully, and put the advice into action. Throughout his life, he forced himself past his comfort zone. No matter what form the challenge took, he simply resolved to do his best.

In the 1979 PBS interview with Bill Moyers, he reminisced about his early life when his family lived "payday to payday." When Dutch got his first job at WOC, he had never been "east of Chicago or west of Clinton, Iowa." Living through the Depression wasn't easy, but, "There was a warmth among the people. A desire to help." That was how he saw the world. It was a perspective he had inherited from his mother. Bess Reagan told a reporter in May 1981, "She tried her best to make ours a more caring society. She was kind to—and generous with—friend and stranger alike. She trusted everyone, sometimes to her own disadvantage. To her, no one had a bad side. To her, everyone was a good person."[20] Ronald Reagan's closest associates describe him in exactly the same terms, almost word for word.

Elected president of the United States when he was sixty-nine, he was the oldest man to serve as president in the nation's two-hundred-year history. He was America's Abraham—his descendants "as numerous as the stars." He lives on as a rallying point and a polestar—a model of a life well-lived. He once said, "What I'd really like to do is go down in history as the president who made Americans believe in themselves again." A 2009 Rasmussen poll found that "being like Reagan" was "the most positive thing you can say about a candidate."

In rooms filled with supercharged egos, dazzling résumés, and platinum-plated credentials, the kid from Dixon held his own. In the end, values, wisdom, and life experience trumped degrees and diplomas. His strength was not in imposing his will on others, but in listening to advice and keeping the lines of communication open and information flowing in both directions.

Reagan's journey was an unlikely odyssey from small-town boy to leader of the free world. From the start he was the kid who refused to give up. The young man aching for a break who buttonholed a college president and pleaded to be given a chance. The skinny kid on the sidelines anxiously waiting to be put in the game. The freshman who gave a rousing, call-to-action speech. The newly minted graduate who, against all odds, chased and caught his dream job. From humble beginnings, he matured into a man who dealt with a terrifying attempt on his life with grace and good humor; who, in the face of tremendous personal cost and pressure, stood by an ally; who confronted tyranny with straightforward words. Rivals, opponents, friends, and advisors might clamor and offer advice, but when it came to the principles he cherished most dearly, he stood firm.

His chief arms negotiator, Ken Adelman, saw Reykjavik as Reagan's "finest moment." Twenty-five hundred journalists hovered, waiting for a historic agreement. On his way to make concessions, Reagan caught sight of the crowd through a window, stopped, paused, turned around, and walked away. Years later Gorbachev conceded that Reykjavik was the turning point in the confrontation between the West and the Soviet Union. The breakthrough came because Reagan stayed his own course. As Prime Minister Margaret Thatcher said, "He won the Cold War without firing a shot."

Secretary of State George Shultz said Reagan's "strongest suit lay in knowing what he believed and why he believed it."

He always had. At the end of his historic presidency, Ronald Reagan was the same man who declared in a 1947 New Year's broadcast, "Whether or not most of the world achieves peace and democracy this year depends greatly on all of us. We must not seem divided over race or religion. Discrimination and hate are the weapons of our enemies. Let's show the world we're strong and united and free." His executive assistant Kathy Osborne, who spent thousands of hours by his side in Sacramento and at the White House, sums him up as the "all-American midwestern boy who just wanted to do the right thing."

Burnished by history, through the prism of time, Ronald Reagan's achievements become ever clearer. Coming into office as the country slipped into a recession, he revitalized the U.S. economy and set America on a path of sustained growth. In an era when totalitarian regimes were on the march, he faced down oppression and unleashed the forces of freedom and democracy around the world. Since his death in 2004, visitors come to his grave at the Reagan Library to honor and contemplate the accomplishments of this extraordinary man. As day draws to a close and shadows lengthen over the purple-sage hills of the West, the setting sun shines on the words of the man from Dixon . . .

I know in my heart that man is good
that what is right will always eventually triumph
and that there is purpose and worth to each and every life.

Notes

Introduction

1. *Time,* March 30, 1980, "Reagan's Rousing Return."

1. Discovering Talents, Developing Strengths

1. Neil Reagan, oral history, p. 3.
2. *Star Courier,* February 8–9, 2003, "Reagan Remembered College Football Days with Kewanee Man."
3. Neil Reagan, oral history, p. 12.
4. Ronald Reagan, *An American Life,* p. 27.
5. Ibid.
6. Ibid., p. 28.
7. Baptized Nellie; as an adult in Dixon, Illinois, she adopted a more sophisticated version of her name, Nelle.
8. Ronald Reagan and Richard Hubler, *Where's the Rest of Me?,* p. 9.
9. *The Star,* June 17, 1980, "Ronald Reagan's Roots."
10. Ronald Reagan, *An American Life,* p. 20.
11. Nancy Reagan, *I Love You, Ronnie,* p. 87.
12. Pastor Scott Porter, Abiding Word Church, Sterling, Illinois, to author, March 2009.
13. *Saturday Evening Post,* May 1, 1985, "The Unflappable Nelle Reagan."

14. Ronald Reagan, *An American Life*, p. 226.
15. Maureen Reagan, *First Father, First Daughter*, p. 64.
16. Presidents James A. Garfield and Lyndon B. Johnson were also members of the Disciples of Christ.
17. Ronald Reagan and Hubler, *Where's the Rest of Me?*, p. 12.
18. Broadcast History—Part I—1910–1920; tape 37, The Paley Center.
19. Ronald Reagan, *An American Life*, p. 31.
20. Ronald Reagan and Hubler, *Where's the Rest of Me?*, p. 17.
21. Ibid., p. 7.
22. Ronald Reagan, *An American Life*, p. 32.
23. In the period from 1902 to 1942, Harold Bell Wright was the first author to sell a million books and to earn more than a million dollars from his writing.
24. Ronald Reagan, *An American Life*, p. 26.
25. Ronald Reagan and Hubler, *Where's the Rest of Me?*, p. 35.
26. Ronald Reagan, *An American Life*, p. 35.
27. Ronald Reagan and Hubler, *Where's the Rest of Me?*, p. 15.
28. Neil Reagan, oral history, p. 11.
29. Ronald Reagan, *An American Life*, p. 35.
30. Ibid., p. 59.
31. Garry Wills, *Reagan's America*, p. 27.
32. *Dixon Evening Telegraph*, February 28, 1981, caption under 1928 yearbook photo of Dixonian Dramatic Club.
33. Ronald Reagan Museum, Eureka College.
34. Ronald Reagan, *An American Life*, p. 46.
35. Ibid.
36. Junius Rodriguez, to author, February 2009.
37. Ibid.
38. Brian Sajko, to author, February 2009.
39. Ronald Reagan and Hubler, *Where's the Rest of Me?*, p. 43.
40. *U.S. Life Saving*, undated photocopy from Reagan Library files, "Dutch Reagan the Lifeguard."

2. Finding Mentors, Setting Goals

1. *Washington Post*, September 30, 1980, "Midwest Fans Tuned in to 'Dutch.'"

2. Ronald Reagan and Hubler, *Where's the Rest of Me?*, p. 44.
3. Ibid.
4. WEAF lives on as a sports radio station. As of 2010 the station is CBS-owned WFAN (660 AM).
5. Edwards, *Early Reagan*, p. 69.
6. Ronald Reagan and Hubler, *Where's the Rest of Me?*, p. 52.
7. Ibid., p. 57.
8. A "clear channel" radio station is defined as one that operates at maximum power (50,000 watts) on a frequency that's exclusive to the station and is designed to reach an extended audience.
9. Skinner, ed., *Reagan, A Life in Letters*, p. 95.
10. Ronald Reagan and Hubler, *Where's the Rest of Me?*, p. 61.
11. Neil Reagan, oral history, p. 13.
12. *Los Angeles Times*, November 28, 1980.
13. Bill Boyarsky, *The Rise of Ronald Reagan*, p. 60.
14. Ibid.
15. Ronald Reagan and Hubler, *Where's the Rest of Me?*, p. 58.
16. John Meroney, to author, January 2010.
17. Bill Boyarsky, *The Rise of Ronald Reagan*, p. 60.
18. Bob Colacello, *Ronnie and Nancy*, p. 68.

3. Evolving into a Brand

1. Approximately $100 in 2010 dollars.
2. MCA agent Richard Steenberg and SAG archivist Valerie Yaros, to author, 2009.
3. Ronald Reagan and Hubler, *Where's the Rest of Me?*, p. 91.
4. Ibid., p. 101.
5. *Los Angeles Times*, November 6, 1940, "Catholic Club to See Film of Celebration."
6. Richard Steenberg, to author, June 2009.
7. Ronald Reagan and Hubler, *Where's the Rest of Me?*, p. 106.
8. *Los Angeles Times*, April 20, 1942, "Ronald Reagan Departs to Report for Army Service."
9. Ronald Reagan and Hubler, *Where's the Rest of Me?*, p. 122.
10. *Los Angeles Times*, June 11, 1945, "Stores Sponsor Bond Premieres."
11. Ronald Reagan and Hubler, *Where's the Rest of Me?*, p. 123.

12. Ibid.
13. *Los Angeles Times,* October 21, 1945, "Jane Wyman Lauded for Her Dramatic Roles."
14. *Los Angeles Times,* June 2, 1942, "Voice Won Reagan Chance."
15. *Los Angeles Times,* March 12, 1947, "Seven Actors' Guild Officers Resign Posts."
16. SAG archivist Valerie Yaros, to author, January 2010.
17. Jack Dales, oral history, p. 29.
18. Grant Schneider, to author, January 2010.

4. Creating a Network of Contacts and Support

1. *Time,* October 13, 1945, "Swan Song."
2. General Electric biography.
3. *Time,* December 28, 1942, "U.S. at War: Tough Babies."
4. Mike Dann, *As I Saw It,* p. 44.
5. Nancy Reagan, *My Turn,* p. 125.
6. Jack Dales, oral history, p. 45.
7. Ibid.
8. Chester Migden, Complete Portrait/Interview, American Film Foundation/Screen Actors Guild Foundation, Legacy Documentation Program, 1989, p. 16.
9. Ibid., p. 14.
10. Ibid.
11. Jack Dales, oral history, p. 29.
12. In its early days, CBS hosted a promotional event at Tiffany's, and the association stuck.
13. Jaquelin Hume, oral history, p. 28.
14. Ibid., p. 45.
15. Earl Dunckel, oral history, p. 1.
16. Thomas W. Evans, *The Education of Ronald Reagan,* p. 3.
17. Earl Dunckel, oral history, p. 10.
18. Kurt Ritter and David Henry, *Ronald Reagan: The Great Communicator,* p. 14.
19. Ibid.
20. Bill Boyarsky, *The Rise of Ronald Reagan,* p. 26.
21. Neil Reagan, oral history, p. 22.
22. Ronald Reagan and Hubler, *Where's the Rest of Me?,* p. 276.

23. Ronald Reagan letter to Earl Dunckel, October 25, 1966, files of Hoover Institute.
24. Ronald Reagan and Hubler, *Where's the Rest of Me?*, p. 296.

5. Turning Point

1. Marianne Mills Spielmann, to author, January 2010.
2. Bob Colacello, *Ronnie and Nancy*, p. 124.
3. Holmes Tuttle, oral history, p. 113.
4. Ibid., p. 114.
5. J. William Middendorf II, *A Glorious Disaster*, p. 209.
6. Ibid.
7. Ronald Reagan, *An American Life*, p. 140.
8. J. William Middendorf II, *A Glorious Disaster*, p. 207.
9. *Los Angeles Times*, November 4, 1964, "GOP Assesses Self in Lieu of Victory Party."
10. *Los Angeles Times*, November 11, 1964, "Young GOP Reaffirms Support of Goldwater."
11. Anne Edwards, *Early Reagan*, p. 444.
12. *Los Angeles Times*, November 14, 1964, "GOP Needs Moderate—Christopher."
13. *Washington Post*, October 29, 1964, "Inside Report by Rowland Evans and Robert Novak."

6. Unleashing the Power of a Team

1. Michael Deaver, oral history, p. 9.
2. Holmes Tuttle, oral history, p. 115.
3. Edward Mills, oral history, p. 71.
4. Ronald Reagan, oral history, p. 5.
5. John Meroney, to author, January 2010.
6. Taped conversation between Ronald Reagan and Myles Martel, 1978, private collection.
7. Holmes Tuttle, oral history, p. 124.
8. Nancy Clark Reynolds, to author, February 2010.
9. *Los Angeles Times*, April 23, 1967, "Ronald Reagan's 'Kitchen Cabinet.'"
10. Stuart Spencer, oral history, p. 26.
11. Ibid., p. 32.

12. Ibid., p. 28.
13. Ronald Reagan, oral history, p. 14.
14. Edward Mills, oral history, p. 70.
15. William Roberts, oral history, p. 22.
16. Ibid., p. 14.
17. Lyn Nofziger, oral history, p. 18.
18. Stanley Plog, oral history, introduction by Stephen Stern, p. i.
19. Ibid., p. 11.
20. Jaquelin Hume, oral history, p. 22.
21. Jack Wrather, oral history, p. 7.
22. Eleanor Ring Storrs, oral history, p. 2.
23. Ronald Reagan, oral history, p. 13.
24. Jaquelin Hume, oral history, p. 38.
25. Stanley Plog, oral history, p. 14.
26. Jaquelin Hume, oral history, p. 38.
27. Stephen Stern, introduction to Stanley Plog oral history, p. i.
28. William French Smith, oral history, p. 28.
29. Aram Bakshian, to author, January 2010.
30. Peter Hannaford, UVA oral history, p. 7.
31. Ibid., p. 7.
32. *Los Angeles Times,* "Reagan Invites 'Hostile' Quiz by Listeners," April 16, 1966.
33. Stuart Spencer, oral history, p. 31.
34. Henry Salvatori, oral history, p. 17.
35. Ibid., p. 16.
36. Ibid.
37. Ronald Reagan, oral history, p. 9.
38. Lyn Nofziger, oral history, p. 37.
39. *Los Angeles Times,* "Reagan Storms From Meeting of Negro GOP Unit," March 6, 1966.
40. *Los Angeles Times,* "School Bussing Unfair, Reagan Tells Parents," October 6, 1970.
41. Ibid.
42. Stanley Plog, oral history, p. 8.
43. Lyn Nofziger, oral history, p. 9.
44. Stanley Plog, oral history, p. 9.
45. Ibid.

46. Gordon Luce, oral history, p. 56.
47. Edward Mills, oral history p. 74.
48. *New York Times,* October 21, 1966, "10 Copley Papers Endorse Reagan in California Race."

7. LEADERSHIP

1. Jaquelin Hume, oral history, p. 16.
2. Ronald Reagan, *An American Life,* p. 156.
3. Ronald Reagan, oral history, p. 21.
4. Ibid.
5. Ronald Reagan, *An American Life,* p. 180.
6. *Los Angeles Times,* "Professors' March Protests Plans to Cut College Budgets," January 15, 1967.
7. *Los Angeles Times,* "Showdown Move by Kerr Prompted Vote, Reagan Says," January 21, 1967.
8. Alex Sherriffs, oral history, p. 66.
9. Ibid., p. 68.
10. Wofsy, oral history, p. 24.
11. *Los Angeles Times,* "Reagan Says GOP's New Rule Makes Him 'Kind of Lonely,'" April 15, 1966.
12. Alex Sherriffs, oral history, p. 89.
13. *Los Angeles Times,* "Meyer Statement on Kerr Dismissal," January 24, 1967.
14. *Los Angeles Times,* "Mail Backs Reagan 3–1 on Tuition, Aide Says," January 19, 1967.
15. Gordon Luce, oral history, p. 13.
16. Ronald Reagan, *An American Life,* p. 161.
17. Ibid.
18. Ibid.
19. Eileen Hultin, to author, November 2008.
20. *Los Angeles Times,* "Reagan Shows Interest in Favorite-Son Role," January 18, 1967.
21. William French Smith, oral history, p. 40.
22. Ibid., p. 42.
23. Jerry Martin, oral history, p. 18.
24. Ibid., p. 30.
25. Nancy Clark Reynolds, to author, March 2009.

26. Michael Deaver, oral history, p. 39.
27. "Bill Moyers: A Conversation with Ronald Reagan," 1979.
28. Ibid.
29. *Los Angeles Times,* November 7, 1974, "Reagan Looks Back on His Two Terms—and to Future."
30. Peter Hannaford, oral history, p. 33.
31. Peter Hannaford, UVA oral history, p. 38.
32. Ibid.
33. Ibid., p. 36.
34. Nancy Clark Reynolds, to author, March 2009.
35. Ibid.
36. Nancy Reagan, *My Turn,* p. 182.
37. Nancy Clark Reynolds, to author, March 2009.
38. Ibid.
39. Mike Deaver, *A Different Drummer,* p. 43.
40. Gerald Carmen, to author, November 2009.
41. Dennis Revell, to author, March 2010.
42. Gerald Carmen, to author, November 2009.

8. The Great Communicator

1. Dan Hickey, to author, April 2009.
2. Edwin Meese, to author, April 2009.
3. Max Friedersdorf, oral history, p. 44.
4. Douglas Brinkley, ed., *Reagan Diaries,* p. 5, February 26, 1981.
5. Ibid., p. 5, February 27, 1981.
6. Max Friedersdorf, oral history, p. 61.
7. Ibid.
8. Michael Deaver, *A Different Drummer,* p. 146.
9. Michael Deaver, oral history, p. 13.
10. Kenneth Adelman, oral history, p. 49.
11. Michael Deaver, oral history, p. 13.
12. Edwin Meese, to author, April 2009.
13. Ronald Reagan, *An American Life,* p. 594.
14. Michael Deaver, *A Different Drummer,* p. 142.
15. Ibid.
16. William Safire, *New York Times,* June 1, 1981.
17. Leonard Silk, *New York Times,* September 23, 1981.

18. George Shultz, oral history, p. 26.
19. Deaver, *A Different Drummer*, p. 121.
20. Ibid., p. 55.
21. Aram Bakshian, to author, January 2010.
22. Ibid.
23. Aram Bakshian, oral history, p. 54.
24. Ibid., p. 38.
25. Anthony R. Dolan, to author, November 2009.
26. Anthony R. Dolan, speech, Heritage Foundation, June 3, 2002.
27. Ibid.
28. Ronald Reagan, *An American Life*, p. 570.
29. *Time*, April 4, 1983, "The Risk of Taking Up Shields."
30. Richard Wirthlin, *The Greatest Communicator*, p. 116.
31. Ibid., p. 119.
32. Ibid., p. 12.
33. George Shultz, oral history, p. 25.
34. Bing West, to author, November 2008.
35. Richard Wirthlin, *The Greatest Communicator*, p. 2.
36. George Shultz, oral history, p. 12.
37. Richard Wirthlin, *The Greatest Communicator*, p. 128.
38. *Boston Globe*, November 12, 1990, "Knowing the Mystery and Suffering of Russia."
39. Michael Deaver, oral history, p. 14.
40. George Shultz, oral history, p. 23.
41. Ibid., p. 22.
42. Ibid., p. 23.
43. Nancy Reagan, *My Turn*, p. 266.
44. Rick Ahearn, to author, April 2009.
45. Deaver, *A Different Drummer*, p. 103.

9. Challenges

1. Michael Deaver, *A Different Drummer*, p. 119.
2. Margaret Thatcher, *The Downing Street Years*, p. 461.
3. *Los Angeles Times*, February 27, 1985, "Donald Regan Taking the Heat."
4. Nancy Reagan, *My Turn*, p. 63.
5. Richard Wirthlin, *The Greatest Communicator*, pp. 20–21.

6. George Shultz, oral history, p. 30.
7. Michael Deaver, *A Different Drummer,* p. 108.
8. Remarks at a Joint German-American Military Ceremony at Bitburg Airbase in the Federal Republic of Germany, May 5, 1985.
9. *Time,* July 1, 1985, "Prime-Time Terrorism."
10. Kenneth Adelman, oral history, p. 52.
11. Edwin Meese, to author, April 2009.
12. Ibid.
13. George Shultz, oral history, p. 15.
14. Nancy Reagan, *My Turn,* p. 331.

10. LEGACY

1. Scott Porter, to author, February 2010.
2. Michael Deaver, *A Different Drummer,* p. 3.
3. *Rockford Morning Star,* February 25, 1976.
4. *Sydney Morning Herald,* November 29, 1986, "The Other Reagan."
5. Dan Hickey, to author, April 2009.
6. *Los Angeles Times,* November 7, 1974, "Reagan Looks Back on His Two Terms—and to Future."
7. William French Smith, oral history, overview.
8. Caspar Weinberger, oral history, p. 4.
9. PBS Interview with Bill Moyers, 1979.
10. Frank Carlucci, oral history, p. 30.
11. Scott Porter, to author, April 2009.
12. Nancy Clark Reynolds, to author, April 2009.
13. John Meroney, to author, January 2010.
14. Scott Porter, to author, April 2009.
15. David Thompson, to author, November 2008.
16. Joan Johnson, to author, February 2009.
17. Edwin Meese, to author, April 2009.
18. Referring to the era's Department of Health, Education, and Welfare.
19. Lyn Nofziger, oral history, p. 29.
20. *Sacramento Bee,* May 10, 1981, "Reagans Influenced by Mother."

Bibliography

Barber, Red. *The Broadcasters.* New York: Dial Press, 1970.

Barletta, John R., and Schweizer, Rochelle. *Riding with Reagan: From the White House to the Ranch.* New York: Citadel Press Books, 2005.

Barnouw, Erik. *The Golden Web: A History of Broadcasting in the United States, Volume II—1933 to 1953.* New York: Oxford University Press, 1968.

Basinger, Jeanine. *The Star Machine.* New York: Alfred A. Knopf, 2007.

Beaman, Jim. *Interviewing for Radio.* London and New York: Routledge, 2000.

Brooks, John. *Telephone: The First Hundred Years.* New York: Harper and Row, 1975.

Brown, Mary Beth. *Hand of Providence: The Strong and Quiet Faith of Ronald Reagan.* Nashville, Tenn.: WND Books, 2004.

Buckley, William F., Jr., *God and Man at Yale.* Washington, D.C.: Regnery, 1986.

——. *The Reagan I Knew.* New York: Basic Books, 2008.

Cannon, Lou. *President Reagan: The Role of a Lifetime.* New York: Public Affairs, 1991.

——. *Governor Reagan: His Rise to Power.* New York: Public Affairs, 2003.

Colacello, Bob. *Ronnie and Nancy: Their Path to the White House—1911–1980.* New York: Warner Books, 2004.

Dann, Mike. *As I Saw It: The Inside Story of the Golden Years of Television.* El Prado, N. Mex.: Levine Mesa Press, 2009.

Deaver, Michael K. *A Different Drummer: My Thirty Years with Ronald Reagan.* New York: HarperCollins, 2001.

——. *Why I Am a Reagan Conservative.* New York: HarperCollins, 2005.

D'Souza, Dinesh. *Ronald Reagan: How an Ordinary Man Became an Extraordinary Leader.* New York: Free Press, 1997.

Duerr, Edwin. *Radio and Television Acting—Criticism, Theory, and Practice.* Westport, Conn.: Greenwood Press, 1950.

Edwards, Anne. *Early Reagan: The Rise to Power.* New York: William Morrow, 1990.

——. *The Reagans: Portrait of a Marriage.* New York: St. Martin's Griffin, 2003.

Eureka College, Elmira Jane Dickinson, ed. *A History of Eureka College with Biographical Sketches and Reminiscences.* St. Louis: Christian Publishing Company, 1894.

Felten, D. Erik. *A Shining City: The Legacy of Ronald Reagan.* New York: Simon & Schuster, 1998.

Flynn, Errol. *My Wicked, Wicked Ways: The Autobiography of Errol Flynn.* New York: Cooper Square Press, 2003.

Hannaford, Peter. *The Reagans—A Political Portrait.* New York: Coward-McCann, 1983.

Hannaford, Peter, ed. *Recollections of Reagan: A Portrait of Ronald Reagan.* New York: William Morrow, 1997.

Hayward, Steven F. *The Age of Reagan.* Roseville: Prima Publishing, 2001.

Holmes, Joseph R., ed. and comp. *The Quotable Ronald Reagan: The Common Sense and Straight Talk of Former California Governor Ronald Reagan.* San Diego: JRH & Associates, 1975.

Johnson, W. Brad, and Ridley, Charles R. *The Elements of Mentoring.* New York: Palgrave Macmillan, 2004.

Kengor, Paul. *God and Ronald Reagan: A Spiritual Life.* New York: Regan Books, 2004.

Kengor, Paul, and Doerner, Patricia Clark. *The Judge: William P. Clark, Ronald Reagan's Top Hand.* San Francisco: Ignatius Press, 2007.

Kessel, John H. *The Goldwater Coalition: Republican Strategies in 1964.* Indianapolis and New York: Bobbs-Merrill, 1968.

Kuhn, Jim. *Ronald Reagan in Private: A Memoir of My Years in the White House.* New York: Sentinel, 2004.

Mayer, George H. *The Republican Party 1954–1966*, 2nd ed. New York: Oxford University Press, 1967.

McDougal, Dennis. *The Last Mogul: Lew Wasserman, MCA, and the Hidden History of Hollywood.* New York: Crown, 1998.

Meese, Edwin III. *With Reagan: The Inside Story.* Washington, D.C.: Regnery, 1992.

Middendorf, J. William II. *A Glorious Disaster: Barry Goldwater's Presidential Campaign and the Origins of the Conservative Movement.* New York: Basic Books, 2006.

Morris, Edmund. *Dutch—A Memoir of Ronald Reagan.* New York: Random House, 1999.

Neal, Patricia. *As I Am.* New York: Simon & Schuster, 1988.

Nofziger, Lyn. *Nofziger.* Washington, D.C.: Regnery, 1992.

O'Sullivan, John. *The President, the Pope and the Prime Minister: Three Who Changed the World.* Washington, D.C.: Regnery, 2006.

Paiva, Bob. *The Program Director's Handbook.* Blue Ridge Summit, Pa.: TAB Books, 1983.

Patrick, Curtis. *Reagan: What Was He Really Like?*, Vol. I, 2007.

Patterson, Ted. *The Golden Voices of Football*, Vol. I. Sports Publishing LLC, 2004.

Petro, Joseph. *Standing Next to History: An Agent's Life Inside the Secret Service.* New York: Thomas Dunne Books, 2005.

Reagan, Maureen. *First Father, First Daughter.* New York: Little Brown, 1989.

Reagan, Michael. *Twice Adopted.* Nashville: Broadman & Holman, 2004.

Reagan, Michael, and Hyams, Joe. *On the Outside Looking In.* New York: Zebra Books, 1988.

Reagan, Nancy, with Novak, William. *My Turn: The Memoirs of Nancy Reagan.* New York: Random House, 1989.

Reagan, Ronald. *An American Life.* New York: Simon and Schuster, 1990.

Reagan, Ronald, and Brinkley, Douglas, ed. *The Reagan Diaries.* New York: HarperCollins, 2007.

Reagan, Ronald, and Hubler, Richard G. *Where's the Rest of Me? The Ronald Reagan Story.* New York: Duell, Sloan and Pearce, 1965.

Reese, David E., Beadle, Mary E., and Stephenson, Alan R. *Broadcast Announcing Worktext—Performing for Radio, Television and Cable.* Boston: Focal Press, 2000.

Regnery, Alfred. *Upstream: The Ascendance of American Conservatism.* New York: Threshold Editions, 2008.

Robinson, Peter. *How Ronald Reagan Changed My Life.* New York: Regan Books, 2003.

Roseboom, Eugene H., and Eckes, Alfred E., Jr. *A History of Presidential Elections: From George Washington to Jimmy Carter,* 4th ed. New York: Macmillan, 1979.

Ryan, Frederick J., Jr. *Ronald Reagan: The Great Communicator.* San Francisco: Perennial, 1995.

Shadegg, Stephen C. *What Happened to Goldwater?* New York: Holt, Rinehart and Winston, 1965.

——. *Winning's a Lot More Fun: An Insider's Report on the Greatest Political Comeback in History . . . and the Story of the Entire 1968 Election.* London: Macmillan, 1969.

Sharp, Kathleen. *Mr. & Mrs. Hollywood: Edie and Lew Wasserman and Their Entertainment Empire.* New York: Carroll and Graf, 2003.

Shearer, Stephen Michael. *Patricia Neal: An Unquiet Life.* Lexington, Ky.: University Press of Kentucky, 2006.

Sinetar, Marsha. *The Mentor's Spirit.* New York: St. Martin's Press, 1998.

Skinner, Kiron K., Anderson, Annelise, and Anderson, Martin, eds. *Reagan: In His Own Hand.* New York: Free Press, 2001.

Strober, Deborah Hart, and Strober, Gerald S. *The Reagan Presidency: An Oral History of the Era,* rev. ed. Washington, D.C.: Brassey's, 1998.

Thatcher, Margaret. *The Downing Street Years.* New York: HarperCollins, 1993.

Valenti, Jack. *Speak Up with Confidence: How to Prepare, Learn, and Deliver Effective Speeches.* New York: Hyperion, 1982.

——. *This Time, This Place: My Life in War, the White House, and Hollywood.* New York: Harmony Books, 2007.

Vaughan, Stephen. *Ronald Reagan in Hollywood: Movies and Politics.* New York: Cambridge University Press, 1994.

Von Damm, Helene. *Sincerely, Ronald Reagan.* Ottawa, Ill.: Green Hill Publishers, 1976.

Wapshott, Nicholas. *Ronald Reagan and Margaret Thatcher: A Political Marriage.* New York: Sentinel, 2007.

Weinberger, Caspar W., with Gretchen Roberts. *In the Arena—A Memoir of the 20th Century.* Washington, D.C.: Regnery, 2001.

White, Theodore. *The Making of the President, 1964.* New York: Athenaeum, 1965.

Wills, Gary. *Reagan's America: Innocents at Home.* New York: Penguin, 1985.

Wirthlin, Dick, and Hall, Wynton C. *The Greatest Communicator: What Ronald Reagan Taught Me about Politics, Leadership, and Life.* Hoboken, N.J.: John Wiley & Sons, 2004.

Wymbs, Norm. *Ronald Reagan & the Holy Spirit.* Oakland: Elderberry Press, 2005.

Oral Histories

Adams, Winifred, "Philosophy and Practice of Government," an interview conducted by Gabrielle Morris in *Appointments, Cabinet Management, and Policy Research for Governor Ronald Reagan, 1967–1974,* Regional Oral History Office, Bancroft Library, University of California, Berkeley, 1982.

Adelman, Kenneth, interview, Miller Center, University of Virginia, Ronald Reagan Presidential Oral History Project, 2003.

Anderson, Annelise, interview, Miller Center, University of Virginia, Ronald Reagan Presidential Oral History Project, 2001.

Anderson, Martin, interview, Miller Center, University of Virginia, Ronald Reagan Presidential Oral History Project, 2001.

Bakshian, Aram, interview, Miller Center, University of Virginia, Ronald Reagan Presidential Oral History Project, 2002.

Beck, Paul, "From the *Los Angeles Times* to the Executive Press Office. 1967–1972," an interview conducted by Gabrielle Morris in 1982 in *The Governor's Office and Public Information, Education, and Planning, 1967–1974,* Regional Oral History Office, Bancroft Library, University of California, Berkeley, 1984.

Carlucci, Frank, interview, Miller Center, University of Virginia, Ronald Reagan Presidential Oral History Project, 2001.

Dales, Jack, "Pragmatic Leadership: Ronald Reagan as President of the Screen Actors Guild," an interview conducted by Mitch Tuchman for the Oral History Program, University of California, Los Angeles, California, 1981, 49 pp.

del Junco, Tirso, "California Republican Party Leadership and Success, 1966–1982," an interview conducted by Gabrielle Morris in 1982 in *Republican Philosophy and Party Activism,* Regional Oral History Office, Bancroft Library, University of California, Berkeley, 1984.

Drake, Joanne, interview, Miller Center, University of Virginia, Ronald Reagan Presidential Oral History Project, 2003.

Dunckel, Earl, "Ronald Reagan and the *General Electric Theater,* 1954–1955," an oral history conducted in 1982 by Gabrielle Morris, Regional Oral History Office, Bancroft Library, University of California, Berkeley, 1982.

Hannaford, Peter, "Expanding Political Horizons," an interview conducted by Gabrielle Morris in 1982 in *The Governor's Office and Public Information, Education, and Planning, 1967–1974,* Regional Oral History Office, Bancroft Library, University of California, Berkeley, 1984.

Hannaford, Peter, interview, Miller Center, University of Virginia, Ronald Reagan Presidential Oral History Project, 2003.

Hume, Jaquelin, "Basic Economics and the Body Politic: Views of a Northern California Reagan Loyalist," an oral history conducted in 1982 by Gabrielle Morris in *Republican Philosophy and Party Activism,* Regional Oral History Office, Bancroft Library, University of California, Berkeley, 1984.

James, Pendleton, interview, Miller Center, University of Virginia, Ronald Reagan Presidential Oral History Project, 2003.

The "Kitchen Cabinet": Four California Citizen Advisers of Ronald Reagan, interviews conducted by Steven D. Edgington and Lawrence B. de Graaf in 1983, California Government History Documentation Project: The Reagan Era. Courtesy of the Center for Oral and Public History, California State University, Fullerton.

Kuhn, James F., interview, Miller Center, University of Virginia, Ronald Reagan Presidential Oral History Project, 2003.

Livermore, Norman B., Jr., "Man in the Middle: High Sierra Packer, Timberman, Conservationist, and California Resources Secretary," an interview conducted by Ann Lage and Gabrielle Morris, 1981–1982,

Regional Oral History Office, Bancroft Library, University of California, Berkeley, 1983.

Luce, Gordon, "A Banker's View of State Administration and Republican Politics," an oral history conducted by Gabrielle Morris in 1982–1983 in *Governor Reagan and His Cabinet: An Introduction*, Regional Oral History Office, Bancroft Library, University of California, Berkeley, 1986.

Martin, Jerry C., "Information and Policy Research for Ronald Reagan, 1969–1975," an interview conducted by Sarah Sharp, 1981–1982 in *Appointments, Cabinet Management, and Policy Research for Governor Ronald Reagan, 1967–1974*, Regional Oral History Office, Bancroft Library, University of California, Berkeley, 1983.

Nofziger, Lyn, "Press Secretary for Ronald Reagan, 1966," an interview conducted by Sarah Sharp in 1978 in *Issues and Innovations in the 1966 Republican Gubernatorial Campaign*, Regional Oral History Office, Bancroft Library, University of California, Berkeley, 1980.

——. interview, Miller Center, University of Virginia, Ronald Reagan Presidential Oral History Project, 2003.

Orr, Verne, "Business Leadership in the Department of Motor Vehicles and State Finance," an oral history conducted in 1982–1983 by Gabrielle Morris in *Governor Reagan and His Cabinet: An Introduction*, Regional History Office, Bancroft Library, University of California, Berkeley, 1986.

Parkinson, Gaylord B., "California Republican Party Official, 1962–1967," an interview conducted by Sarah Sharp in 1978 in *Issues and Innovations in the 1966 Republican Gubernatorial Campaign*, Regional Oral History Office, Bancroft Library, University of California, 1980.

Plog, Stanley, "More than Just an Actor: The Early Campaigns of Ronald Reagan," an interview conducted by Stephen Stern in June 1981 for the Oral History Program. Available through the UCLA Department of Special Collections in the Charles E. Young Research Library.

Reagan, Neil, "Private Dimensions and Public Images: The Early Political Campaigns of Ronald Reagan," an interview conducted by Stephen Stern in 1981, Oral History Program. Available through the UCLA Department of Special Collections in the Charles E. Young Research Library.

Reagan, Ronald, "On Becoming Governor," an oral history conducted in 1979 by Sarah Sharp in *Governor Reagan and His Cabinet: An Introduction,* Regional Oral History Office, Bancroft Library, University of California, Berkeley, 1986.

Roberts, William E., "Professional Campaign Management and the Candidate, 1960–1966," an interview conducted in 1979 by Sarah Sharp in *Issues and Innovations in the 1966 Republican Gubernatorial Campaign,* Regional Oral History Office, Bancroft Library, University of California, Berkeley, 1980.

Ryan, Frederick J., Jr., interview, Miller Center, University of Virginia, Ronald Reagan Presidential Oral History Project, 2004.

Sheriffs, Alex D., "Education Advisor to Ronald Reagan and State University Administrator, 1969–1982," interviews conducted in 1981 and 1982 by Gabrielle Morris and Sarah Sharp in *The Governor's Office and Public Information, Education, and Planning, 1967–1974,* Regional Oral History Office, Bancroft Library, University of California, Berkeley, 1984.

Shultz, George, interview, Miller Center, University of Virginia, Ronald Reagan Presidential Oral History Project, 2003.

Smith, William French, "Evolution of the Kitchen Cabinet. 1965–1973," an oral history conducted in 1988 by Gabrielle Morris, Regional Oral History Office, Bancroft Library, University of California, Berkeley, 1989.

Spencer, Stuart, "Developing a Campaign Management Organization," an interview conducted in 1979 by Gabrielle Morris in *Issues and Innovations in the 1966 Republican Gubernatorial Campaign,* Regional Oral History Office, Bancroft Library, University of California, Berkeley, 1980.

Storrs, Eleanor Ring, "Parties, Politics, and Principles: 'It's at the Local Level,'" an interview conducted by Sarah Sharp in 1983 in *Republican Philosophy and Party Activism,* Regional Oral History Office, Bancroft Library, University of California, Berkeley, 1984.

Tuttle, Robert H., interview, Miller Center, University of Virginia, Ronald Reagan Presidential Oral History Project, 2003.

Weinberger, Caspar, interview, Miller Center, University of Virginia, Ronald Reagan Presidential Oral History Project, 2002.

Wofsy, Leon, "Professor Emeritus in Immunology and Political Activist," an oral history conducted in 1999 by Lisa Rubens, Regional Oral History Office, Bancroft Library, University of California, Berkeley, 2008.

Wrather, Jack, "On Friendship, Politics, and Government," an oral history conducted in 1982 by Gabrielle Morris, in *Republican Philosophy and Party Activism,* Regional Oral History Office, Bancroft Library, University of California, Berkeley, 1984.

Acknowledgments

For an author, a book is a journey, a winding road of random encounters, hushed libraries, and off-the-beaten-path historic sites. That's what makes it fun.

The unsung heroes who traveled with Reagan, spent his birthdays with him, and called to him from hotel corridors—"Nancy says to turn out the lights!"—have been invaluable resources for *Reagan's Journey*. My brother, Jim Morrell, inadvertently opened the door to Reagan's inner circle by mentioning this project to lifelong friend Jim Casey, who introduced me to his friend, Dan Hickey, whose father, Ed Hickey, was one of Ronald Reagan's closest associates.

Many, many thanks to Dan Hickey and General Herbert Temple, who were indispensable guides through the labyrinth of Reagan connections. Ronald Reagan led such an enormous life, it proved impossible to follow up on all their introductions. With Ronald Reagan, there will always be one more person to talk to, one more conversation to have, one more page to turn.

This book was made possible by conversations with Reagan insiders Edwin Meese, Nancy Clark Reynolds, Peter Hannaford, William Clark, Dennis Revell, Gerald Carmen, Kathy Osborne, Philip Manuel, Anthony R. Dolan, Aram Bakshian, Barbara Cook Fabiani, Jay Hoffman, and John Meroney. I very much appreciated the insights of Thomas P. O'Neill III into his father's working relationship with President Reagan. Their generosity made this project a joy to work on.

For a memorable trip to Illinois that encompassed Springfield, Eureka, Galesburg, Monmouth, Dixon, Tampico, and Chicago, thanks go to Susan and Greg Townsend, the hospitable staff of Eureka College—Junius Rodriguez, Tony Glass, Brian Sajko, and John Morris—and delightful tour guides Joan Johnson, at Reagan's birthplace in Tampico, and Bill Jones, of the Dixon Historic Center.

For help, suggestions, and input along the way, many thanks to Diane Barrie, Martha Van Heyde Huggins, and Steve Branch at the Reagan Library and Mike Greco and Sheila Blackford at the University of Virginia's Miller Center. This project wouldn't have been possible without the great work done by the Miller Center and, a generation ago, by the able staff of the Regional Oral History Office at the University of California at Berkeley. Their interviews with key Reagan staffers provided a rich trove of material. In particular I'd like to thank Gabrielle Morris for her spot-on interviews and for generously sharing memories of long-ago conversations.

I appreciated Jonathan Schmitz, archivist at the Chautauqua Institute, taking time late on a Friday afternoon to explain the origins of the Chautauqua movement and the impact this program had on rural Americans thirsting for knowledge. A conversation with Andrew McFarlane, executive director of the Dixon, Illinois, YMCA, brought alive how important and valuable the YMCA was to young Dutch Reagan.

Ronald Reagan's involvement with the Screen Actors Guild had a profound affect on him. Today this impressive organization bears witness to the generosity of its founders and storied ranks of board members. Many thanks to Davidson Lloyd, Richard Baldwin, and awe-inspiring archivist Valerie Yaros.

For bringing the world of radio alive, many thanks to Greater Media's Peter Smyth, Grace Blazer, and Michael Graham, and to Salem Communications' Joe Davis and David Spady. For expertise on branding, I'm very grateful to Jodi Ordioni of BrandeMix and Grant Schneider of Time, Inc.

For sharing memories of their firsthand encounters with Ronald Reagan, thanks go to Jim and Cyndie Quist, Andrew Chaveriat, David

Leffler, Mary Blackwood Collier, Bing West, Eileen Hultin, and early member of Friends of Ronald Reagan Californian Louise Dougherty.

I thoroughly enjoyed a lengthy conversation over a leisurely breakfast with Marianne Mills Spielmann, who reminisced about her father, Ed Mills, a founding member of the kitchen cabinet who played a key role in Ronald Reagan's transformation from Goldwater supporter to full-throttle politician. Marianne brought to life the earliest days of Ronald Reagan's political career.

Many thanks to David Blews, Jim Hawkins, and Barbara Holton for reading early drafts of *Reagan's Journey* and offering feedback and suggestions.

A special thanks to Scott Porter for sharing the story of his memorable visit with President Reagan in 1998.

Finally, a book is a team effort, and I am very grateful to have crackerjack literary agent Doug Grad as a partner on this project and the enthusiastic support of Carolyn Reidy, Louise Burke, Anthony Ziccardi, Dan Smetanka, Mary McCue, Lisa Litwack, and Andrea DeWerd at Simon & Schuster's Threshold Editions.

Margot Morrell
New York, N.Y.
October 2010